Twayne's United States Authors Series

Sylvia E. Bowman, *Editor*

INDIANA UNIVERSITY

James Thurber

JAMES THURBER

by **ROBERT E. MORSBERGER**

Michigan State University

 62

Twayne Publishers, Inc.   ::   New York

MANUFACTURED IN THE UNITED STATES OF AMERICA BY
UNITED PRINTING SERVICES, INC.
NEW HAVEN, CONN.

To
MY MOTHER AND FATHER
CHAPTER IV TO GRACE

Preface

THIS BOOK is the first full-length study of the work of James Thurber. Perhaps no other distinguished contemporary has been so neglected critically: for, in spite of his immense popularity at home and abroad, he has received little serious critical attention and that only in book reviews or brief articles. One difficulty for reader and critic is that most of Thurber's pieces are short and are scattered over thirty years of periodicals and more than two dozen books. Most of his public read him intermittently, relishing the individual selections but failing to survey the whole of his achievement.

The critic of a humorist labors under several disadvantages. He must make his subject convincingly significant; but, if he overstresses the serious side, he may make him appear ponderous or pretentious. Humor inevitably loses in critical translation. The critic can examine irony, satire, paradox, and character; but, if he tries to tell the reader why or when he should laugh, he is apt to appear an embarrassing rib-nudger or a tedious pedant. The point of wit can be blunted and the edge of irony dulled by excessive analysis. Wolcott Gibbs wrote of Max Eastman's *The Enjoyment of Laughter*: "It seems to me Eastman has got American humor down and broken its arm."[1] Sometimes reviewers expect the critic to write humorously himself, but studies of Twain and Shaw are not notably funny. To have any insight, the critic must possess a sense of humor, but his job is to interpret—not to imitate his subject. Still he is tempted; and he may, therefore, become anecdotal at the risk of being superficial or he may borrow humor by quotations chosen to amuse rather than to enlighten.

Sometimes academic readers insist that an author be reduced to a single thesis, but such an approach can lead to rigid oversimplification. Few artists are so consistent or so confined, and criticism can be more challenging when it examines the complex variations of artistic perception and performance. Thurber's humor succeeds with a brilliant balance of style and content, covering an entire spectrum of human behavior. *The New Yorker* found his work "largely unclassifiable." E. B. White wrote that "There were at least two, probably six Thurbers. His thoughts have always been a tangle of baseball scores, Civil War tactical problems, Henry James, personal maladjustments, terrier puppies, literary rip tides, ancient myths, and modern apprehensions. Through this jungle stalk the unpredictable ghosts of his relatives in Columbus, Ohio."[2]

Thurber himself was wary of being forced into a critical mold. In 1955 he challenged one "intrepid young literary explorer" who tried to organize his work "lying sprawled and unburied on the plain." Over the years he wrote to various professors "that the academic dedication is to order, importance, intensity, but that the so-called creative man likes to mingle his most serious with the just plain amusing, since one's life, day, month, and year are ordered that way."[3] Accordingly, one obstacle to criticism is the casual variety of Thurber's work.

Thurber was one of his own best critics; and since he has made a good many statements about his methods and objectives, I have quoted extensively to let him speak in his own voice. As it is impracticable to give close reading and individual analysis to his hundreds of short selections, I have approached them thematically, not trying to superimpose any tight scheme, but examining some of their major and recurrent issues as they are indicated in general by my chapter titles. Some of the more prominent fiction is examined at length and put in the perspective of Thurber's larger work, but many of his essays are credos that lend themselves more to thematic commentary than to aesthetic analysis. Stories, fables, drama, essays, fantasies, brief biographies, cartoons and drawings—all these play a subtle counterpoint and contribute to James Thurber's unique accomplishment.

ROBERT E. MORSBERGER

Michigan State University

Acknowledgments

I should like to thank the following for permission to quote from copyrighted material.

Henry Brandon and Doubleday and Company, Inc., for Henry Brandon, *As We Are.*

Malcolm Cowley for "James Thurber's Dream Book," *The New Republic,* Vol. 112, March 12, 1945; "Lions and Lemmings, Toads and Tigers," *The Reporter,* Vol. 15, December 13, 1956; "Salute to Thurber," *The Saturday Review,* Vol. 44, November 25, 1961; and *The Literary Situation,* New York: The Viking Press, Inc., 1954.

Harcourt, Brace and World, Inc., for e. e. cummings, *Poems 1923-1954* and *The Autobiography of Mark Van Doren.*

Harper and Row, Inc., for Frederick Lewis Allen, *Since Yesterday, The Nineteen-Thirties in America.*

Alfred A. Knopf, Inc., for Albert Camus, *The Rebel* and Henry Bamford Parkes, *The American Experience.*

The Macmillan Company for William E. Bohn, *I Remember America.*

Walter Rumsey Marvin and the Martha Kinney Cooper Ohioana Library Association for *Ohio Authors and Their Books,* 1796-1950, ed. William Coyle.

Random House, Inc., for William Faulkner's Nobel Prize Address. Reprinted from *The Faulkner Reader,* Copyright 1954, by William Faulkner.

Charles Scribner's Sons for F. Scott Fitzgerald, *The Great Gatsby, This Side of Paradise, The Short Stories of F. Scott Fitzgerald.*

Simon and Schuster, Inc., for Romain Gary, *The Roots of Heaven.*

The Viking Press, Inc., for *Writers at Work,* ed. Malcolm Cowley.

The World Publishing Company for Harvey Breit, *The Writer Observed.*

All quotations from James Thurber's books and uncollected pieces are used by permission of Mrs. James Thurber and are copyrighted © 1929, 1930, 1931, 1932, 1933, 1934, 1935, 1936, 1937, 1938, 1939, 1940, 1941, 1942, 1943, 1944, 1945, 1946, 1947, 1948, 1949, 1950, 1951, 1952, 1953, 1954, 1955, 1956, 1957, 1958, 1959, 1960, 1961 by James Thurber. *Credos and Curios,* copyrighted © 1962 by Helen Thurber.

I am grateful to Elliott Nugent and E. B. White for information about their collaboration with James Thurber on *The Male*

Animal and *Is Sex Necessary?* respectively. Ronald John Williams, editor of *The Bermudian,* provided information about Thurber's contributions to his magazine; and Mrs. Harriet H. Crowley furnished some data about his publications in the *Detroit Athletic Club News.* Kenneth MacLean kindly sent me a copy of his article, "James Thurber—a Portrait of the Dog Artist," which appeared in the Spring, 1944, issue of *Acta Victorana.* Terence Tobin sent me a bibliography of Thurber works translated into other languages. I should like to thank the staff of the Martha Kinney Cooper Ohioana Library, the Ohio State University Library, the State University of Iowa Library, and the University of Chicago Library for their assistance. My research and manuscript preparation were greatly helped by two grants from Michigan State University.

I am particularly indebted to Mrs. James Thurber for giving me permission to quote from her husband's works, for showing me some of her husband's unpublished and uncollected writings, and for lending me typescripts and tearsheets of unavailable critical material. Despite her own busy schedule, she took time to answer a great many questions. My meeting her and my correspondence with her were among the most pleasant results of my research.

I should also like to thank Bartholow Crawford, Frederick McDowell, and John Gerber of The State University of Iowa and Don Hausdorff of Michigan State University for reading and criticizing parts of my manuscript, and Sylvia Bowman for her editorial assistance. Thanks are inadequate for my wife, who read and criticized my manuscript a dozen or so times and has not undergone such an ordeal since repairing her great aunt's crazy quilt. The fact that she can still read the book with appreciation is my best hope that I have written an acceptable volume.

Contents

Chronology

1894　James Grover Thurber born December 8, in Columbus, Ohio, to Mary Fisher Thurber and Charles L. Thurber.

1901　Family moved temporarily to Washington, D.C. Thurber blinded in left eye when older brother William accidentally shot him with an arrow.

1903　Returned to Columbus, Ohio. Attended Sullivant School.

1908　Attended Douglas Junior High School.

1909　Entered East High School.

1913　Entered Ohio State University.

1916　Met Elliott Nugent; began to join campus activities.

1917　Began writing for campus paper, *The Ohio State Lantern*, and for *The Sun-Dial*, the student monthly.

1918　Became editor-in-chief of *The Sun-Dial*. Joined Phi Kappa Psi fraternity. Left Ohio State University in June, without taking a degree. Became code clerk for the State Department, first in Washington, D.C., and then at the American Embassy in Paris, from November, 1918, to March, 1920.

1920　Returned to Columbus and began work as a reporter for the Columbus *Dispatch* at $25.00 a week.

1921　Began writing and directing musical comedies for the Scarlet Mask Club of Ohio State University, working on five of them between 1921 and 1925.

1922　Married Althea Adams of Columbus.

1923　Wrote Sunday halfpage, "Credos and Curios," for the Columbus *Dispatch*.

1924　Resigned from the Columbus *Dispatch* to try free-lance writing. Was central Ohio correspondent for *The Christian Science Monitor*; contributed notes on Ohio politics to the Wheeling *Intelligencer*.

1925　Went in May to France to write a novel, which never materialized. Was hired as reporter for the Paris edition of the Chicago *Tribune*. Later switched to the Riviera edition.

1926　Returned to the United States in April. Wrote 25,000 word parody, *Why We Behave Like Microbe Hunters*, which was rejected by publishers. Began work as a reporter for the New York *Evening Post* at $40.00 a week.

1927　In February, met E. B. White and Harold Ross. Was hired for staff of *The New Yorker*.

1929　First book published—*Is Sex Necessary?*—in collaboration with E. B. White.

1931   First cartoons published in *The New Yorker. The Owl in the Attic and Other Perplexities* published. Daughter Rosemary born October 7.

1932   *The Seal in the Bedroom and Other Predicaments* published.

1933   *My Life and Hard Times* published.

1934   One-man show of drawings at the Valentine Gallery, New York.

1935   Divorced from Althea Adams. Married to Helen Wismer. *The Middle-Aged Man on the Flying Trapeze* published. Gave up *New Yorker* staff job to free-lance.

1937   *Let Your Mind Alone!* published. One-man shows of drawings at the Storran Gallery, London, and the Putzel Gallery, Hollywood.

1937-   Traveled in France.
1938

1939   *The Last Flower* published. Father died. Collaborated with Elliott Nugent on *The Male Animal.* "The Secret Life of Walter Mitty" published in *The New Yorker.*

1940   One-man shows of drawings at Vassar College, the Shaw Gallery in Boston, the Marie Harriman Gallery in New York, and the Museum of Art of the Rhode Island School of Design. Drawings included in "American Humor in Prints and Drawings," the Weyhe Gallery, New York. *Fables for Our Time and Famous Poems Illustrated* published. *The Male Animal* produced successfully at the Cort Theatre, New York.

1940-   Series of eye operations for cataract and trachoma.
1941

1942   *My World—and Welcome to It* published; *The Male Animal* filmed.

1943   *Men, Women and Dogs* and *Many Moons* published. One-man show of drawings at Pomfret School.

1944   *The Great Quillow* published. One-man shows of drawings at Princeton University, Cornell University, and the Arts Club of Chicago. Drawings included in exhibitions at M. H. DeYoung Memorial Museum, San Francisco; Portland, Oregon Art Museum; Carnegie Institute, Pittsburgh; City Art Museum, St. Louis; and Philadelphia Museum of Art.

1945   *The Thurber Carnival* and *The White Deer* published. *The White Deer* given the Ohioana Juvenile medal. Drawings included in "Some Ohio Moderns" exhibition at Cincinnati Modern Art Society, Dayton Art Institute, and Columbus Gallery of Fine Arts.

1946   Drawings included in "American Cartoonists" exhibition shown in Paris by the Office of War Information.

1947   "The Secret Life of Walter Mitty" filmed.

1948   *The Beast in Me and Other Animals* published.

1949   Received Laughing Lions of Columbia University Award for Humor.

1950   Awarded honorary Doctor of Letters degree by Kenyon College. *The 13 Clocks* published.

1951   Awarded honorary degree of Doctor of Humane Letters by Williams College. Did last drawing.

1952   "The Unicorn in the Garden" filmed. *The Thurber Album* published.

1953   Awarded honorary Litt. D. by Yale University. Given Sesquicentennial Medal of the Ohioana Library Association. *Thurber Country* published.

1955   *Thurber's Dogs* published. Revisited France. Mother died on December 20.

1955   Drawing included in "American Cartoons" exhibition in Latin America and Europe, sponsored by the United States Information Agency and run by the American Federation of Arts.

1956   Appeared on *Omnibus* TV program. Received American Cartoonists' Society T-Square Award. *Further Fables for Our Time* published.

1957   *Further Fables* received American Library Association's Liberty and Justice Award. *The Wonderful O* and *Alarms and Diversions* published.

1958   Visited England. Was first American since Mark Twain to be "called to the table" for *Punch's* Wednesday luncheon.

1959   Received Distinguished Service Award from the Press Club of Ohio. Appeared on *Small World* and *Jack Paar* TV programs. *The Years With Ross* published.

1960   A *Thurber Carnival* produced successfully at the ANTA Theatre, New York. Gave speech in May dedicating Ohio State University's Denny Hall. "The Catbird Seat" filmed as *The Battle of the Sexes*. Joined cast of A *Thurber Carnival* in September for eighty-eight performances. Won Antoinette Perry Award from the American Theatre Wing for distinguished writing of A *Thurber Carnival*.

1961   *Lanterns and Lances* published. Received Certificate of Award from Ohio State University Class of 1916 for "Meritorious Service to Humanity and to Our Alma Mater." Revisited Europe. Appeared on TV program *Open End*. Stricken with blood clot on brain on October 4; underwent emergency surgery. Rallied but caught pneumonia. Died November 4. Buried November 9 at Green Lawn Cemetery in Columbus.

1962   *Credos and Curios* published posthumously.

CHAPTER 1

Predicaments and Perplexities

> ". . . laughter is surely
> The surest touch of genius in creation."
> —Christopher Fry,
> *The Lady's Not for Burning*

IT IS A COMMONPLACE that great literary humorists are not merely entertainers but use laughter to criticize their society or at least to present an authentic image of certain aspects of their world and time. If its targets are only passing fads or follies, comedy quickly becomes dated and of interest mainly to literary historians. To have enduring substance, it must reach below externalities to explore the essential nature of man himself. Still, as man's nature is seen in relation to the manners and morals of his day, comedy is more apt than tragedy to reflect the changing surface of society. Oedipus, Hamlet, and Ahab are more clearly akin than Molière and Mark Twain or Cervantes and Shaw. Man's tragic dilemma is essentially unchanged. So is his folly; but he finds different outlets to express it. Yet insofar as his folly is part of the tragedy, we find that the memorable characters of comedy also dramatize the graver issues of their generation.

I *Humor and the Changing American Scene*

In American writing, the change between nineteenth-and twentieth-century humor has been particularly marked. Though Mark Twain's work evolved from the high-spirited horseplay of the frontier to the savage scorn of embittered age, most American nineteenth-century humor is notable for its robust vigor and gusto. Reflecting the confidence of a new and expanding nation and expressing the unintellectual animal spirits of the frontier, it specialized in Yankee shrewdness, cracker-barrel wisdom, tall tales, and extravagant farce. Its characters were not noted for sensitivity, though they might have a crude cunning. If they expressed the frustrations of the frontier or of growing industrialism, it was only by aggressive practical jokes; and, if they were aware of Darwinism, they enacted the survival of the fittest. Their modern descendants are in Dogpatch or among Faulkner's Snopeses.

By contrast, a prominent trend of modern humor is to dramatize a sense of inadequacy, impotence, and defeat before the complexities and destructive potential of the century. Instead of roistering Davy Crocketts and Mike Finks, its protagonists are repressed, squeamish, and hypersensitive. Such figures recur frequently in James Thurber's work, particularly during the 1930's.

In Thurber there is a strong current of melancholy balancing the absurdity, for he had a painful awareness of the defects of contemporary life—a perilous life abounding with predicaments and perplexities. It is filled with malignant machines, with unpredictable monsters called automobiles, with domestic tragedy, with the insanity of world wars, and with scared, bewildered people leading illogical patterns of life with logical consistency. In Thurber's world the dividing line between humor and tragedy is perilously thin; and humor is not merely an aspect but a necessity of life—a vital element in human endurance and survival.

The downbeat of Thurber's humor is attributable to a changing view of both man and his environment. Rejecting any optimistic faith in the essential goodness and perfectibility of man, Thurber, like many contemporary thinkers, rediscovered human fallibility and depravity. The abysses of human nature are too appalling for comedy, so Thurber concentrated on the social conventions, shams, pretentions, and status-seeking that emasculate the modern male or drive him to furtive rebellion.

His most typical protagonists present a comic version of the modern anti-hero who fails to respond to traditional pious and patriotic platitudes. Finding society's official values hollow and hypocritical or simply too demanding, Thurber's men become reluctant rebels who retreat from the pressures of conformity and responsibility. Despite its slogan of rugged individualism, America has been traditionally suspicious of the unorthodox and sensitive individual; its hero is the "practical," aggressive businessman with "a healthy contempt for the arts." Even Emerson and Holmes felt that education and intellectuality sapped one's strength and animal vigor. Thoreau, Melville, Henry Adams, and Henry James were all alienated from a materialistic society that stressed commercial aggressiveness and suppressed artistic sensitivity. Though Thurber's characters are not artists, they are emphatically not Organization Men. In them, ambition has been replaced by apprehension, a fear of failure. A sense of some personal deficiency drains their vitality.

In a sense, Mr. Monroe, Walter Mitty, and similar characters are an implied criticism of industrial, competitive, acquisitive society. The antithesis of the ideal of Dale Carnegie, Napoleon Hill, and Norman Vincent Peale, they do not think positively nor compete with confidence. They lack executive energy and have no aspirations except some anodyne for their anxieties. Something has jarred loose their equanimity and chipped away the edges of their self-assurance so that they shun the spotlight and evade responsibility, lest they create some new catastrophe to add to their humiliating recollections. In a society that believed, and to some extent still does, that success is a sign of strength and salvation and that failure is the mark of weakness and unworthiness, they become abject and disconsolate. Thurber's characters would lose out in the survival of the fittest and are emphatically not in a state of Calvinist-Capitalist-Darwinian grace.

The change from Mike Fink to Walter Mitty parallels that from a free frontier and a basically agricultural society to that of urban industrialism. The Thurber characters who keep their vitality and have no need to hide their idiosyncracies are in turn-of-the-century Columbus, which retains an old-fashioned and rustic atmosphere. The Columbus gang resemble something from the early Mark Twain, and most of them can "wrassle" with life and pin it down. But Thurber was not really in the tradition of frontier humor; he claimed he never read anything by Twain except one story during his school days. Instead, he was an enthusiastic admirer of Henry James; and his characters, alienated in urban exile, are comic offspring of James's isolated and hypersensitive individuals. Their fastidious introversion is a sharp contrast to the swaggering half-horse, half-alligator; to the sadistic pranks of Sut Lovingood; and to the violent practical jokes of the frontier.

Instead, Thurber's characters are terrorized by technology and menaced by the machine. Though not so explicit or slapstick, some of Thurber's writings form a counterpart to Chaplin's *Modern Times,* and his pathetic protagonists are upper middle-class cousins of Chaplin's little tramp. It is perhaps significant that most of Thurber's accounts of frustration and failure were written during the Depression. "We're all disenchanted," says the wife in one cartoon, and certainly the Depression was a disenchanted decade. The Thurberian male's losing struggles with appliances show the displacement of men by machines on the domestic level. More seriously, the lives of his urban characters in the 1930's seem pointless and unrewarding. They have no financial worries but are caught in the strange, dismal grayness of the time. On the sophisticated skids, they suffer from a slow sense of futility and attrition. Their wives nag because the husbands are not aggressive enough, not sufficiently competitive. The men compensate by furtive flights into fantasy. They are not escaping from the Depression itself but from some of the things that caused it—the acquisitiveness and materialism. Money is no problem; as in Henry James, they seem to have an adequate income from some unstated source. We never see them at work or engaged in business, but they are sensitive souls retreating from a more sophisticated Babbittry.

Like some of the characters in Gogol and Dostoevsky, they feel themselves superfluous; and to a degree the comedy of their dilemma resembles Camus' sense of the absurd. They seem important to nobody—not even very much so to themselves. One cannot imagine them holding positions of responsibility. Their world is a sort of wasteland, spiritually empty, impotent, and sterile. There is no religion nor any transcendent consolations or goal. Instead of Eliot's tarot or game of chess, these hollow people play aggressive, unpleasant little parlor games or backbite at cocktail parties. There is little love between spouses or toward children: children appear only as stubborn and reluctant offspring, and the parental relation is about as tender as that in the W. C. Fields movies. About the only affection is for animals.

II *The Comic Catharsis*

But the total picture is not at all oppressive. Though prominent, the subdued husbands and disapproving wives do not dominate Thurber's work. His pages are filled with irrepressible characters who enliven his stories and cavort in his cartoons. Even the fearful characters, by turning predicament into catastrophe, create situations that explode with a good deal of energy. Moreover, Thurber felt that he sometimes helped the reader endure his own difficulties through a feeling of superiority to the dilemmas in which Thurber's people are involved—"in the comforting feeling that one has had, after all, a pretty sensible and peaceful life, by comparison." This effect is described by Henri Bergson and practiced by such artists as Charlie Chaplin and Al Capp. Writing about Chaplin, Capp observes: "The utter defeat of Chaplin as a lover made our own unsatisfactory romances seem less humiliating. Nothing that ever happened to any of us could possibly be as disappointing as what always happened to him. We are such a hell of a lot better than he is that he has made us feel secure and protected and we laugh."[1]

Thurber once stated that "Humor is a kind of emotional chaos told about calmly and quietly in retrospect," and this technique of reminiscence gives a perspective that eases the mind by rendering painful experience comic. "The sharp edges of old reticences are softened . . . by the passing of time—a man does not pull the pillow over his head when he wakes in the morning because he suddenly remembers some awful thing that happened to him fifteen or twenty years ago," observed Thurber, "but the confusions and the panics of last year and the year before are too close for contentment. Until a man can quit talking loudly to himself in order to shout down the memories of blunderings and gropings, he is in no shape for the painstaking examination of distress and the careful ordering of event so necessary to a calm and balanced exposition of what, exactly, was the matter." But when such experience can be seen dispassionately and humorously, a comic catharsis is achieved. In Thurber's words, "The things we laugh at are awful while they are going on, but get funny when we look back. And other people laugh because they've been through it too. The closest thing to humor is tragedy."[2]

In effect many of Thurber's pieces illustrate the theme that man's reason is unable to save him from confusion and chaos. He therefore portrayed man not as heroic in the traditional sense but as prey to bafflement and humiliation. There was some dignity in being frustrated by Life with its dome of many-colored glass, but not by a Mixmaster. A man can maintain his pride when the universe falls around his head but not when he cannot get the chains off his car. Thurber handled minor and not major catastrophe and explained that "His gestures are the ludicrous reflexes of the maladjusted; his repose is the momentary inertia of the nonplussed. . . . He talks largely about small matters and smally about great affairs." Thurber commented that authors of such pieces have a genius for getting into minor difficulties. "To call such persons 'humorists,' a loose-fitting and ugly word, is to miss the nature of their dilemma and the dilemma of their nature. The little wheels of their invention are set in motion by the damp hand of melancholy." "This type of writing," he explained, "is not a joyous form of self-expression but the manifestation of a twitchiness at once cosmic and mundane." Thurber usually let the cosmic pass and concentrated on the innumerable little episodes of everyday life in which man is bewildered or trapped by reality. "I think humor is the best that lies closest to the familiar which is humiliating, distressing, even tragic," he stated.[3]

Some of Thurber's humor, especially his early work, resembles Robert Benchley's but without being imitative. *My Ten Years in a Quandary*—the title of one of Benchley's books—sounds rather like *My Life and Hard Times* in its narrative of predicament, and Walter Blair points out that both authors are victimized by inanimate things and ruined by tremendous trifles. J. Bryan III calls Benchley's humor a study in professional frustration: "He sees himself . . . not the master of high comedy, but the victim of low tragedy. King Lear loses a throne; Benchley loses a filling. Romeo breaks his heart; Benchley breaks his shoelace. They are annihilated; he is humiliated. His whole life has been spent as a dupe of the total depravity of inanimate things." This statement would be equally accurate if applied to many of Thurber's writings. Several years after Thurber defined humor as "emotional chaos told about calmly and quietly in retrospect," Mr. Bryan explained Benchley's humor in almost identical terms: "A Benchley short is simply the refinement of a Benchley humiliation. It is commotion recollected in tranquillity. Yesterday's tragic ineffectuality has become today's comic effect."[4]

The chronicling of dilemma is only one aspect of Thurber's versatile writing, but it is prominent and provocative. Marriage and disparity between the sexes is a particularly fertile ground for producing irritations, anxieties, and embarrassment, especially at the expense of the male, whose tendency toward bewilderment and perplexity allows his personality to be dominated by his more confident spouse.

III *Menace ex Machina*

Besides their wives, Thurber's men have to contend with the hazards of the machine age. They are especially baffled by the mysteries of the automobile, which their wives drive with annoying competence. Thurber reported that "the automobile and I were never in tune with each other. There was a fundamental incompatibility between us that amounted at times to chemical repulsion." His battle with machines is more than a result of the innate cussedness of inanimate objects, for the machine seems to have a conscious malignancy: "I have felt the headlights of an automobile following me the way the eyes of a cat follow the ominous activities of a neighbor's dog." After a number of embarrassing experiences with cars, Thurber developed a theory about his. "The thing possessed, I decided, a certain antic intelligence, akin to that of a six-month-old poodle. . . . Whenever I tried to put chains on a tire, the car would maliciously wrap them around a rear axle. If I parked it ten feet from a fire plug and went into a store, it would be only five feet from the plug when I came out. If it saw a nail in the road, the car would swerve and pick the nail up." Similarly, the automobile baffled almost every Thurber male who encountered one, from Grandfather Fisher with the electric runabout that he drove as if it were an untamed horse, through the old Reo belonging to Thurber's father, which had to be pushed until it was finally smashed by a streetcar, down to Walter Mitty, Tommy Trinway, and Mr. Pendly with the Poindexter, not to mention Olympy Sementzoff, a French-speaking Russian to whom Thurber attempted to teach driving in an incredible bi-lingual jaunt (reminiscent of the Keystone Kops) along the shore road at Antibes. Thurber concluded that "Neither the motor car nor myself would greatly mourn if one of us were suddenly extinguished."

Though the automobile seems to be the peculiar nemesis of Thurber's men, his women too are wary of technology. His mother's greatest dread was the Victrola, which she thought might blow up; and his grandmother feared that electricity leaked through the house from empty wall sockets. Thurber himself (in his fictional role) was afraid to let some needles run down the sink drain because they might cause a short circuit. "I know nothing about electricity and I don't want to have it explained to me," he wrote. Most of his characters are equally inept. One hypothetical husband tried to cook a simple meal for himself only to get panic stricken when entangled in a confusion of unfamiliar gadgets and utensils, the uses of which perplexed him so much that he almost tried to open a can of peaches with a Mixmaster. "Every person carries on his consciousness the old scar, or the fresh wound, of some harrowing misadventure with a contraption of some sort"; and man must display "a natural caution in a world made up of gadgets that whir and whine and whiz and shriek and sometimes explode."

Clearly Thurber did not believe that mankind will be saved by building better mousetraps. In fact, it is man who is trapped; "trapped inside an inadequate animal body, trapped within the poor limitations of the human spirit." This modern age has its particular hazards, for man faces the danger of losing his identity in a world of ever-growing complexity—the intricacies of science, the labyrinths of red tape, the omnipresent forms that must be filled out and regulations that must be followed—at the same time that his individuality is shrinking into a statistic.

Thurber was quite sensitive to this predicament, and he felt at times persecuted by impersonal forces like those in the nightmarish fiction of Kafka. To the state of Connecticut, he was merely No. 3902090, the operator of a motor vehicle; and he pictured the state as laying wary traps to catch him making a mistake in renewing his driver's license. Once he created a mental image of Connecticut as "a fat gentleman with thinning hair and octagonal glasses whom no motorist has ever heard of or ever seen, a Goebbels of red tape, a Göring for discipline." Similarly he visualized one Rudwooll Y. Peffifoss, an official of the Connecticut Telephone Company, who took a fiendish glee in changing simple numbers like 905 Ring 4 to Pussymeister W-7 Oh 8 Oh 9 6 J-4.

Far from engaging in traditional heroics, Thurber said that he and his characters were preoccupied with the smaller enormities of life and overwhelmed by minor tyrannies and persecutions. The paraphrase of Wordsworth's "emotion recollected in tranquillity" particularly fits his burlesque autobiography, *My Life and Hard Times*, which recounts a series of emotionally chaotic events that are usually humiliating and sometimes border on the disastrous. This book is a study in anticlimax, a series of variations on the theme of much ado about nothing. In most chapters there is some great commotion over fears that prove groundless. Each episode develops a sequence of chain-reaction misunderstandings building up to a climax of bedlam. Thus, when the army cot on which Thurber was sleeping tipped over on top of him, his mother thought that the heavy headboard of the old wooden bed in which her husband was sleeping in the attic that night (to be away where he could think) had crashed down on his head and killed him. At the same time, Briggs Beall, a visiting cousin who had the nightly dread that he would suffocate in his sleep, thought his fears were realized, poured a glass of camphor over himself, and smashed the windowpane to get fresh air. The rest of the family tried frantically to force open the attic door and rush to the aid of the supposedly dying man. In the uproar, the family dog jumped for Briggs and had to be forcibly restrained. When Thurber's father at last descended safe and sound from the attic, "The situation was finally put together like a gigantic jigsaw puzzle."

In most of the chapters of *My Life and Hard Times*, the characters have lurking fears and quickly jump to the conclusion that they are realized. The ensuing chaos more than vindicates them. The supreme example is the day the dam broke. Actually East Columbus escaped the worst of the 1913 Ohio flood, but utter confusion broke out when the town *thought* the dam had broken. Within a few moments thousands of people, stricken with "fine despair and grotesque desperation," were racing for the hills. The chapter, a comic study in mass hysteria, shows that few persons are capable of rational behavior in moments of fearful crisis; for "some of the most dignified, staid, cynical, and clear-thinking men" gave way to panic. The supposed break of the dam was a leveling event; people making their little boasts and gestures all succumbed to the general alarm, and the proud and pompous outran many of their fellow citizens.

In this and other chapters. Thurber deflated self-esteem, continually belittling his figures and recounting the family adventures in a mock-heroic manner. He remarked that, while many autobiographers describe earthquakes and other spectacular incidents they had experienced, he was unable to do so because his family was never in an earthquake, though they went through a number of things in Columbus that were a great deal like earthquakes. Inevitably the episodes created by the eccentricities or even by the normal activities of the Thurbers ended up in humiliating bedlam. There is the comic apprehension of a peculiar fate visiting the family, to whom things happened in a way that they never did to anybody else. Great-uncle Zenas was the only person in history to die of the chestnut-tree blight. Thurber himself got into trouble because he was the only student at college who could never see through a microscope. In particular the Thurbers had a knack for employing erratic servants. There was Dora Gedd, who shot at a man in her room; Juanemma Kramer, who was remarkably susceptible to hypnosis; Vashti, who thought she was being wooed by an imaginary stepfather; Mrs. Doody, who thought Mr. Thurber was the Antichrist and went after him with a bread knife; and Edda Millmoss, who during a dinner party accused Mr. Thurber of having done her out of her rights to the land under Trinity Church in New York.

My Life and Hard Times and many of Thurber's other reminiscences and personal essays are anything but factual autobiography. One has only to read *The Thurber Album* to see that most of the characterizations in the earlier work, especially that of the half-insane grandfather, are completely fictitious. Thurber even altered names in his comic autobiography, calling his brothers Roy and Herman instead of their actual names, William and Robert. E. B. White remarked that, "James Thurber never used to claim that his memories were wholly factual. . . . It is easy to believe the Thurber household was an unusually active one, but surely the most tempestuous and busy spot in the whole place was the mind of little Jamie."[5] Thurber explained: "Historicity lies so close to legend in my world that I often walk with one foot in each area, with side trips, or so my critics declare, into fantasy. That is because of my unenviable talent for stumbling from one confusion into another. . . . Looking back from this distance I can't always distinguish between reality and the dream."

IV *The Real Thurber*

As he appears in his writings, Thurber often has many of the fears, hesitations, neuroses, and fragmentation of character found in numerous contemporary writers and/or their literary creations.

Not only is he unsure of his identity, but people even mistake his name for Thurberg, Thumber, Thurl, Ferber, Thorber, Thalberg, Thurman, and Jane Thurber. But we must remember that this picture of Thurber is itself a literary creation like the Mark Twain persona or the incompetent Geoffrey whom Chaucer presents in his poetry. This distinction is borne out by Thurber's drawings; for the typical man in his pictures—diminutive, bald, and pince-nezed—bears no resemblance at all to Thurber, even when appearing in illustrations for pieces in which Thurber is the central character. Thurber was six foot, one and a half inches tall, with a short, cropped mustache and a thick head of often unruly hair. James E. Pollard noted his youthful look and erect carriage at sixty-six.

Despite the frustrations suffered by many Thurber characters, most of his audience do not find the bulk of his work depressing. Though he sometimes wrote about distressing events, he explained that "You have to enjoy humorous writing while you're doing it. ... You can't be mad, or bitter, or irate. If you are it will be no good."[6] Those modern artists who take themselves too seriously may become too closely involved in their dilemmas to see themselves in humorous perspective and maintain a wholeness and equilibrium. "I can't remember any humor in old Scott Fitzgerald," observed Thurber despite his admiration for *The Great Gatsby.* "Humor would have saved him. It seems to me the great novelists have humor in them, even if it isn't predominant. The Russians had it; Gogol had it, and Dostoevsky. It seems to me Fitzgerald strangled humor because he was caught in the romantic tradition."[7] Actually Fitzgerald's writings reveal a fair amount of humor. More accurately, Thurber was referring to what Fitzgerald called his habit of taking things hard, so that at the last (as he observed during his crack-up) he became identified with the objects of his horror or compassion.

Consequently, Thurber's reminiscences should not be read as straightforward accounts, and he should not be identified with the frustrated people of his fiction. George Plimpton and Max Steele, who interviewed him for *The Paris Review,* remarked

> After years of delighting in the shy, trapped little man in the Thurber cartoons and the confused and bewildered man who has fumbled in and out of some of the funniest books written in this century, we, perhaps like many readers, were expecting to find the same frightened little man in person. Not at all. Thurber by his firm handgrasp and confident voice and by the way he lowered himself into his chair gave the impression of outward calmness and assurance.[8]

Wolcott Gibbs wrote of Thurber:

> I have been familiar with his outward presence for something like a
> quarter of a century, and the idea that he would be helpless in the
> face of any known social situation seems very humorous to me.
> There have been times when I thought that he dealt a little more
> erratically with life than most of the men I know, but I have
> certainly never seen him defeated, or even perceptibly disconcerted
> by it. The essence of Mitty and Monroe is that they are, so to
> speak, driven underground by more confident personalities; the
> essence of Thurber is such that in any real contest of personalities
> everybody else would be well advised to take to the hills.[9]

Henry Brandon found that "Thurber's gaunt figure and his flat,
commanding voice were a little intimidating at first. This was not
the 'little-man-what-now' type trapped between the 'hard covers'
of life, this was a man who knew what he wanted, who had
learned and obviously succeeded in overcoming many vicissitudes
of life."[10] But Brandon, like almost everyone who interviewed
Thurber, spoke of his being gracious and entertaining and of his
uncanny ability to put people at ease. Even his blindness was no
obstacle; W. J. Weatherby noted that "His eyes did not look blind
behind his glasses, they had not got that look of eyes washed in
milk that many blind people's have, and he found his whisky and
his cigarettes unerringly. . . ."[11] Even when blind, he welcomed
people with "I'm glad to see you."

A probable though not so obvious inspiration for some of Thurber's fictional characters was *The New Yorker*'s editor Harold Ross
in his "God how I pity me" phases. Thurber noted Ross's "monu-
mentally magnified trivialities" and called him "the Great Multi-
plier of Menace," who—despite his gusty extroversion—spent a
great deal of time worrying about commas, sex, and other editorial
nightmares; was afraid to fire people; hated to be seen in the ele-
vator; and tried to sneak unobserved to the men's room. But
essentially the middle-aged man on the flying trapeze is a product
of the artistic imagination.

Still, Thurber's childhood and undergraduate days may have
furnished some background for the self-conscious, nervous characters of his pictures and prose. Blinded in one eye in a childhood
accident, he fell behind in school, had to avoid active sports, and
became rather withdrawn and introspective. His sixth-grade
teacher, Miss McElvaine, recalled that he was quiet, studious, and
so nervous that "When I call on him to recite and he stands on
his feet, his adam's apple rolls around so wildly that he can hardly
speak."[12] A skinny, gangling boy with thick-lensed, steel-rimmed

glasses and bushy hair pasted down like Woodrow Wilson's, he was not very imposing, though he later became quite distinguished looking. By 1913, he had overcome his nervousness sufficiently to become president of his high school senior class; but, when he entered Ohio State University in the fall of that year, his myopic, preoccupied look, sheep-dog haircut, and shy deportment caused him to be overlooked by his fellow students; and he shambled around the campus in a rather forlorn manner. Since he lived at home, some miles from the university, he got to know few of the students until he became friends with Elliott Nugent—star actor in the dramatic society, fraternity man, and president of the junior class—who took him in hand, spruced him up a bit, and drew him into campus activities.

Thurber was sufficiently self-reliant and soon became an important person on campus in his own right. When he returned to Columbus after World War I to work as a reporter for the *Dispatch,* he had a great many friends, several of whom became well-known writers. Thurber was an accomplished journalist but had great frustration getting started as a more creative writer. His early efforts were rejected, an attempted novel was abortive; he was in his early thirties before he joined *The New Yorker.* Not until several years after that did he begin to achieve a literary reputation.

Thurber endured enough hardships in his life to have crushed a person of less tenacity and courage. In 1940, at the height of his career, his remaining eye began to lose its sight. During 1940-41, he underwent five operations for cataract and trachoma. For some months he was almost totally blind, with only about one-fiftieth vision in his right eye. Despite temporary improvement, his eye required subsequent operations and, at best, had little more than threshold vision. By 1946, he could see shapes but not faces; and, for practical purposes, he was blind for the last fifteen years of his life, though he could still see "a soft diffusion of light." Other illnesses plagued him too. Between 1941 and 1956, he had by his count "cataract, glaucoma, sympathetic ophthalmia, pneumonia, ruptured appendix, peritonitis, and toxic thyroid."

Despite incredible handicaps ("What a writer needs is handicaps," he said), his literary output did not diminish. Finding that "the imagination doesn't go blind," he taught himself new methods of writing and brought out more books in his last ten years than in any other decade. He refused to become an invalid and continued to lead an active life, going to the theater, vacationing in Bermuda, traveling frequently to Europe, and even acting on Broadway. Kenneth MacLean reported that "In spite of fortune, Thurber's spirits are magnificent ."[13] Like some of Ellen Glasgow's characters (Miss Glasgow was an ardent Thurber enthusiast), Thurber managed to "live gallantly without the light," literally as well as metaphorically. W. J. Weatherby found him basically as pessimistic as Faulkner: "And in conversation what he says is often deeply gloomy and yet—like his work—is expressed with such verve and pell-mell vitality that the final impression is optimistic, of a man engaged in life to the hilt, whose desperation comes from seeing so many missed opportunities for living."[14] As for his sight, he wrote in 1950: "My one-eighth vision happily obscures sad and ungainly sights, leaving only the vivid and the radiant, some of whom are my friends and neighbors. My pleasures are clean and simple. I like to sit around at night holding untenable positions against logical and expert assault, playing the match game, listening to ball games on the radio, and romping with my wife and daughter and our female French poodle who is nine but doesn't look a day over five."

In his later work, Thurber stopped using the bewildered little man, just as Chaplin gave up his tramp role. No longer a stumble-footed, repressed incompetent, Thurber's protagonist became a sardonic and caustic cosmopolitan. As listener and critic, he is witty and given to aphoristic wisecracks as defense against a tenacious *Weltanschauung*. Halfway between essays and short stories, many of the later writings are conversation pieces, told in the first person by a narrator who is either nameless or is supposed to be Thurber himself. Whoever he is, his tone and manner are similar. Like the earlier protagonist, he is not really the author but another person. This one is much closer to Thurber, though he is not blind and is a good deal more irascible. No longer frustrated by gadgetry or by his spouse, he has to survive various social and political imbecilities. The conversation pieces usually occur at a party or bar, where unacquainted table hoppers insist on telling the story of their life or where the narrator and others sit down and talk over the state of the world, finding some gallows humor from man's putting his neck in the noose, and hoping that the next time they discuss the subject it won't be at an autopsy or a wake. Liquor is ever present as an anesthetic against the intrusions of sound and folly. The later protagonist does not have to cope with a sense of inferiority; his troubles are more external—harassment by visitors, bad jokes, and stale situations—and he drinks to deaden the familiar dialogue. An old pro, he is automatically on guard and is good— almost too good—at verbal infighting. With an aging man's experience and knowledge of human nature, he has the exasperation of a person who has been through it all before and who needles his conversationalist while the latter doesn't know what is happening to him. His wife is now the one who is long-suffering; her attitude is usually, "Oh God, here we go again."

V *The Nature of Man*

One reason for the frustrations of his characters is Thurber's view of human nature. "Humorists of 100 years ago thought that reason was basic," commented John Gerber. "Today humorists are saying a man of reason is a man of pretense."[15] Walter Blair makes essentially the same point in *Horse Sense in American Humor*, reducing reason to a reliance upon common sense and homespun logic. Taking Thurber by contrast as the best representative of modern humor, Mr. Blair notes, somewhat unfavorably, that Thurber gives a very unflattering picture of man, baffled and even terrified by the perplexities of life from which he is incapable of extricating himself through the exercise of his rational powers.

In presenting his picture of man, Thurber was reacting against the doctrine of progress and human self-sufficiency, which reached a peak in the nineteenth century. By contrast we find in Thurber a revolt from reason and from the glorification of man. This revolt is rather widespread in the twentieth century; for the theories of Freud, the horrors of total war, totalitarian atrocities, scientific developments, the growing complexity of mass civilization, and the widespread loss of faith in religious or moral certainties have done much to weaken the belief in progress that was held so confidently by many people of earlier generations. Their optimism has proved to be too facile, and it appears that reason alone is inadequate to keep man from acting irrationally. On the other hand, Thurber did not belong in the ranks of futilitarians who see life as a hopeless blunder. A prey neither to bland optimism nor to a dour and somber pessimism, Thurber was acutely aware of the perversity in man's nature. He also knew that people can be admirable and wonderful in many ways; and the fact that man is capable at all of love and aspiration indicates that he is not utterly damned.

Thurber traced part of his own disillusionment and growing awareness of the duality of man's nature in an essay about Doc Marlowe, one of his youthful heroes. Marlowe, a medicine-show man, claimed to have been an adventurer in the Far West; and he looked the part, being six foot, four inches tall with long hair and a drooping mustache like that of General Custer. When Thurber was a boy, Doc Marlowe told him stories of Indian warfare and showed him his remarkable collection of Indian relics and six-shooters. Thurber reported that at first Marlowe represented the

Wild West to him, and there was nobody he admired so much. But on closer intimacy, Thurber found that Doc cheated at gambling with marked cards and crooked dice. The boy was outraged, but Doc seemed merely to enjoy his indignation. It turned out that Doc would not scruple at swindling people who were fond of him, such as the Hardmans, to whom he fraudulently sold an old wreck of an automobile especially doctored up for the occasion. When he heard how the car broke down, leaving the Hardmans with a piece of junk, Doc simply laughed and invited Thurber to play cards with him. "Not with a cheater like you!" the boy shouted in bitter disillusionment. On his deathbed, Doc Marlowe bequeathed to Thurber a two-headed quarter and chuckled the advice, "Never let the other fella call the turn, Jimmy, my boy." After his death, it even turned out that all of Doc's tales of adventure in the Far West were lies and that he had been born in Brooklyn.

But Doc always had a twinkle in his eye and a chuckle in his voice, and he was often generous to people. Occasionally, he used the two-headed quarter to win money from Thurber, but he befriended the boy and once gave him a whole dollar to buy fireworks on the Fourth of July. Even so, Thurber's hero worship changed to disillusionment and anger when he learned of Doc's dishonesty. "For a long time I didn't like to think about it, or about Doc Marlowe, but I do now," he wrote. For with maturity, he came to understand both sides of man's nature and to sympathize with his dilemma. This ambivalence furnishes the subject for artistic tension; as Thurber told Henry Brandon in 1958, "the dichotomy of the very nature of our species . . . makes it interesting and also terrifying."[16]

Thurber was neither complacent nor despairing about the human condition. He stated, in fact, that he was "intensely dedicated to opposing the perilous wrongs and injustices of this bad earth. . . ." Though aware that man will not attain perfection, he felt that man can and must be better than he is. Because Thurber was a disillusioned idealist who still held to his ideals, he satirized human follies and crimes with a moral indignation of almost Swiftian intensity.

In one fantasy a lemming being interviewed by a Thurberian scientist calls mankind "murderous, maladjusted, maleficent, malicious and muffle-headed." "You kill, you mangle, you torture, you imprison, you starve each other," says the lemming. "I know that you are cruel, cunning and carnivorous, sly, sensual and selfish, greedy, gullible and guileful—" The scientist agrees. "You could go on all night like that," he says, "listing our sins and our shames." Meanwhile, he has been studying lemmings and knows all about them except why they all rush down to the sea and drown themselves. "How curious," the lemming replies. "The one thing I don't understand is why you humans don't." Likewise, when a Thurber dinosaur is insulted by a proud, arrogant human, the beast replies, "There are worse things than being extinct, and one of them is being you."

It is man's glorification of himself as a supreme and rational being which particularly angered Thurber. Man has reason, yes, but his perversion of it makes him worse than the dumb animals, whose instincts may sometimes lead them to kill yet who are incapable of conscious malevolence. In this view Thurber is like Mark Twain or Swift's Houyhnhnm master, who "looked upon us as a sort of animals to whose share, by what accident he could not conjecture, some small pittance of reason had fallen, whereof we made no other use than by its assistance to aggravate our natural corruptions, and to acquire new ones which nature had not given us." For Thurber as for Swift, man's deification of reason is largely the basis of evil; and both conclude that abstract reasoning is inferior to instinct. Unimpressed by man's pretensions, Thurber wrote: "Abstract reasoning, in itself, has not benefited Man so much as instinct has benefited the lower animals. In moving into the alien and complicated sphere of Thought and Imagination he has become the least well-adjusted of all creatures on the earth and, hence, the most bewildered."[17]

In denying the supreme efficacy of reason, Thurber was not entirely unlike the humorists of the last century, for they too objected to the analytics of the abstract intellect. While criticizing the misuse of reason, Thurber frequently championed common sense, though it too could not always prevent confusion and dilemma. Rather than human reason, Thurber admired the instinctive sense of the dogs and other animals that appear in his pages: "It may be the finer mysteries of life and death can be comprehended only through pure instinct; the cat, for example, appears to Know. . . . Man, on the other hand, is surely further away from the Answer than any other animal this side of the ladybug. His mistaken selection of reasoning as an instrument of perception has put him into a fine quandary."[18]

Thus Thurber found that he could not go along with the sanguine premises of the late Dr. Frederick Tilney, the eminent brain specialist, who, reporting that man is using only one-fourth of his brain cells, believed that, when man begins to use them all, "he will become wise enough to put an end to wars, depressions, recessions, and allied evils." On the contrary, Thurber asked in "Footnote on the Future" (1940),

What . . . is to keep Man from becoming four times as ornery, four times as sly and crafty, four times as full of dovilishly ingenious devices for the extinction of his species? In the history of mankind the increase of no kind of power has, so far as I can find out, ever moved naturally and inevitably in the direction of the benign. It has, as a matter of fact, almost always tended in the direction of the malignant. . . . This tendency, it seems to me, would be especially true of the power of the mind, since it is that very power which is behind all the deviltry Man is now up to and always has been up to . . . Man, as pacifist and economist, has gone steadily from bad to worse with the development of his brain power through the ages.

When Thurber wrote these statements, World War II had broken out in Europe. This was the climax produced by man's supposed rationality. Thurber observed in 1939 that man lacks even the sense to preserve his species; that, while the lower social animals cooperate constructively, man often does so for destruction. In 1961, he still echoed this statement. Reading that dolphins may in some respects have superior mental powers, he felt that they, "all gaiety, charm, and intelligence . . . might one day come out of the boundless deep and show us how a world can be run by creatures dedicated not to the destruction of their species but to its preservation."

Relying on their instinct, the animals struggle to keep alive. Most of them are incapable of hatred; and, according to W. C. Allee, whom Thurber quoted, they hardly ever participate in group warfare. Thurber therefore found it unfortunate that man "developed Reason, Thought, and Imagination, qualities which would get the smartest group of rabbits or orioles in the world into inextricable trouble overnight." In 1958, he told Henry Brandon, "I often think it would be fine if the French poodles would take over the world because they've certainly been more intelligent in the last few years than the human being. . . . My old poodle, who died at 17, had genuine comic sense. . . . But, as I say, when I spoke to the poodle about her species taking over, she said: 'The hell with it!' They don't want to get mixed up in it."[19] Here again Thurber resembles Swift, who considered "human understanding below the sagacity of a common hound, who has judgment enough to distinguish and follow the cry of the ablest dog in the pack, without being ever mistaken."

Man, on the other hand, took to following the war lords, who exploited the resources of science for torture, genocide, and carnage. After the war, Justice Robert Jackson at the Nürnberg trials observed: "It is one of the paradoxes of our time that modern society needs to fear . . . only the educated man. The primitive peoples of the earth constitute no menace. The most serious crimes against civilization can be committed only by educated and technically competent people."[20]

This statement is similar to Thurber's charge, but it is not wholly accurate because the uneducated man is not necessarily the primitive one. Mobs or pressure groups of ignorant people in society can dominate and enslave the educated, but the technology of the latter is needed for modern scientific warfare. Thurber probably would have made this qualification also, for he recognized that the excesses either of intellectualism or of militant and wilful ignorance can be equally dangerous. He therefore championed learning but deplored the abuse of it. He considered that man's intellect is not wholly a liability; it has, after all, produced Art, "the one achievement of Man which has made the long trip up from all fours seem well advised."[21] Unfortunately, "Human Dignity has gleamed only now and then and here and there, in lonely splendor, throughout the ages, a hope of the better man, never an achievement of the majority."[22] And with the tragedy of World War II beginning, Thurber felt that "The dignity of Man and the Divine Destiny of Man are two things which it is at the moment impossible for me to accept with whole-hearted enthusiasm."[23]

Thus he wrote in 1939 that he was beset with the temporary doubt that life has any meaning and with the suspicion that the power moving the world is purposeless. When he considered Hitler and Chamberlain, he would conclude that "there can be no God watching over the sorrowful and sinister scene, these menacing and meaningless animals." But Thurber never attacked or abused religion; and even in 1939 he would have believed if he could. He commented that, if it is hard to Believe, it is just as hard, as Browning's Bishop Blougram points out to the cynical Mr. Gigadibs, to "guard our unbelief." "There is always Browning's 'grand Perhaps,'" he admitted. "Why not," asks Blougram, "'the Way, the Truth, the Life'?" To which Thurber replied, "Why not indeed? 'It is all right with me,' I say over my wine. But what is all this fear of and opposition to Oblivion? What is the matter with the soft Darkness, the Dreamless Sleep?"[24]

Nevertheless, Thurber continued his work. When the rest of the lemmings (in a later Thurber fable) plunged hysterically into the sea, one solitary scholarly lemming remained behind; and, although he tore up what he had written through the years about his species, he did not surrender but started his studies all over again. "Unfortunately, I have never been able to maintain a consistent attitude toward life or reality or toward anything else," Thurber has written. "My attitudes change with the years, sometimes with the hours."[25] And so he managed to overcome extreme pessimism and to accept a more affirmative outlook in which the tragic elements of life are lightened by love and laughter and by the ideals for which men still strive. "Human dignity, the humorist believes, is not only silly but a little sad," he wrote. "So are dreams and conventions and illusions. The fine brave fragile stuff that men live by. They look so swell, and go to pieces so easily."[26] Even though they do sometimes go to pieces, they are still fine and brave; and Thurber believed in them.

One of the finest fables, "The Moth and the Star," tells of a young and impressionable moth who yearned for a certain star and kept flying toward it in spite of the admonitions of his parents and relatives and despite the fact that the star was four and one-third light years away. "He never did reach the star, but he went right on trying, night after night, and when he was a very, very old moth he began to think he really had reached the star and he went around saying so. This gave him a deep and lasting pleasure, and he lived to a great old age. His parents and his brothers and his sisters had all been burned to death [against various lamps] when they were quite young."

VI *Thurber and Religion*

The difficulties with his vision that left Thurber increasingly blind after 1940 seem, after an initial breakdown, to have tempered him and given him renewed patience and calmness. He commented that blindness is a challenge, not a handicap; and he managed to continue writing and (for a time) drawing in spite of obstacles. "There must be an amiable God," he said in 1943, "who had it in mind for me to do these drawings and is not opposed to them." But in a television appearance in June, 1959, he said that we cannot count on miracles for medical cures. Later on this same program, Thurber remarked that there must be a God to make Bosman's Potto and the human being. In his later work he nowhere questioned the existence of a deity; in fact, he made numerous references to God and His providence, though perhaps like Ross, he had "two gods, Upper Case and lower case."

Named for a Methodist minister and brought up in a fairly conservative religious environment (his grandfather Fisher once interrupted a sermon to inform the minister, "I go to church to hear the Word of God, not the word of Emerson"), Thurber seems to have retained a religious if not a doctrinal attitude. He recalled that there was a cartoon submitted to *The New Yorker* "whose central figures were two divinity students, their eyes bright with recognition, walking toward each other in Grand Central Station with outstretched hands, above the caption 'Well, Judas Priest!' I substitute the name for that of the deity because I share Ross's deep conviction that major blasphemies have no place in comedy." Once he wrote that he wished to live within reasonable distance of "a grocery, a drugstore, a church, a library, and a movie house"; and a Methodist service was held at his funeral.

Thurber therefore had no quarrel with God but only with men who claim to be glorious, if not divine, and then commit appalling atrocities and depravities. In reply to a questionnaire from *The Humanist*, Thurber wrote in 1951 that "naturalistic philosophy must be a little bit like naturalistic religion; or an effort to make a philosophy out of the wrong materials. I don't see how a man can be lifted up by any system of thought that does not have some idea of super in it rather than sub. . . . The perfect philosophy, I should think, might do well to get away from a word like 'humanism,' which is ⅝ths human."[27]

In effect, Thurber recognized original sin, though he did not describe it in theological terms. "The Christian insight into the nature of sin is not the monopoly of Christian theologians. It is discerned by many sharp students of contemporary culture, like James Thurber," wrote a religious scholar.[28] This sin is not an inheritance from the mythical scene in Eden but an innate imperfection of man (recognized by theologians and psychologists alike); whose very mortality—making him prisoner to pain, death, hunger, and desires—creates fears, hatreds, and aggressions that cannot always be controlled. The deadliest sin of all in the Christian catalogue is pride, as shown by thinkers who consider man supreme master of his fate and potential ruler of the universe. Hence Thurber said that:

> If I have run down the human species, it was not altogether unintentional. . . . it has occurred to me that Man's arrogance and aggression arises from a false feeling of transcendency, and that he will not get anywhere until he realizes, in all humility, that he is just another of God's creatures, less kindly than Dog, possessed of less dignity than Swan, and incapable of becoming as magnificent an angel as Black Panther. I have grown a little tired of the capitalization of Man, his easy assumption of a dignity more apparent than real, and his faith in a high destiny for which he is not fitted by his long and bloody history. The most frightening study of mankind is Man.[29]

Similarly Swift observed, "how diminutive, contemptible, and helpless an animal was man in his own nature: . . . how much he was excelled by one creature in strength, by another in speed, by a third in foresight, by a fourth in industry."

Man is, however, one of God's creatures; and Thurber had a compassionate sympathy for him as well as anger at his pride and perversity. "I'll tell you something," he said, "that is hard to believe when we think of all the cruelty and selfishness in the world. Ten men in the United States and one in England, strangers to me, have offered me an eye in the belief that an eye could help me." He believed that "The human species is both horrible and wonderful. Occasionally, I get very mad at human beings, but there's nothing you can do about it. I like people and hate them at the same time. I wouldn't draw them in cartoons, .. I didn't think they were horrible, and I wouldn't write about them if I didn't think they were wonderful."[30] In view of this remark, it is perhaps significant that Thurber considered himself primarily a writer and only casually a cartoonist.

In the summer of 1941, Thurber asked Mark Van Doren whether his blindness "was not a punishment for the kind of writing he had done. 'I have done nothing,' he said, 'but make fun of weakness and folly; wisdom, strength, goodness have never been my subjects as they ought to be for anybody—as they are for you. I have been pitiless, trivial, destructive. And now this trouble comes.'" Van Doren replied that the language of satirists is the reverse language of scorn. A few months later Thurber wrote him that he was "all straightened out again." Van Doren stated that Thurber "has never pitied himself for being blind, though his rages—terrible, fantastic—could be traced to that condition. In my own opinion they are a satirist's indignations: savage, like Swift's, and with as deep a source. These rages end as suddenly as they begin, and a great sweetness follows. Thurber is tiger, then is turtle dove."[31]

Despite his occasional bursts of temper, many writers have paid tribute to Thurber's gift for friendship. Lewis Gannett said that he "had a vast capacity for affection," and E. B. White wrote of "the intensity of his interest in others and his sympathy for their dilemmas...." David Holloway called him a humorist "who believed so strongly in human beings and based his humor in his faith in them...." And Henry Brandon found that "Thurber's real secret...is a warm heart and an angry mind."[32]

Sometimes his satire sounds as sweeping as Mark Twain's on "the damned human race"; but, if so, his anger came not from misanthropy but from his awareness of man's inhumanity to man. Ronald Searle said on the BBC (British Broadcasting Corporation) that "Thurber was no kindly old charmer, and his exasperation and occasional bitterness arose more out of concern for humans than out of his dislike for them." Often a satirist as savage as Twain has far deeper affection for people than an idealist like Emerson, who glorified mankind in the abstract but did not care for individuals. "I like man, but not men," Emerson wrote, and his acquaintances spoke of his aloofness and incapacity for friendship. By contrast, both Twain and Thurber, while denouncing mankind in general, had a great fund of feeling for individuals. Praising his friend McNulty for his "delight in human beings," Thurber found it important that "McNulty's love of humanity was not expressed at a distance, from a platform," but in active personal relationships.

VII *Thurber and Intellectualism*

Thurber's anti-rationalism should not be confused with anti-intellectualism except in the sense that nineteenth-century romantics objected to the dry logic of their predecessors. Of course, Thurber disliked intellectual arrogance and exhibitionism. Such display is a form of snobbery which has nothing to do with genuine intelligence and learning, and too often it takes the form of contempt for those whose opinions are uncongenial. "An intellectual hatred is the worst," wrote Yeats.

Despite his reputation for whimsy, Thurber was very much an advocate of logic and clear thinking. He intensely disliked being tagged with coy labels and protested, "How anyone can be zany and an intellectual, I don't know." To one interviewer he said, "I'm laying in wait for the next person that calls me elfin. If it's a woman, I'll walk out of the room. If it's a man, I'll propose to kick him to death."[33] Apparently he missed the column in which Ben Hayes called him a pixie. Clifton Fadiman said on the BBC, "I would think of Jim as an intellectual; essentially his interest lay in ideas. It was astonishing how much reading he had digested in the course of his life." Thurber had an extensive knowledge of literature; his work is full of literary anecdotes and allusions, some of them quite recondite. With his insatiable curiosity, he did extensive research on radio soap operas, bloodhounds, police dogs, the Hall-Mills case, the Loch Ness Monster, Harold Ross, turn-of-the-century Columbus, and other topics that interested him. In the course of these investigations he exploded many popular misconceptions. He was quite well informed on a great variety of subjects but wore his learning lightly.

What he objected to was a reliance on mere facts and an overemphasis on abstractions resulting in an impersonal intellectualism. Like Swift, he championed learning and intelligence but criticized their abuse when they are wasted in absurd exercises or deified as ultimate ends in themselves. Some of his most delightful characters have little education and limited intellectual development—people like the Somentzoffs, various servants, Aunt Wilma and other Columbus kin. Sometimes they are eccentric; a balance is not always maintained between head and heart, and comedy results from their irrational behavior; but, if one faculty is to be off balance, it is better for the heart to be sound. "Sometimes I think (hell, always I think)," wrote Thurber, "that a world of friendliness would be better for what ails us than a world of surprising strokes of intelligence."

Thurber often showed the seemingly foolish confounding the wise. Aunt Margery Albright frequently defied the gloomy prognostics of doctors and cured herself and others by an application of common sense when these learned men had given up hope. Thurber's daughter once outwitted *The New Yorker,* which could not identify the cartoon hippopotamus that devoured Dr. Millmoss. His daughter, "who was 2 years old at the time, identified the beast immediately. 'That's a hippotomanus,' she said. *The New Yorker* was not so smart. They described the drawing for their files as follows: 'Woman with strange animal.' *The New Yorker* was nine years old at the time."

In particular the fairy tales, recalling the simplicity of some biblical stories and medieval fables, show the wise being confounded by the foolish. In *Many Moons,* the Jester and Princess Lenore had more insight than the Lord High Chamberlain, the Royal Wizard, and the Royal Mathematician. In *The Great Quillow,* Quillow the toymaker and storyteller has a position like that of the town jester and fool. He was not a member of the town council, who made fun of him and considered his work a rather pretty waste of time. But when the town was threatened by a wicked giant, Quillow was the only man who could outwit and destroy him. Similarly the rather simple-minded Golux in *The 13 Clocks* was the one who brought about the downfall of the wicked duke. Some rationalists might dismiss Thurber's fantasies as sentimental irrelevancies, but Edmund Wilson wrote that *The White Deer* "has the essence of poetry, and it ought to be read in preference to almost any best-selling novel."[34]

In the idealism of these fairy tales, Thurber certainly was not a cynic. Though some people, seeing mainly the melancholy in his work, concluded that he was a lugubrious if not a somber writer, he maintained a sane balance between the extremes of hopefulness and gloom. He considered himself essentially an optimist, and he appears as a man of faith, though not in conventional terms. During a discussion of *The Cocktail Party,* he challenged one controversialist's morbid interpretation.

"What makes you think, Codd, that the meaning of the play to you, or last night's dream, is sure to show a sinister significance?" I asked.

Charles stared at me in horror. "Great God!" he cried. "Are you looking for the bluebird of happiness? Do you think there are actually hinges on chimneys so the stars can get by? Do you believe Love will slay the dragon and live happily ever after?"

I was as cool as steel. "I believe in the sudden deep greenness of summer," I said. In the fifteen years I have known Charles, his skepticism has always shattered against my affirmation, and he knows it.

In point of fact Thurber wrote five fairy tales in which there are hinges on chimneys and Love does slay the dragon. His attitude is like that of the Golux in *The 13 Clocks:*

> "Half the places I have been to, never were. I make things up. Half the things I say are there cannot be found. When I was young I told a tale of buried gold, and men from leagues around dug in the woods. I dug myself."
> "But why?"
> "I thought the tale of treasure might be true."

The skeptic and man of mere facts would argue that the Golux himself could not be true. " 'There isn't any Golux. I have been to school and know,' the captain said." Nevertheless, Thurber's Golux is a fully rounded and describable character; the only Golux in the world, and not a mere device, platitude, or Golux *ex machina*.

If, as W. J. Weatherby found, Thurber's outlook could be as gloomy as Faulkner's, it must be remembered that Faulkner was also a superb humorist and that in his Nobel Prize address he spoke of mankind's ability not merely to survive but to prevail because man has an immortal soul capable of love, pride, and compassion. This answer is essentially Thurber's too. But in order to appreciate man's best qualities, both writers had to examine man's pathetic shortcomings and tragic flaws, to dramatize the dark side of human nature in order to bring forth the light.

Thus along with his lantern, Thurber carried the satirist's lance. As early as 1923, he challenged the creed of militant complacency and smiling sentimentality. "The greatest accomplishments, the most beautiful poems, the most important writings," he insisted, "have been done by men and women who suffered and out of whose vast pain or great unbelief or stupendous grief have come the fine things born of such conditions. Out of the cult of the content has come nothing and nobody.... There is a majesty in melancholy and a glory in sadness which the idiotic tutti-frutti vending of joy shouters cannot begin to aspire to." Thirty-eight years later in his dedicatory speech for Denny Hall he maintained that "The heart in which there is no fighting is as barren as the soul without conflict or the mind without anxiety or the spirit without struggle."

VIII   *The Decline of Comedy*

But Thurber did not confuse melancholy with morbidity nor tragedy with decadence. In the last years of his life he became increasingly disturbed at the "mass mental projection of gloom" and at the vogue of "modern morbid playwrights and sex novelists, who are more interested in the sordid corners of life than in the human heart." Too many of them, he found, indulged in impotent self-pity or found release in callous and gratuitous violence or perversion. The result was that "human stature, hope and humor," as well as the state of literature, are "dwindling and diminishing." Having overcome incredible obstacles himself, Thurber fought against "The trend of the modern temper . . . toward gloom, resignation, and even surrender. . . ." Kenneth MacLean wrote that, "One of Thurber's strongest themes is survival: it is strongly written into these last pieces. He himself will speak of the adjustability of the human being to almost any situation."[35] Perhaps that is why Thurber was, as Alistair Cooke noted, one of Dag Hammarskjöld's abiding passions.

But Thurber seemed to feel, toward the end, that he was fighting a rear-guard action, and once told a friend that "a species living under the threat of obliteration is bound to produce obliterature—and that's what we are producing."[36] Thurber considered that even comedy was going crazy, identifying itself "with the very tension and terror it once did so much to alleviate. . . . If we cannot tell evil, horror, and insanity from nonsense," he wrote, "the future of humor and comedy is cryptic. They require, for existence, a brave spirit and a high heart. . . ." Thurber's spirit remained brave, but he too had difficulty keeping his heart high; and he wrote to Robert Connelly that, while he hated the decline of comedy into "terror, horror, morbidity, ghastliness, and decadence," he had to admit that "it fits the Zeitgeist."

Thurber's own work after World War II shows the situation undergoing at first an imperceptible but increasing change for the worse. There was a sense of real and not merely imaginary horror closing in. During the fossilization of the cold war, his pages became sprinkled with fallout; McCarthyism and the H-bomb replaced the nagging wife. Humor, he wrote, "was suffering from acute hysteria, pernicious fission, recurring nightmare, loose talk, false witness, undulant panic, ingrown suspicion, and occlusion of perception."

Earlier projections of pessimism like "Footnote on the Future" (1940) are actually and intentionally quite funny as well as foreboding; the humorist has dominated his material. In some late pieces he barely manages to hold his own. Though he complained of sick dramatists and comedians, by burlesquing them one better, he joined them as a fringe member. His answer was to beat them at their own game, by inventing even madder garblings, episodes, and examples of crazy reactions and impossible psychoses; and, by fighting fire with fire, he sometimes got burned. If the decadent theater confuses *avant-garde* with *fin de siècle*, why not have plays called *Abie's Irish Neurosis, I Dismember Mama, They Slew What They Wanted, The Glands Menagerie, The Manic Who Came to Dinner,* and *Oklahomosexual!* To "exorcise the howling devils of [his] nightmares," Thurber filled his pages with such precarious punning until the reader is a bit punchdrunk. "For God's sake, tell me something truly amusing," says one of his fictional companions.

In its lucid commentary on a mad world, even the voice of sanity sometimes seems cracked; and Thurber's final midnight meditations have a giddy feeling as in the title of Anthony Newley's *Stop the World, I Want to Get Off.* Objecting to the morbidity of the midcentury, Thurber found some of it contagious. The comedy of "The Future, if Any, of Comedy," "The Manic in the Moon," "Afternoon of a Playwright," or "Carpe Noctem, if You Can" is touched with cyanide; the total impact is as depressing as it is amusing. John Updike found in them "an irritation with the present state of things so inclusive as to be pointless."[37] Actually only half a dozen of Thurber's last pieces have an oppressive gloom; and it is often broken by a lance of wit or a lantern light of affirmation, though of courage rather than confidence.

What Mr. Updike did not know, nor Thurber either, was that for two years prior to the cerebral stroke that brought on his final illness, he probably had a series of minor strokes. Something was severely wrong, but he did not know what it was; and a man unaware that he is slowly dying cannot be blamed or held entirely accountable if an occasional irritability intrudes or even dominates his work. Even so, like Cyrano giving his gazette, Thurber resisted not only with gallantry but with grace. In his last letter to Peter de Vries, he "spoke strongly of the general human obligation to gaiety." "If there is no human comedy it will be necessary to create one. How long can the needle of the human gramaphone stay in the rut of *Angst* without wearing out and ending in the repetition of a ghoulish gibbering?" he asked in "The Future, if Any, of Comedy." His answer was that man can overcome *Angst*: "By rising above it. . . . By the lifting of the spirit. . . . It takes guts to be happy, make no mistake about it; and I don't mean slap-happy, or drink-happy, or drug-happy."

Those who endure and prevail in Thurber's world are stoics who bear their burdens with fortitude and do not surrender their ideals to cynicism or despair. "I salute any man who can carry into his middle years, untarnished and undiminished, those first fine affections of his youth," wrote Thurber. As a toast, he gave, "God rest you tranquil, gentlemen, whom life did not dismay."

Some of the reasons for the difference between Thurber's humor and that of nineteenth-century America should now be clear. Both Thurber and his predecessors reflect, in large part, the spirit of their respective epochs. The difference, then, is not the superficial distinction that much of our earlier humor dealt with unlettered frontiersmen and was written in dialect or with errors in grammar and spelling as a pretense of illiteracy. The American scene has changed, both externally and psychologically; and humor has changed with the times. Thurber remarked that the time of writers like himself is not Walter Lippmann's time, or Stuart Chase's time, or Professor Einstein's time: "It is his own personal time, circumscribed by the short boundaries of his pain and his embarrassment, in which what happens to his digestion, the rear axle of his car, and the confused flow of his relationships with six or eight persons and two or three buildings is of greater importance than what goes on in the nation or in the universe." Still, the unheroic Thurberian protagonist is representative of a part of modern man, involved in anxieties both cosmic and mundane. One critic for the Manchester *Guardian* remarked that Thurber's characters recall T. S. Eliot's Sweeney or James Joyce's Mr. Bloom. Another called him "a Joyce in false-face." Yet another wrote that, "It is hard to think of anyone who more closely resembles the Prufrock of Eliot than the middle-aged man on the flying trapeze. There is, for instance, the same dominating sense of Predicament. The same painful and fastidious self-inventory, the same detailed anxiety, the same self-disparagement. . . ."[38] T. S. Eliot himself commented that Thurber's

is a form of humor which is also a way of saying something serious. There is a criticism of life at the bottom of it. It is serious and even somber. Unlike so much humor, it is not merely a criticism of manners—that is, of the superficial aspects of society at a given moment—but something more profound. His writings and also his illustrations are capable of surviving the immediate environment and time out of which they spring. To some extent they will be a document of the age they belong to.[39]

CHAPTER 2

The Romantic Imagination

THURBER'S "The Secret Life of Walter Mitty" is not only his most popular story but one of the best-known short stories of the twentieth century. Mitty has entered the language; one continually finds allusions to him. The *Lancet* has recognized the "Walter Mitty syndrome," and Lewis Gannet even discovered that an editorial in a Pakistani newspaper referred to "Walter Mitty types," assuming the readers knew what was meant. Even more than Prufrock, Mitty has been taken as representing the dilemma of modern man, frustrated by increasing chaos and competitiveness and feeling himself superfluous except in his daydreams. Triumphing over a sense of inadequacy and a nagging wife, Mitty takes refuge from the pressures and doldrums of middle-class existence by escaping into the world of the imagination. There he does all the things that others would like to think themselves capable of doing: he sails through hurricanes, performs miracles of surgery, is admired by his colleagues and adored by lovely women, and is supremely calm in moments of incredible danger, even facing the firing squad with dauntless courage. In real life he is also like many of us, entangled with trivia—overshoes, puppy biscuits, bicarbonate, Kleenex, razor blades, and the mysteries of automobile engines.

I *Walter Mitty and Lord Jim*

In his attempts to escape from painful reality into the realms of romance, Mitty has overtones of Conrad's Lord Jim, who also needed to envisage himself as a dashing hero overcoming all dangers and winning universal acclaim for courage and prowess. The closing passages of Conrad's novel and Thurber's story have a striking resemblance:

Jim stood stiffened and with bared head. . . . They say that the white man sent right and left at all those faces a proud and unflinching glance. Then with his hand over his lips he fell forward, dead . . . He is gone, inscrutable at heart . . .[1]

He put his shoulders back and his heels together. . . . He took one last drag on his cigarette and snapped it away. Then, with that faint, fleeting smile playing about his lips, he faced the firing squad; erect and motionless, proud and disdainful, Walter Mitty the Undefeated, inscrutable to the last.

In his introduction to *The Owl in the Attic*, E. B. White jocularly compared Thurber to Lord Jim; and Thurber himself continued the comparison in his epilogue to *My Life and Hard Times*, finding, alas, that he was incapable of achieving the high romance which finally befell Jim, though it defeated him as well. Harassed by commonplace reality, Thurber thought of wandering around the South Seas, "like a character out of Conrad, silent and inscrutable. But the necessity for frequent visits to my oculist and dentist has prevented this. . . . Furthermore, my horn-rimmed glasses and my Ohio accent betray me, even when I sit on the terrasses [sic] of little tropical cafes, wearing a pith helmet, staring straight ahead, and twitching a muscle in my jaw."

When Thurber spent one summer in the West Indies, no dark girl looking like Tondelaya in *White Cargo* offered to go to pieces with him; instead the native women tried to sell him baskets, beads, and postcards. As usual Thurber found his adventures anticlimactic; for, when he reboarded his ship, he discovered that someone had stolen the pants to his dinner jacket. He observed that "There was, of course, even for Conrad's Lord Jim, no running away. The cloud of his special discomfiture followed him like a pup, no matter what ships he took or what wildernesses he entered. In the pathways between office and home and the houses of settled people there are always, ready to snap at you, the little perils of routine living, but there is no escape in the unplanned tangent, the sudden turn."

Though there is no permanent escape from reality, one can find a temporary relief in the realms of his imagination, just as Walter Mitty did. In spite of those who insist that man must face Life, this imaginative escape seems to have a wide appeal, as the success of "Walter Mitty" indicates. Reprinted in *The Reader's Digest*, the story was remarkably popular with the troops in World War II, who —themselves bogged down in foxholes, trapped in the dreary and demanding routine of behind-the-lines tedium, or harried with the nervous tension of combat—found in Mitty a kindred spirit, the little man with the big idea, daydreaming himself from routine living into the realm of heroic romance. Faced themselves with awful experiences which tensed both mind and body, the troops were cheered by the fantasy of daredevilish Mitty, Commander of a Navy hydroplane, who was not afraid of hell. Prepared to take off on a suicidal flight behind enemy lines, Captain Mitty of the dawn patrol stood up and strapped on his Webley-Vickers automatic. " 'It's forty kilometers through hell, sir,' said the sergeant. Mitty finished one last brandy. 'After all,' he said softly, 'what isn't?' " While emergency battlefield operations were going on in reality, master surgeon Mitty performed nerve-racking surgery with cool, unruffled competence. Pocketa-pocketa-pocketa, went the cylinders of the hydroplane; pocketa-pocketa-pocketa went the the flame throwers—but Mitty remained dauntless. Somehow his bravado cheered the troops and helped them to whistle in the dark. (It has been reported that during the Battle of the Bulge, General Hoge, Commander of the 4th Armored Division, made his entire staff read Thurber's "The Day the Dam Broke."[2]) A Mitty International was formed in Europe and a Mitty Society in the South Pacific, with the password "Pocketa-pocketa-pocketa" and a crest of two Webley-Vickers crossed automatics. Here again is the comic catharsis.

"Mitty" is so skillfully written that despite its stream-of-consciousness, it seems simple and perhaps therefore superficial to critics seeking symbolic and philosophical profundities. Actually Mitty himself is one of the most effective symbols of the century. The story is pivotal to Thurber's work: as the meeting ground of his escapist fantasy and his pungent social criticism, it is his most representative piece, though not necessarily his most subtly rendered. Still, it is a perfect performance, beautifully developed, in which every word counts. Not the least skillful touch is the superbly connotative White Rabbit quality of Walter Mitty's name. As the story begins in a daydream, both the reader and Mitty are simultaneously jarred back to reality, and the succeeding transitions have an absurd but inescapable logic and symmetry. Each episodic escape is set off by some corresponding frustration. Mitty is so well done, with such structural and verbal inevitability, that it unfortunately tends to eclipse other equally skillful but less familiar and universal Thurber stories.

Mitty has a number of honorable literary antecedents; his romantic dreaming and gallantry, as well as his pathos, recall Don Quixote and Cyrano; he has something of d'Artagnan's gasconades; his adventurous fantasies resemble Tom Saywer's; and his irresolute sensitivity plus his longing for heroic action make him even a remote and comic kin to Hamlet. Thurber's own biography shows a considerable background for Mitty. His mother's frequent disguises and pretended identities may have been an influence; and his older brother William—an irrepressible ham who seized any opportunity to perform and who took up fencing, rope twirling, and wanted to prospect for uranium in Alaska—was a model for Mitty. The melodramatic clichés of the story's dream sequences no doubt owe something to Thurber's youthful fondness for Wild Bill Hickok and such nickel novels as *Jed the Trapper, The Liberty Boys of '76, The Rover Boys, Young Wild West, Frank Merriwell, Old King Brady,* and *Fred Fearnot,* as well as to more recent Hollywood derring-do of *The Dawn Patrol* (which furnished the episode of Mitty's flying alone behind Von Richtman's lines to bomb the ammunition dumps) and *The Prisoner of Zenda* (cf. the cartoon "Who are you today—Ronald Colman?"). Like Mitty, Thurber himself endured a great many frustrations, but he managed to overcome them, turn them into symbols, and recreate them as literature. His eyesight set him as a boy somewhat apart from his fellows, stimulated a withdrawn inner life, and forced him to compete under considerable handicaps.

Thurber, who had an essential toughness of character, did not make a comeback only in dreams, yet we find him casting himself in a Mitty role in the prophecy he wrote for his eighth-grade class. In this extended narrative, the class takes a trip in a Seairoplane. They are approaching Mars, when disaster threatens, in the very cadences used thirty years later in "Walter Mitty": "Unless that rope is gotten out of the curobater we will all be killed," cried one of the boys. These awful words astounded us and we all became frightened. Suddenly amid all of our lamentations a cry from Harold was heard and we all looked up. What was our surprise to see James Thurber walking out on the beam. He reached the end safely and then extricated the rope...." The class then learns that Thurber had been a tightrope walker for Barnsell's and Ringbailey's circus.

Mitty not only is the essential character of Thurber's fiction but also is the culmination of his work in the 1930's. Mr. Monroe, Mr. Bruhl, Mr. Pendly, Mr. Bidwell, all foreshadow him, as do a number of other stories and essays dealing with the anxieties of anti-heroes who attempt an imaginary or escapist refuge from their repressions. But except for Mr. Bruhl, who finds a final transfiguration, the others remain trapped by their inadequacies: "Human voices wake us, and we drown." Mitty, however, has a wistful gallantry; and, of all of Thurber's ineffectual men, only he and Mr.

Martin in "The Catbird Seat" manage to beat the system. Mitty's appeal is more universal, and the final impression we have of him is not of the henpecked husband but of the dashing and undaunted swashbuckler—"Walter Mitty the Undefeated, inscrutable to the last." The imaginary alter egos of his daydreams confront dangerous situations far more harrowing than any on the road to Waterbury, but they master them; or, if they go, they exit jauntily, whistling "Auprès de ma Blonde," and end not with a whimper but a bang.

II *The Need for Escape*

Thurber was often an escapist because, like all good humorists, he was basically serious and knew that living can be a grim, sober experience. Speaking of *The 13 Clocks*, he remarked that he wrote it in Bermuda, where he had gone to finish another book: "The shift to this one was an example of escapism and self-indulgence. Unless modern Man wanders down these byways occasionally, I do not see how he can hope to preserve his sanity." The rabbits who believed their friends' advice that this is no world for escapists were killed by wolves, and Thurber's moral is: "Run, don't walk, to the nearest desert island." For, "Who flies afar from the sphere of our sorrow is here today and here tomorrow."

While he felt the need to escape occasionally, Thurber could point out the absurdity of carrying escapism to extremes, as in "A Box to Hide In":

> "I didn't feel strong, and I'd had this overpowering desire to hide in a box for a long time," he explained.
> " 'Whatta you mean you want to hide in this box?' one grocer asked me.
> " 'It's a form of escape,' I told him, 'Hiding in a box. It circumscribes your worries and the range of your anguish. You don't see people either.' "

The worries and the anguish may be real; but hiding in a box is, of course, a ridiculous way out. As it was, none of the groceries had a box big enough.

The one satisfactory though temporary method of escape is through the imagination—through seeing things in a suggestive and picturesque light. For instance, the idiosyncracies of speech of his colored maid Della, whose mispronunciations resulted in such statements as "They are here with the reeves," (meaning wreaths) were a rare delight to Thurber's powers of imagination and conjured up a host of fantastic images. "I share with Della a form of escapism that is the most mystic and satisfying flight from actuality I have ever known," he wrote. "It may not always comfort me, but it never ceases to beguile me." Thurber was a connoisseur of mispronunciations and gathered quite a collection of amusing verbal trivia. In a critical article, Otto Friedrich considered this interest of Thurber's a weakness; but Thurber explained that "Mr. Friedrich has confused my armor with its chink." This trivia provided a protection, and its purpose was "the side-tracking of worrisome trains of thought."

Thurber's imagination both saved him and led him into trouble. He wrote of himself, "His ears are shut to the ominous rumblings of the dynasties of the world moving towards a cloudier chaos than ever before, but he hears with an acute perception the startling sounds that rabbits make twisting in the bushes along a country road at night. . . . He can sleep while the commonwealth crumbles but a strange sound in the pantry at three in the morning will strike terror into his stomach." He was essentially a Romantic in his use of the imagination; he scoffed, as he said, at "scientists, statisticians, actuaries, all those men who place numbers above hunches, figures above feelings, facts above possibilities, the normal above the phenomenal. . . . with their eyes on the average, they fail to discern the significant."

In this statement is another reason for Thurber's anti-rationalism. Traditionally Romanticists have protested that the scientific insistence upon precise fact is destructive to the creative imagination. "Well, if you're like me, you loathe all science and mathematics," says Father Darcy to Fitzgerald's romantic egotist Amory Blaine.[3] "I'd rather learn from one bird how to sing/than teach ten thousand stars how not to dance," wrote E. E. Cummings.[4] Unable to see flower cells through a microscope in his botany course at Ohio State, Thurber protested that the microscope took away the beauty of flowers. "We are not concerned with beauty in this course," his instructor informed him. "We are concerned solely with what I may call the mechanics of flars [sic]."

Thurber, like Wordsworth, disliked the analytical reason of scientists for what the poet called its "callow unawareness of the mystery that lies at the heart of all reality." Wordsworth thought that "All science which waged war with and wished to extinguish Imagination in the mind of man, and to leave it nothing of any kind but the naked knowledge of facts, was . . . much worse than useless. . . ."[5] Making essentially the same point, Thurber in *Let Your Mind Alone!* satirized various scientists who would have their readers "get a precise and dogmatic meaning out of everything they read, thus leaving nothing to the fantasy and the imagination." Thurber related: "I remember that, as a boy of eight, I thought

'Post No Bills' meant that the walls on which it appeared belonged to one Post No Bill, a man of the same heroic proportions as Buffalo Bill. Some suspicious-minded investigator cleared this up for me, and a part of the glamour of life was gone." "It is respectable to have no illusions—and safe—and profitable—and dull," wrote Conrad. "Yet you, too, in your time must have known the intensity of life, that light of glamour in the shock of trifles, as amazing as the glow of sparks struck from a cold stone—and as short-lived, alas!"[6]

III *Criticism of Science*

Many scientists, Thurber said, "withdraw from the world and devote themselves to the study of the inanimate and the impalpable." Accordingly, he ridiculed Lord Hailsham's saying that all good scientists are poets and Alfred North Whitehead's "attempt to find the scientist in Tennyson, Wordsworth, and Shelley.... If Shelley was a scientist," wrote Thurber, "then I am a neurosurgeon. ... Any scientist knows that the moth cannot desire the star for the simple scientific reason that the moth cannot see the star." Actually, the scientist may have as great a sense of wonder as the literary critic, and he often displays a creative imagination. Thurber was not against scientific progress *per se,* despite his guerrilla warfare with the machine; but his objections to science were in part a protest against materialism. He felt that human nature in the space age is not "measurable in terms of speed, momentum, weightlessness, or distance from earth, but is a matter of the development of the human mind." This mental development could, of course, include scientific perception; but, when some Russians wrote to *Izvestia* that Gagarin's orbital flight had destroyed their religious faith and "proved that science is God, and only man is truly super and supernal," Thurber replied: "I don't happen to be a phrenetically religious man myself, but I flatly refuse to accept Gagarin as the Son of a new God."

With his reservations about human nature, Thurber naturally did not share science's customary confidence nor care for its occasional self-glorification. In the heroic age of science, Thurber's irresolute and intimidated anti-heroes are a striking contrast to scientific swagger, assurance, and even arrogance. C. P. Snow praises Lord Rutherford's trumpeted retort to the envious statement, "Lucky fellow Rutherford, always on the crest of the wave," "Well, I made the wave, didn't I?"[7] Mr. Bidwell just sees how long he can hold his breath. Thurber was glad to find one scientist apprehensive about bloodhounds. "Poor, frightened little scientist," he rejoiced. "I have never liked or trusted scientists very much, and I think now that I know why: they are afraid of bloodhounds. They must, therefore, be afraid of frogs, jack rabbits, and the larger pussycats. . . . I have arrived at what I call Thurber's Law, which is that scientists don't really know anything about anything. I doubt every thing they have ever discovered."

Thurber was, of course, exaggerating; but behind his statements is a genuine criticism, neither burlesque nor petulant, shared by such serious thinkers of our times as Carl Jung, who feared that scientism, if carried to extremes, can reduce the individual to a statistic and create what Thurber called "the dehumanization of our species." With a future-directed optimism, many scientists accuse the humanities of indulging in a tragic sense that is archaic and defeatist. But Thurber was not so enthusiastic about the atomic age and said that "The score is Strontium 90, humanity 13." If tragedy is dismissed as mere sentimentality, then literature becomes, as some scientists regard it, comparatively trivial and irrelevant. Many scientists, of course, recognize the tragic condition of the individual but consider the social condition optimistic. In *Science and the Humanities,* Moody E. Prior writes that science "explores a reality which finds its ideal expression in mathematical relations, and cares for the individual experience only as it becomes a clue to the possibility of an impersonal formulation in which the individual instance loses its identity in an all-powerful generalization."[8] Very much involved with individual experience, Thurber did not care for a scientific detachment that could become indifference. Society does not exist apart from individuals; and, if they suffer or are enslaved, there is no utopia in saving mankind in the abstract.

There is, of course, no scientist in the abstract either; many individual scientists share Thurber's concern, his sense of wonder, and his rebellion against pedestrian reality. After all, modern science is making us increasingly aware of the difference between reality and appearances; but it is not therefore likely to pursue Thurber's white deer nor see with his bifocal vision. One day Thurber broke his glasses and, venturing into town without them, found the view much more interesting than when he could see with precision: "With perfect vision, one is extricably trapped in the workaday world, a prisoner of reality. . . . For the hawk-eyed person life has none of those soft edges which for me blur into fantasy; for such a person an electric welder is merely an electric welder, not a radiant fool setting off a skyrocket by day."

So when the husband in Thurber's fable found a unicorn in his garden, his wife snorted that "The unicorn is a mythical beast." But a unicorn is an inspiring sight, and its presence cheered the husband's heart. His skeptical and intolerant spouse called the police and a psychiatrist, but, by a twist anticipating the ending of "The Catbird Seat," she was the one who ended up in the booby hatch. "Moral: Don't count your boobies until they are hatched." Writers as diverse as St. Paul and Emily Dickinson have claimed that the world considers the imaginative nonconformist mad, but Thurber for once turned the tables.

IV The Stimulus of Fear

In Thurber's world there are grotches in the woods and warbs in the garrick, and telephone bells ring without benefit of human agency. "Both my poodles and I myself believed ... in fiends, and still do," he stated. "Fiends who materialize out of nothing and nowhere, like winged pigweed or Russian thistle." An imagination which can visualize grotches and believe in fiends may find life hazardous but will never find it dull.

Fear plays an important part in the works of many Romantics and Thurber for essentially the same reason—it arouses the imaginative faculties. According to Raymond Dexter Havens, "A principal reason for Wordsworth's unusual emphasis on fear is that it stimulates the imagination. . . . Like fear, wonder and the sense of the mystery in all things rouse us from the lethargy into which familiar scenes and similar experiences are ever leading us. . . ."[9] Thurber recognized this, and in a study of L. Frank Baum's Oz books he criticized Mr. Baum's intention of omitting heartaches and nightmares from his fairy tales: "I am glad that, in spite of this high determination, Mr. Baum failed to keep them out. Children love a lot of nightmare and at least a little heartache in their books."

Thurber's own books are full of fears, and he frequently had a sense of "stealthy doom" creeping over him. This usually results in high comedy, as in the case when he feared that his wife's Siamese cats Circe and Jezebel planned to murder him and dispose of his body. When Circe was killed by a Scottish terrier, Thurber was afraid she would return to earth in some guise and be revenged on him. One time, after reading Clarence Day's story about females who were half human and half cat, he suddenly imagined with horror that a young lady with whom he was dancing was a reincarnation of Circe and that he was dancing with the cat who swore to kill him. This was only one of Thurber's fears; he listed other horrors which should not be overlooked. Some of them are quite real like the personal income tax and the mobile investigatory units of Congress; but others include "the bears under the bed, the green men from Mars, the cats sealed up in the walls, the hearts beating under the floor boards, the faces of laughing girls that recede, float past, and come back again." He claimed that he was in constant dread of "boats coming down rocks, people being teleported, statues dripping blood, old regrets and dreams in the form of Luna moths fluttering against the windows at midnight." Sometimes he omitted to bank the furnace because he heard funny noises in the cellar all evening and was scared to go down there. Both he and his poodle Christabel were afraid of thunder—"the growling monster of the menacing skies." And he stated that he never drove at night out of the fear that he might turn up at the portals of some mystical monastery and never return.

Charles Addams' cartoon world is one in which Thurber's fears have come true; but, except in his fairy tales, Thurber did not give his fears an objective existence. He brought them up purely for their power to arouse the imagination above the commonplace, and he would doubtless agree with Wordsworth's lines:

> Yet rather would I instantly decline
> To the traditionary sympathies
> Of a most rustic ignorance, and take
> A fearful apprehension from the owl
> Or death watch: and as readily rejoice
> If two auspicious magpies crossed my way:
> To this would rather bend than see and hear
> The repetitions wearisome of sense,
> Where soul is dead, and feeling hath no place.[10]

"Indeed," comments a distinguished Wordsworthian critic, "with most of us such survivals of primitive feelings and ways of thought are much more common than is generally realized. The belief in charms, lucky days, and unlucky numbers, the half-jocular allusions to the total depravity of inanimate things are but a few of these vestigial remains."[11]

Thurber's characters often feel themselves stalked by menace— by their own particular Beast in the Jungle. Afraid of "an alien and nameless terror," they wait for some lurking, unknown doom. These hypersensitive, introspective men, abjectly overwhelmed by a sense of inadequacy, may derive in part from Thurber's favorite author Henry James; but their fears can also be connected with their own time. Just as James's protagonists of fine conscience seem ill at ease in the vulgarities of the Gilded Age, with its "Gospel of Greed," so Thurber's ineffectual men are an implied criticism of an industrial, acquisitive society and its breakdown in the Depression. Though they seem to have no financial problems, in the aggressive competitiveness of American life they are failures, anti-heroes who want to be heroic but who are dreamers rather than men of action and so find in fantasy their escape to Walden, to some privacy and dignity which social pressures deny them. Their escapism resembles Tom Wingfield's nightly flight to the movies in Tennessee Williams' *The Glass Menagerie*, set in the Depression. "You live in a dream; you manufacture illusions!" his mother tells him. He explains that he goes to the movies because he likes adventure and can't find it in his work. Escapism in this play is represented also by the fire escape, " a structure whose name is a touch of accidental poetic truth, for all of these huge buildings are always burning with the slow and implacable fires of human desperation."[12]

Thurber may not have had the Depression intentionally in mind; he had overcome his own financial problems before it struck, and his work at that time usually avoids political references, though Ed Keller, the villain of *The Male Animal,* is a militant Roosevelt-hater. Just as Henry James's novels do not customarily confront the explicit economic and social problems of their day, so Thurber wrote nothing about labor except some mild satire on proletariat fiction. He was not a social evangelist, and he observed that *The New Yorker* had no ax to grind and "just didn't give a good goddam."

Nevertheless, the fear and frustration in Thurber's fiction may have found such a deep public response because of what Frederick Lewis Allen calls the "undercurrent of fear" during the Depression.[13] Masculine pride and confidence were shaken; Charles M. Schwab of Bethlehem Steel was quoted as saying, "I'm afraid, every man is afraid. I don't know, we don't know, whether the values we have are going to be real next month or not."[14] Allen writes of "panic: a dreadful fear of inadequacy which was one of the Depression's commonest psychopathological results. A woman clerk, offered piecework after being jobless for a year, confessed that she almost had not dared to come to the office, she had been in such terror lest she wouldn't know where to hang her coat, wouldn't know how to find the washroom, wouldn't understand the boss's directions for her job."[15]

In the popular arts, the Depression was an escapist era that preferred *Anthony Adverse, Gone with the Wind,* the Lone Ranger, Charlie McCarthy, Snow White, Shangri-La, Andy Hardy, and Errol Flynn to socially conscious books and films that reminded people of their predicament. The jittery and hysterical reaction to Orson Welles's broadcast of *The War of the Worlds* was a sign, according to Allen, that "A feeling of insecurity and apprehension, a feeling that the world was going to pieces . . . had never quite left thoughtful Americans since the collapse of Coolidge-Hoover prosperity in 1929 and 1930."[16] Accordingly, the anxieties of Thurber's characters may have made his readers feel that their own were more endurable.

Despite his cartoon of "The Collapse of Civilization," Thurber's work was not so disheartening. Even while life could frighten him (or rather his persona), Thurber displayed a great gusto for living; he found something romantic and wildly adventurous in the daily details of existence. Kenneth MacLean writes that "The real and full Thurber story is the story of fear turning into joy. He is one writer who has been able intelligently to carry happiness into our own time, and he does this by laying out the provisions of the imagination."[17]

V   *Facts and Fantasy*

"Dis morning bime by," said his hired man Barney Haller, "I go hunt grotches in de voods." Such a statement set Thurber's mind on fire. "If you are susceptible to such things, it is not difficult to visualize grotches. They fluttered into my mind: ugly little creatures, about the size of whippoorwills, only covered with blood and honey and the scrapings of church bells." The grotches turn out to be nothing more than crotched branches of trees, but a world without grotches is a duller place. "There is no person," wrote Thurber, "whose spirit hasn't at one time or another been enriched by some cherished transfiguring of meanings"; and he gave as an example the youngster who thought that the first line of the Lord's Prayer was, "Our Father, who art in Heaven, Halloween be thy Name." "There must have been for him in that reading a thrill, a delight, and an exaltation that the exact sense of the line could not possibly have created."

A militant realist might scoff at such a mind as Thurber's; but, in so doing, he would miss much of the charm of life—like the patient bloodhound who went through the world with his eyes and nose to the ground and so missed all its beauty and excitement. The realist worries about heredity and environment, depression and taxes; Thurber too knew that life is perilous, but he worried about being "softly followed by little men padding along in single file, about a foot and a half high, large-eyed and whiskered." (For a picture of these little men, see *The Seal in the Bedroom*.) "Fantasy is the food for the mind, not facts," wrote Thurber; and one of his cartoons shows a social gathering in the midst of which sits an austere, scholarly looking man, chin in hand, scowling; while behind his back, one woman explains to another, "He doesn't know anything except facts."

Robert Louis Stevenson expressed what is essentially Thurber's position:

> There are moments when the mind refuses to be satisfied with evolution, and demands a ruddier presentation of the sum of man's experience. Sometimes the mood is brought about by laughter at the humorous side of life. . . . Sometimes it comes by the spirit of delight, and sometimes by the spirit of terror. At least, there will always be hours when we refuse to be put off by the feint of explanation, nicknamed science; and demand instead some palpitating image of our estate, that shall represent the troubled and uncertain element in which we dwell, and satisfy reason by the means of art. Science writes of the world as if with the cold finger of a starfish. . . .[18]

Thurber recognized the dangers of carrying the imagination to extremes. While commenting that "Realists are always getting into trouble," he went on to say that "I do not pretend that the daydream cannot be carried too far." "You can't live in a fantastic dream world, night in and night out, and remain sane," he explained. Charlie Deshler in "The Curb in the Sky" tried to do just this and ended up in an asylum. In "A Friend to Alexander," Mr. Andrews, who took to dreaming constantly about Aaron Burr, withdrew farther and farther into his imagination, dreaming of finally wreaking vengeance on Burr, for whom he felt an intense hatred because the face of Alexander Hamilton resembled that of Andrews' dead brother. When he finally faced Burr's phantom in an imaginary duel, Andrews, identifying himself with Hamilton, dropped dead.

For all of his fantasy, Thurber satirized those who mistook illusion for reality. In his study of soap opera, he told of listeners who thought that radio characters were real and sent in wedding gifts and layettes to the studio when "Big Sister" got married or the daughter on "Just Plain Bill" had a baby. When another actor took over the role of the husband in "Pepper Young's Family," "Indignant ladies wrote in, protesting against these immoral goings on." Another woman listener, recognizing that Kerry Donovan, the husband in "Just Plain Bill," and Larry Noble, the husband in "Backstage Wife," were played by the same actor, wrote to the studio that she was aware of this double life and threatened to expose the bigamy. Such a confusion of fact and fiction Thurber found pathetically absurd.

Thurber himself was certainly well grounded in reality. His work even more than Wordsworth's is full of concrete details and observations, sometimes interesting and informative, sometimes dead wood. Thurber had total recall, and once commented about himself: "He can tell you to this day the names of all the children who were in the fourth grade when he was. He remembers the phone numbers of several of his high school chums. He knows the birthdays of all his friends and can tell you the date on which any child of theirs was christened. He can rattle off the names of all the persons who attended the lawn fete of the First M. E. Church in Columbus in 1907." As a result, he filled his work with a mine of incidental information which, while sometimes irrelevant, helped give his writings verisimilitude. Henri Bergson noted that "Humor delights in concrete terms, technical details, definite facts. . . . This is not an accidental trait of humor, it is its very essence."[19]

The Romantic element is only one aspect of Thurber's work and is balanced by a great deal of skillful satire, a genre traditionally associated with Classicism. However, Thomas Wolfe observed that "The best fabulists have often been the greatest satirists. . . . Great satire needs the sustenance of great fable."[20] As examples, Wolfe cited Aristophanes, Voltaire, and Swift; to these we might add Rabelais, Samuel Johnson, Mark Twain, Aldous Huxley, George Orwell, and Thurber himself. Sometimes Thurber combined romanticism and satire, as when he attacked the excesses of scientists and psychologists in their efforts to direct or control the imagination.

Perhaps psychiatrists have helped bring about the decline of fantasy (except in science-fiction) by making it too much a subject for analysis. One psychiatrist told Mrs. Thurber that if he had her husband under treatment for a few weeks, he would cure him of all his drawings. Thurber shrugged this incident aside, but he was highly incensed when the psychiatrist Dr. Paul Schilder analyzed Lewis Carroll and concluded that *Alice in Wonderland* is full of "cruelty, destruction, and annihilation." If carried to their illogical extreme, views such as Dr. Schilder's would destroy imaginative literature almost entirely. "Dr. Schilder's work . . . is cut out for him," wrote Thurber. "He has the evil nature of Charles Perrault to dip into, surely as black and devious and unwholesome as Lewis Carroll's. He has the Grimms and Hans Christian Andersen. He has Mother Goose, or much of it. He can spend at least a year on the Legend of Childe Rowland, which is filled with perfectly swell sexual symbols—from (in some versions) an underground cave more provocative by far than the rabbit hole in Wonderland to the sinister Dark Tower of the more familiar versions. This one piece of research will lead him into the myth of Proserpine and into

Browning and Shakespeare and Milton's *Comus* and even into the dark and perilous kingdom of Arthurian legend. . . . When he is through with all this, Dr. Schilder should be pretty well persuaded that behind the imaginative works of all the cruel writing men . . . lies the destructive and unstable, the fearful and unwholesome . . ." Dr. Schilder would probably think that Lewis Carroll would have done better to devote himself solely to mathematics or to some other aspect of Reality; but Thurber believed that *Alice* is more valuable; and he wrote that, after all of Tenniel's political cartoons, the illustrations for *Alice in Wonderland* had given him something important to do. In reply to Dr. Schilder, Thurber quoted Dr. Morton Prince, "a truly intelligent psychologist," who says of the creatures of artistic imagination that "Far from being mere freaks, monstrosities of consciousness, they are in fact shown to be manifestations of the very constitution of life."

Certainly Thurber, an extremely careful craftsman and conscious critic of his work, which often underwent two dozen revisions, would not endorse the Freudian theory of the unconscious origins of art as a product of sublimated neurosis. As for Freud's study of humor, Thurber wrote in 1949: "I strongly believe that the analogy between dreams and wit rests on a similarity more superficial than basic, and the psychic explanation of wit fails to take in the selectivity of the artist whose powers of rejection and perfection are greater than his vulnerability to impulse."[21] "Don't you think the subconscious has been done to death and that it's high time some one rediscovered the conscious?" he wrote as caption for a cartoon advertisement of S. N. Berhman's *Rain from Heaven* (1935).

"I have not always, I am sorry to say, been able to go the whole way with the Freudians, or even a very considerable distance," he wrote in 1937. His first book, *Is Sex Necessary?* spoofs the sort of sex books that transform love into nothing more than an inherited behavior pattern with a heavy dose of neuroses. Never caring for the attitude that cherishes neuroses and even considers them a sign of superior sensitivity, Thurber wrote that through the early part of this century "neuroses were staved off longer, owing to the general ignorance of psychology." Accordingly he found little use for the theories of Dr. Louis E. Bisch, the "Be-Glad-You're-Neurotic" man, whose concepts he dismissed as mere mysticism. Thurber refused to indulge in psychic hypochondria and maintained that the analysts could not have him while he still kept his strength. "We worry so much about being neurotic that we never really delve into our minds," he told W. J. Weatherby in 1961.[22] "Modern psychology and psychiatry have made us all afraid of ourselves," he wrote in the same year. "*Angst* is spreading, and with it mental ailments of whose cause and cure, one authority has recently said, we know little or nothing. But the terminology of psychiatry proliferates to the point that almost everybody now seems to think he is schizophrenic, schizoid, or schizo."

VI *The Literature of Living*

His ideal teacher of literature, Joseph Russell Taylor (whose portrait appears in *The Thurber Album*), believed that "the artist is a normal man" and "was interested not in a search for depravity but in finding signs of spiritual increase and of fine sensibility in the world around him"; and Thurber in his final years increasingly criticized the so-called "sick literature" with its often depraved characters and fashionable cult of despair. By contrast, Thurber's fables, like the poetry of E. E. Cummings, urge the reader to accept and embrace life. Tennessee Williams, Thurber complained, "confused the heart, both as organ and as symbol, with the disturbed psyche, the deranged glands, and the jumpy central nervous system. I'm not pleading for the heart that leaps up when it beholds a rainbow in the sky, or for the heart that with rapture fills and dances with the daffodils. The sentimental pure heart of Galahad is gone with the knightly years, but I still believe in the heart of the George Meredith character that was not made of the stuff that breaks." Certainly Thurber had a tragic awareness, as we have seen, nor would he dismiss all despair as merely the product of a cult; but like Conrad, Hemingway, Faulkner, and Camus, he would have man confront it with courage rather than capitulate.

Thus he considered psychology's morbid preoccupations a sort of evasion of responsibility. As early as 1930 in "The Future of Psychoanalysis" he challenged its moral relativity. In *The American Character,* D. W. Brogan also commented on the new laissez-faire in manners and morals: "More people than was really necessary reacted, reacted by divorce, by neurosis, by an affected gloom that was no more impressive or convincing than so much real-estate optimism. And it was not a moment too soon that one of the acutest American sociologists issued his manifesto called *Let Your Mind Alone.*"[23]

A paradoxical counterpart to psychology's moral relativity was, in Thurber's view, its conformity to the "normal." Calling himself one of the "non-institutionalized," Thurber disliked any sort of regimentation. At Ohio State he refused to attend military drill, and in the 1930's he attacked mental adjustment and sex *ex machina*. Writes William E. Bohn: ". . . James Thurber is a persistent and pertinent protest against mechanization. He hates what science and the belt line threaten to do to human nature. He is equally at odds with Ford and Freud. Ford makes a man stand in one place and do one thing. Freud attempts to analyze mysteries of his inner being and hopes to produce a state of normalcy devoid of hallucination. Thurber prefers inefficiency and dreams to high production levels and sanity."[24]

In *Let Your Mind Alone!* Thurber not only satirized Freudianism but also punctured the pretensions of current books and theories that dabbled with men's minds to teach them to attain Masterful Adjustment, to Worry Successfully, to Grow into Life, and to Wake-Up-and-Live. He found a similarity between these mental inspiration books and Marxist philosophy: both believe they can solve everything, a belief that can lead to madness.

It was a painful irony that such success books came out by the dozens in the Depression decade, when it was impossible for many people to succeed by any panacea. Through no fault of their own, millions of willing and able workers were unemployed; and the success books, with their bland assurances that anyone with energy and initiative could make good, merely intensified the individual's sense of failure and frustration. By a similar paradox the Horatio Alger books flourished during the age of moguls, trusts, wage slavery, and the depression of the 1890's, when most people had no chance to succeed by Alger's formula. The books Thurber attacked ignored the reality of poverty and suffering; while people starved, struck, and stood in bread lines, Dr. Mursell wrote how to overcome difficulties in escorting a young lady to a restaurant table. Though Thurber did not specifically challenge this aspect of the inspirationalists, he did create his most vivid anti-success characters during the 1930's.

A provocative commentary on success can be found in Thurber's story "The Greatest Man in the World," written in 1931, one of the worst years of the Depression. This sardonic tale tells of Jack ("Pal") Smurch, who flew nonstop around the world in July, 1937, thus becoming the greatest national hero of all time. Thurber remarked that Lindbergh and Byrd had been gentlemen who wore their laurels gracefully and quietly retired from the awful weather of publicity. Smurch, however, was an arrogant, vulgar punk with a criminal record that included the knifing of his high school principal and the bashing of a sacristan over the head with a pot of Easter lilies when that unfortunate man tried to stop him from stealing an altarcloth. Ignorant of all this, the sensation-hungry public demanded Smurch as an American hero. The nation's politicians, who knew his real character, kept him locked up and hid his unsavory background from the press; for the Pantheon of national heroes must not be smirched. In final desperation, the politicians, at the President's nod, pushed Smurch out of a window, killing him to preserve his reputation as a spotless symbol. His tomb at Arlington Cemetery became a pilgrims' shrine. This caustic story is a triple-barreled satire upon the contemptuous arrogance of Smurch, the hero-worshiping public, and the politicians who stop at nothing for the sake of reputation.

But its satire may go even deeper as a commentary on acquisitive values. A vulgar nonconformist, Smurch is the antithesis of the American success figure. He is not the clean-cut, well-bred gentleman (actually neither were many millionaires of the Gilded Age nor the Babbitts after them), but he is part of American democracy. He is, in fact, like some disreputable characters in the Depression fiction of Steinbeck or Erskine Caldwell. In the eyes of the Establishment such a person is a threat; he cannot be allowed to represent America. When a person like Smurch succeeds, in defiance of all the Alger doctrines, he sets the whole Protestant-capitalist image on its ear. Since the Bitch Goddess is an illegitimate offspring of Calvin, success should be reserved for the clean, frugal, tidy, pious, and worthy. Thus the official outrage at Smurch's success. A science fiction narrative of sorts, Thurber's story has sinister implications of potential domestic fascism: the press is completely censored, and Smurch is murdered by right-wing totalitarian bureaucracy.

A proletarian who wants his share of the plutocracy, Smurch thoroughly accepts the system, but he is honest in his greed and doesn't conceal it by Puritan euphemisms and pious platitudes. "'Come awn, come awn. . . . When do I start cuttin' on de parties, huh? And what's they goin' to be *in* it?' 'Money!' exclaimed a state senator, shocked, pale. 'Yeh, money,' said Pal. . . . 'An' big money.'" Actually, Thurber seemed to like Smurch, even with his coarseness (cf. Thurber's fondness for impersonating Jeeter Lester), and he is certainly preferable to the faceless conformists who do him in.

Like excessive scientism, the success myth struck Thurber as being too materialistic, too hostile to the romantic imagination and the artistic temperament. This point is made in several of the fables. In "The Shrike and the Chipmunks," "The male chipmunk thought that arranging nuts in artistic patterns was more fun that just piling them up to see how many you could pile up. The female was all for piling up as many as you could." Insisting that her mate be healthy and wealthy, she drove him to be killed by a shrike. And it was better for the male guinea pigs to escape to Tahiti than to be browbeaten by busybodies.

VII   *Undisciplined Thinking and Common Sense*

In *Let Your Mind Alone!* Thurber's main objection was the pressure for pedestrian conformity. The masterful adjustment writers
generalized too much, overlooking individual idiosyncracies and
unexpected upsets like stepping on a sleeping Boston terrier while
assisting a young lady into a canoe. Mrs. Brande and other mental
disciplinarians failed to account for perverse, frustrating, and fantastic variables. Undeterred by the imposing credentials of Dr.
Bloch, Dr. Mursell, Dr. Shellow, Dr. Bisch, Professor Pitkin, and
their confreres, Thurber challenged their attempts to regiment the
processes of thought and imagination and concluded that "The
undisciplined mind runs far less chance of having its purposes
thwarted, its plans distorted, its whole scheme and system wrenched
out of line. The undisciplined mind, in short is far better adapted
to the confused world in which we live today than the stream-
lined mind."

He announced that in his own case "I show any and all thoughts
to their seats whether they have tickets or not. They can be under-
age and without their parents, or they can be completely cockeyed,
or they can show up without a stitch on: I let them in and show
them to the best seats in my mind. . . ." Thus he gave his imagination free rein when his colored maid frightened him by announcing
that there was a "doom-shaped" thing in the kitchen, meaning the
new dome-shaped electric refrigerator. "I am all for the wholesome,
the healthy, and the vital," explained Thurber, "but sometimes I
think one's mind can become, if one is of the guardian type, too
wholesome, healthy, and vital to be much fun. Any mind, I say
boldly here and now, which would not let a doom-shaped thought
come in and take a seat is not a mind that I want around."

As a result of this undisciplined thinking, Thurber often found
himself unable to stick to the exact point; his mind led him through
a maze of random associations. For instance, thinking about General Grant's horse would remind him of General Grant's beard,
which would remind him of Charles Evans Hughes, who would
remind him of the NRA, and so on. This sort of thinking results in
frequent digressions in his essays and reminiscences—as when writing about his family's old automobile, he thought about the car
owned by the Get-Ready Man and proceeded to give a hilarious account of that peculiar gentleman before returning to the history
of the Thurbers' old Reo.

In *Horse Sense in American Humor*, Walter Blair misreads
Thurber's intention in *Let Your Mind Alone!*. He claims that

Thurber is an enemy of common sense, who "batters down one principle after another set forth in such recent 'Bibles of Common Sense' as *Wake Up and Live!*, *Streamline Your Mind,* and *How to Win Friends and Influence People*."[25] But Thurber's very point is that the principles advocated in such books are the reverse of common sense. For instance, Dr. Mursell in *Streamline Your Mind* tells of a professor and his family who wanted to reroof their house but could not measure the roof because they did not have a ladder. "You and I have this problem solved already," said Thurber; "we would get a ladder." But the professor and his family are stumped for days until a guest tells them how to measure the roof by Pythagorean geometry. Thurber found this reliance upon abstract reasoning absurdly impractical. "I think this places Dr. James L. Mursell for you; at any rate it does for me," he commented: "he is the man who would use the theorem of Pythagoras in place of a ladder . . . It seems to me that borrowing a ladder from next door, or buying one from a hardware store, is a much simpler way to go about measuring a roof than waiting for somebody to show up who knows the theorem of Pythagoras. . . . With a ladder of my own, and the old-fashioned technique of thinking, I could get the job done in no time. This seems to me the simplest way to live." Here is the very sort of horse sense which Mr. Blair says Thurber opposed.

Actually Thurber combined Tom Sawyer's romantic Mitty syndrome with Huck Finn's horse sense and then added a Jamesean ambiguity for appropriate occasions. Far from being a foe to common sense, he had "the kindliness of a man who brings logic to bear on an ailing and illogical world."[26] He sought for sanity in a bizarre world rather than for strange sensations in a world of ennui. Francis Downing points out that what Thurber has done "is to endow this illogical world of ours with logic."[27] Frequently he did so by taking a fantastic proposition and carrying it to a logical conclusion, with ludicrous consequences. This is done with a straight face in the manner of Mark Twain and the tall-tale tellers. In his study of wit, Sigmund Freud explains that, "sense in nonsense transforms nonsense into wit." Thurber did so and also demonstrated another theory of Freud's, "advancing something apparently absurd or nonsensical which, however, discloses sense that serves to illustrate and represent some other actual absurdity and nonsense."[28]

A choice example of this technique is "The Civil War Phone Number Association." Having heard the suggestion that people memorize phone numbers by associating them with dates in the Civil War, Thurber proceeded to see what would happen if this technique were attempted consistently; and he came up with a logical but fantastic solution.

> The way I finally got Algonquin 9618 fixed in my mind . . . was to bring in the World War. I saw that by subtracting 4 from the last 2 digits—18—and adding it to the first two—96—I could make an even 100 of the first two. This made 14 out of the last two. I now had 10014 as a key number. This was useless unless I could plant in my memory some story . . . which would break 10014 down into the proper arrangement of digits. The story I invented was this: that I had ended the war—that is, made '18 out of '14 —by sending overseas a male quartet from my company of 100 men. . . . This gave me logically and smoothly 9618.

In his satires on inspirational books, Thurber took their proposals and considered their probable conclusions, which invariably turn out to be highly absurd. One inspirational remedy was "The Worry Play"—write a play to dramatize your worries. Thurber did so and came up with a play which was almost as long as *Mourning Becomes Electra* and which he then had to adapt to movies with the result that a Mr. Sam Maschino, a movie agent, kept bobbing up in his dreams, hectoring him. He also visualized himself in the main role —having rejected Leslie Howard, John Gielgud, and Lionel Barrymore—and was lousy in the part, which fact worried him further. When Abercrombie and Fitch advertised, "Can't you picture yourself in the middle of the stream with the certain knowledge that a wise old trout is hiding under a ledge and defying you to tempt him with your skillfully cast fly?", Thurber proceeded to create the picture and visualized himself drowning in the current, snagging picnickers with his skillfully cast fly, and being baffled by the intricacies of the rod and reel. And what would happen if owls were let loose at ceremonial events? Henri Bergson observes that "Théophile Gautier said that the comic in its extreme form was the logic of the absurd. . . . What makes us laugh is alleged to be the absurd realized in concrete shape, a 'palpable absurdity.' "[29] And this is what Thurber achieves.

Although he created romantic fantasy, Thurber sometimes used his imagination in a literal way. Bergson again explains that "A comic effect is obtained whenever we pretend to take literally an expression which was used figuratively"; or, to put it another way, "Once our attention is fixed on the material aspect of a metaphor the idea expressed becomes comic."[30] Thus in Thurber's youthful imagination, businessmen who phoned their wives to say that they were tied up at the office did sit tied and gagged in their swivel chairs; and life was peopled with old ladies who were always up in the air, with men who lost their heads during fires but were able to run around yelling, and with young ladies who were really soiled doves. This reaction diminished as he grew up; but he claimed that a remark such as, "It's a common lock. A skeleton will let you in," still aroused nameless horrors in his mind and left him with wide eyes and open mouth. In his satiric illustrations for certain famous poems, Thurber put this sort of imagination to good use by giving literal pictures of the poetic situations in order to make them appear palpably absurd.

This technique was used with a straight face. "We all have flaws," says the wicked Duke of Coffin Castle, "and mine is being wicked." This Duke always wore gloves, "which made it difficult for him to pick up pins or coins or the kernels of nuts, or to tear the wings from nightingales." It is the placid coupling of tearing the wings from nightingales with the perfectly normal action of picking up nuts and pins that gives this line its abrupt shock of humor. And by having the Duke feed his victims to the geese, Thurber created a jocose effect much more horrible than if they were fed to lions.

"If you can touch the clocks and never start them, then you can start the clocks and never touch them," said the Golux. "That's logic, as I know it and use it." And this is the sort of illogical logic which Thurber used to advantage in his writings.

Unfortunately, man's logic leads him into dilemmas that are tragic as well as absurd. Thurber was painfully conscious of both sides of life, and his tragic awareness gave his comedy its poignancy. It also made it necessary for him to take refuge in his fancy. "Some day, I suppose, when the clouds are heavy and the rain is coming down and the pressure of realities is too great, I shall deliberately take my glasses off and go wandering out into the streets. . . . I imagine I'll have a remarkable time wherever I end up." And his parting words in *The 13 Clocks* are: "Remember laughter. You'll need it even in the blessed isles of Ever After."

CHAPTER 3

Men, Women and War

TWO OF THE MAJOR ELEMENTS in Thurber's work are what might be called the Mitty motif—the bewilderment and exasperation of the American male and his efforts to escape through the imagination—and the domination of the American male by the American female. These two recurrent themes are often inter-twined, for the Mitty-like nature of the male permits the female to dominate him. The treatment of men and women has many subtle variations on a single theme; it is almost fugue-like.

The tone of Thurber's treatment of sex and marriage is set in his very first book, *Is Sex Necessary?*, the theme of which is "the mel-ancholy of sex."

> Herein are examined . . . both men and women, male and female, Man and Woman—not only in themselves, but in their curious reactions to each other. The term "reaction" seems to be used in this book to include not only those quick, unpremeditated reflexes which cause so much trouble but also those slowly formulated prejudices, doubts, and suspicions which cause even more trouble.

Here and in many of his later stories and drawings, Thurber traced the development of matrimonial quarrels and incompatibilities, but he was not hostile toward marriage itself. "Marriage, as an instrument, is a well-nigh perfect thing. The trouble is that it cannot be successfully applied to the present-day emotional relationships of men and women. It could much more easily be applied to something else, possibly professional tennis." The main targets in Thurber's part of the book (Preface, chapters I, III, V, VII, and Glossary) are the inhibitions of the genteel tradition and the Freudian rebellion from it to the point that sex becomes an exclusive obsession. When Viennese therapy is applied to such Victorian and Midwestern maladies as Pedestalism and the Lilies-and-Bluebird delusion, the cure is vintage Thurberian confusion. He attacks the myth of motherhood and the mystery of women, the false delicacy that erects an antimacassar barricade between the sexes, the sweeping generalizations that divide them and keep them from recognizing each other as intellectual and moral equals. As he wrote some twenty years after, "The wife who keeps saying, 'Isn't that just like a man?' and the husband who keeps saying, 'Oh, well, you know how women are,' are likely to grow farther and farther apart through the years. These famous generalizations have the effect of reducing an individual to the anonymous status of a mere unit in a mass."

I *Sex and The Monroes*

Is Sex Necessary?, though thoroughly amusing, is merely a spoofing of the sex books then current; and Thurber shared the authorship with E. B. White. With *The Owl in the Attic,* Thurber started on his own, doing more original work and presenting his first collection of short stories, a series of eight pieces concerning Mr. and Mrs. Monroe. Though not so mature as many of his later stories, those on the Monroes contain Thurber's most extended character studies. And a highly unattractive pair are the Monroes. Petite and cute, little Mrs. Monroe (as she is always called, sarcastically) is coolly and exasperatingly competent, and she mothers her bungling husband as if he were a little boy, except when she has had too many cocktails. Mr. Monroe is Thurber's most extreme specimen of the helpless, frustrated, ineffectual male, so much so that he evokes a shudder as often as a smile. In Thurber's own words, "Mr. Monroe didn't really have any character. He had a certain charm, yes; but not character. He evaded difficult situations; he had no talent for firm resolution; he immolated badly; and he wasn't even very good at renunciation, except when he was tired or a little sick." He represents the ultimate in pathetic impotence of personality, and both Thurber and the reader are a bit sickened by him.

In his daydreams Mr. Monroe visualized himself as a masterful individual: "he enjoyed giving the impression of a strong, silent man wrapped in meditation." Actually, he was terrified of customs inspectors, panic-stricken by a bat, afraid of imaginary burglars, and unable to cope with decision. Even as an adulterer, he was ineffectual. His wife destroyed one affair by revealing to the other woman, a Miss Lurell, an account of her husband which reduced him to a childish, gibbering fool, crying, "Woo! Woo!" when things went wrong with mechanical gadgets. But Mr. Monroe continued to imagine himself as a romantic figure and to dabble in adultery. His wife, apparently having decided he was not worth the bother, no longer made any objections, just so he did not make a fool of himself. "That, in her charmingly humorous way, was all little Mrs. Monroe had ever required of him in the event of an—ah

—of a communion with anyone. Just so he selected a lady that a wife need not be ashamed of." But while thinking about another affair one evening, he delayed, brooded, and lost his nerve. He began reading *The Golden Bowl,* which only made him sleepy. Finally, after stalling, inventing excuses, and rationalizing himself into a state of irresolution, he gave up and went to bed. It almost seems that Monroe would have done better to consummate the act than to resign himself to futility, like the would-be lovers in Browning's "The Statue and the Bust."

Much has been written about the aggressive menace of Thurber women; but, while Mrs. Monroe is not very admirable, her husband is even worse. His irresolution forced her to make the decisions and to get things done. When she left him to supervise the moving of furniture from their house, "Mr. Monroe's indecision and evident nervousness began to show up in the movers' attitude toward him. The 'chief' and 'mister' with which they had first addressed him changed to 'buddy' and 'partner' and finally, as Mr. Monroe strove desperately for an air of dignity and authority, to 'sonny.' " The movers finally had to make all of the decisions themselves, and Monroe stood crushing his cigarette in his hand in a gesture of helpless despair. "Then he cried aloud. He couldn't remember the [transfer] man's name. He couldn't remember anything."

Here is Thurber's contribution to the much-discussed impotence of modern man in the literature of the 1920's and early 30's, and it is perhaps the most frightening of them all. It is difficult to identify oneself with the Fisher King (*The Waste Land*), Jake Barnes (*The Sun Also Rises*), or Popeye (*Sanctuary*); but Monroe's is a domesticated, existential predicament in which anyone might find himself. Unredeemed by any poetic grandeur or Gothic horror, his situation is brought much closer to home and is therefore more appalling as personality, though less powerful as literature. Jake accepts his physical wound with stoic equilibrium, and he is seen against a background of Paris and festive Spain; Popeye shares the grotesque violence of Faulkner country; Dick Diver takes his fall against the glamorous settings of Paris, Rome, and the Riviera; but Monroe, while less impressive, is far more familiar and less easy to pass off as symbolic. Thurber's least attractive protagonist, he makes the reader squirm uncomfortably.

A similar but more good-natured relationship between man and woman appears in Thurber's picture parable, "The Race of Life." At the beginning of this sequence (in which a man, woman, and child journey over a barren country to reach at last a heavenly gate on a high hill), the woman starts out with a hopeful look in her eye, but her mate slumps behind her, looking uncertain about it all. For a brief while they proceed at equal speed; but, after taking the lead in hurdling a water jump, the woman consistently outpaces the man. Her expression is always cheerful or boldly resolute; he at best looks blank or hesitant. At one point he becomes winded, and the woman has to carry him. She leaps confidently down precipices, while he cautiously descends backwards, lagging behind. When encountering a bear or an eerie figure entitled "Menace," the woman advances to the fight, leaving her man to cower behind with the child. She sits guard at night while the others sleep, and, at the end, she races on with whoops of joy, pointing to the angelic gates, while the man behind her collapses on his knees in a rainstorm.

II *Soap Opera Syndromes*

Thurber's drawings are satiric; and he became sharply critical when the inferiority and dependence of man upon woman were taken seriously, as they seemed to be in many radio soap operas. In his extensive study of soap opera, Thurber found that its men were regularly afflicted by a series of special ailments—temporary blindness, amnesia, and temporary or permanent paralysis of the legs. "When their men are stricken, the good women become nobler than ever. A disabled hero is likely to lament his fate and indulge in self-pity now and then, but his wife or sweetheart never complains. She is capable of twice as much work, sacrifice, fortitude, endurance, ingenuity, and love as before." Thurber found this fiction pretty revolting but observed that, "The soap-opera males who go blind or lose the use of both legs or wander around in amnesia are, as the psychologists put it, symbols that the listening women demand. As long as the symbols are kept in the proper balance and the woman is in charge and the man under her control, it does not make a great deal of difference to the female listeners whether the story is good or not." Such situations bear an uncomfortable resemblance to *The Shrike*, a play in which a husband who attempts to commit suicide is given the choice of being confined in the mental ward of a hospital or committed to the care of his domineering wife, who exploits the situation to make him totally dependent upon her. The comparison is borne out further by the fact that many of Thurber's drawings contain a shrike (sometimes with a woman's face) hovering overhead preparing to strike.

Even when the soap-opera men were not stricken with some crippling disease, the heroines attempted to render them subordinate and dependent. Thurber commented that the chill Helen Trent has her men frustrated to a point at which a mortal male would smack her little mouth, so smooth, so firm, so free of nicotine, alcohol, and emotion. Suitors in Soapland are usually weak, and Helen's frustration of them is aimed to gratify the listening housewives, brought up in the great American tradition of female domination. Snivelled one of the cold lady's suitors, "I'm not strong, incorruptible, stalwart. I'm weak." Helen purred that she would help him find himself. The weak men continually confess their weakness to the good women, who usually manage to turn them into stable citizens by some vague and soapy magic. The weak men and the good men often confess to one another their dependence on the good woman. In one serial, a weak man said to a good man, "My strength is in Irma now." To which the good man replied, "As mine is in Joan, Steve."

Many of Thurber's own stories and drawings show a weak man dependent upon a strong woman; but such a situation appears deplorable rather than to be desired. The men sometimes revolt, but they are handicapped by weakness of both character and body. Thurber noted that, even as babies, males have far less chance than females for survival. In adult life the physiognomy of the Thurberian male displays "an air of uncertainty, an expression of futility," whereas the female "has her eyes on an objective; you can feel the solid, sharp edges of her purpose." Women are even living on forever, singing, dancing, riding in airplanes, playing kettledrums, and chinning themselves at 114 years of age, while men die in relative youth. Thurber concluded that, "Socially, economically, physically and intellectually, Man is slowly going ... to hell ... Man's day is indeed done; the epoch of Woman is upon us."

Thurber wrote such statements partly in sarcasm and partly in melancholy earnest. He did not hold the women entirely to blame, for his men are equally at fault by apathetically accepting their weakness. Henry Adams anticipated Thurber by several decades when he wrote that "The task of accelerating or deflecting the movement of the American woman had interest infinitely greater than that of any race whatever, Russian, Chinese, Asiatic, or African." At dinners Adams would ask a lady whether she could explain why the American woman was a failure. "Without an instant's hesitation, she was sure to answer: 'Because the American man is a failure!'"[1] Consequently, woman emancipated herself and took over man's functions, often learning to handle his automobiles and machinery better than himself, and learning to scorn him in the process. Like Thurber, Adams observed that the modern American woman "was free; she had no illusions; she was sexless; she had discarded all that the male disliked; and although she secretly regretted the discard, she knew that she could not go backward. She must, like the man, marry machinery. Already the American man sometimes felt surprise at finding himself regarded as sexless; the American woman was oftener surprised at finding herself regarded as sexual."[2] Thus Malcolm Cowley wrote in reviewing *The Thurber Carnival* that, "The women in his [Thurber's] stories are hard, logical, aggressive; they have all the virtues and vices that [Henry] James assigned to businessmen."[3]

Thurber's social criticism is often more implied than overt; but his treatment of men and women, if worth considering at all, must have more basis than a comic feud. If his women have the businessman's aggression, the men display a singular lack of it and, accordingly, of the values of Puritan, frontier, and capitalist folklore. Henry Bamford Parkes's diagnosis of the industrial mind is a striking parallel to the impotence of the Thurberian male:

> Above all [writes Parkes] the Americans believed that the individual should struggle to improve his condition and conquer his environment, that if he had energy, courage, and initiative he would surely succeed, and that if he failed it was because of some deficiency within himself. Yet in the new industrial system it was wholly impossible for more than a small minority of the total population to achieve what society regarded as success. . . . Thus insofar as the American people were committed to the American ideology of personal success, they were attempting to accomplish something that for most of them was impossible. Judged by the prevalent standards of American society, most Americans were compelled to regard themselves as having failed and to attribute their failure to some shortcoming within themselves.[4]

Parkes shows further how the failure to succeed is often seen as a lack of virility and results in nervousness and mental breakdowns. "And," he continues, "the emotional immaturity of so many American men led to a further increase in the relative influence of American women. . . . The man of the industrial age was apt to have a neurotic dependence, first upon his mother and afterwards upon his wife, owing to his own insecurity and lack of masculine self-assurance."[5]

Most of Thurber's men are as far removed as it is possible to conceive from the character of virile hero. On the other hand the women are massively aggressive, large and muscular, and quite capable of outwrestling their mates. ("Two Best Falls Out of Three—Okay, Mr. Montague?" says a hefty woman in one cartoon.) Consequently the difference between the real nature of these men and women and their characters as they imagine them is highly ironic.

"I think of you as being enormously alive," says one woman to a flabby and apathetic-looking man. In another cartoon, an oversized woman reading a novel looks gaily at her scowling, underdeveloped husband and comments, "It's our *own* story *exactly!* He bold as a hawk, she soft as the dawn." "Yoo-hoo, it's me and the ape man," announces a wife cheerfully on arriving at a party with her diminutive spouse. "Mother, this is Tristram," says a young lady introducing a timid, undersized little man, whose romantic name is an ironic contrast to his sorry appearance.

Frequently the woman takes the initiative in courting a reluctant male. "I love the idea of there being two sexes, don't you?" an eager young woman inquires of a man who seems taken aback. Another cartoon shows a hopeful woman crouched upon a sofa like a purring pussycat, to whom the surly object of her affection replies, "My heart has been a stick of wood since May, 1927, Miss Prentice." When other means fail, the women resort to Neanderthal tactics. "You're going a bit far, Miss Blanchard," complains an unwilling swain as a hungry-looking woman is carrying him off in her arms.

On the other hand, some Thurber women deflate their husbands when the latter attempt to imagine themselves heroic. "Who are you today—Ronald Colman?" snarls a wife as her husband, lunging with a cane at a floor lamp, skewers an imaginary swordsman. On another occasion a husband dressed as an Indian chief is belittled by his wife. "You haven't got the face for it, for *one* thing," she tells him.

III *The Matrimonial Trap*

Once snared by marriage, most of Thurber's men lead a harried and frustrated existence, bullied and badgered by nagging wives who consider themselves omniscient. In effect, Thurber's men seem married to their own mothers-in-law. The males seek escape from the battleground of married life by imagining a triumph over their humiliations. Many of them are would-be explorers and adventurers, restrained by their wives; and, like Mitty, they find refuge in their imaginations, though not always even there. Mr. Pendly, whose wife chauffeured his car, got over his feeling of inferiority by dreaming of descending in an autogyro, snatching her away from a garden party, and zooming off into space. Charlie Deshler, in "The Curb in the Sky," would "begin some outlandish story about a dream he had had, knowing that Dorothy could not correct him on his own dreams. They became the only life he had that was his own." But Charlie could not escape permanently, for his wife visited him at the asylum and corrected even the details of his dreams.

Rarely do the husbands manage to assert themselves and regain their wives' respect. Tommy Trinway in "Smashup" is one of the few who succeed at least in part. Tommy lacked the self-confidence to drive, so his wife Betty drove the family car. Because of her husband's phobia, Betty bossed him around scornfully. Finally a time came when she sprained her left wrist and Tommy had to drive. Taking over the wheel, he succeeded in maneuvering through a large city and by quick action managed to miss a woman who stepped right in front of his wheels. Everyone congratulated him on his skillful driving. Everyone but Betty, who continued to belittle him and take the credit for herself. But, having regained self-confidence, Tommy asserted his independence by ordering separate bedrooms at their hotel. Having thus partly overthrown his wife's domination, he went out whistling jauntily. "Smashup" bears a resemblance to Hemingway's "The Short Happy Life of Francis Macomber"; a chief difference between the two stories is that Thurber's characters are not involved in spectacular adventure in a romantic setting but enact their little drama under relatively unexciting circumstances in commonplace surroundings.

Less successful than Tommy Trinway, most of Thurber's married men have to go home, home being seen by an apprehensive husband in one drawing as the personification of a threatening wife. Home life gets worse and worse until some of the men can take no more and are shown strangling their mates or trying to lure them into the cellar in order to bash them over the head with a coal shovel and bury them. "I'm wearing gloves because I don't want to leave any fingerprints around," one husband explains to his wife. Usually these attempts at murder are botched and bungled; and, when they succeed in the cartoons, the effect is comic and no more deadly than when someone shouts, "Bang, you're dead!" in a children's game. Thurber explains that there is obviously no blood to speak of in the people he draws and that no one who looks at his cartoon victims will believe them really dead. They will, of course, be alive again for the next round.

Murder is treated comically in such stories as "Mr. Preble Gets Rid of His Wife" and "The Catbird Seat," but in "The Whip-poor-will" it is deadly serious. This begins like many of Thurber's caustic stories of incompatibility between husband and wife, but it proceeds with a gradual revelation of horror. The reader is led by almost imperceptible steps from domestic squabbling to frenzied insanity and murder. Mrs. Kinstrey acts with authority, maddening poise, and imperturbability while her husband's irritability and insomnia, aggravated by the weird shrieking of a whippoorwill, turns from neurosis to insanity. With the surrealism of the dream world, the story shifts in and out of the stream of Mr. Kinstrey's consciousness as his wife's mocking superiority, the suspected super-ciliousness of the servants, and the cry of the bird chip away the edges of his reason and goad him into uncontrollable paranoia in which he stabs his wife, servants, and finally himself. One of Thurber's most skillfully executed pieces, "The Whip-poor-will" shows the gradual transition from irritability to madness, from a brittle temper to triple murder and suicide.

The effect of "The Whip-poor-will" is one of sheer horror, but there is only a shade of difference between it and such stories of domestic discord as "The Case of Dimity Ann," "The Interview," and "The Breaking Up of the Winships." In these stories and others Thurber shows a constant needling and exchange of gibes between husbands and wives who are unable to converse and only argue. He portrays marriage at the combustible stage when only a spark is needed to ignite a quarrel. Often the causes for antagonism and divorce are quite absurd, but minute irritants constantly rubbing can produce eventual disaster. "It is a commonplace that the small annoyances of the marriage relationship slowly build up its insup-portabilities, as particles of sediment build up great deltas," Thur-ber explained. Thus the breaking up of the Winships is caused by a trivial argument on the comparative merits of Garbo and Donald Duck, which leads to a crescendo of sarcasm, vituperation, and misunderstanding climaxed by divorce. Thurber commented that the whole business is miserable and ridiculous. Equally so is the case of the Bidwells, between whom there is a growing antagonism resulting in divorce because of Mr. Bidwell's amusing himself by seeing how long he could hold his breath.

Sex, rarely an issue in Thurber's accounts of marital frustration, is involved mainly in the Monroe pieces, in "The Interview," and in the ending of "Smashup." Though his repressed men may reflect the competitive pressures of a materialistic society, his work has nothing else in common with D. H. Lawrence or with Sherwood Anderson's *Many Marriages;* and, unlike Lawrence, he offered no solution for the inhibited male. ("I am, by God, going to keep sex out of this office—sex is an incident," blustered Harold Ross, the *New Yorker's* eccentric editor.)

Instead, Thurber showed remarkable skill in tracing the mounting incompatibility between nagging wife and imprecating husband who take a perverse delight in annoying each other. Like the Lock-horns in "The Interview," most of Thurber's couples are very ir-ritable, neurotically temperamental, and often given to excessive drinking. They exemplify "those high-strung, sensitive couples who make up such a large percentage of present day families." Mrs. Lockhorn corrects and regulates her husband, trying to supervise and restrict his drinking, while he sneers insults back at her. There is little healthy emotion in such a marriage, and Lockhorn complains to a visitor that sexual intercourse is only for holidays.

In "The Case of Dimity Ann" Mr. Ridgeway, having insulted and abused his departed guests, sits up until the small hours of the morning drinking Scotch and snarling at his wife, who goads him in turn by analyzing him with amateur psychology. The reader can sense this (Ridgeway's second) marriage breaking up. Ridgeway repeatedly jeers at his wife's former beau, nags, and glares at her. She replies in kind. "I never started a story in my life," he says, "but what you heard something, or saw something, or remembered something. 'I just remembered something' has broken up more marriages than anything else.... And don't keep saying, 'Get it over with.' What the hell kind of attention is that, anyway?" he demands. The story concludes with their going to bed, but the reader senses that this is not the end and that a great deal happened previously to bring about such a heavily charged atmosphere.

Thurber often showed marriage *in medias res,* revealing neither courtship nor the final breakup but some point at which friction is wearing the marriage through and a crisis is anticipated. Again he might show only the end of the affair, as in "The Whip-poor-will," leaving the reader to guess at much that went before. "Take more'n a whip-poor-will to cause a mess like that," commented the police.

A Freudian interpretation might assume that in some of his pieces Thurber was releasing his own pent-up hostility toward women and that in those wherein men murder their wives, he was revealing his own subdued desires. (Mrs. Thurber recalls with amusement that after "The Whip-poor-will" appeared, anxious friends warned her to be on guard and to take protective measures.) Thurber, however, was quite conscious of what he did and was well in control of his work; he had the objectivity to see his art in dispassionate perspective. Instead of being amused at the idea of murdering a woman, Thurber showed such an attempt as grotesquely absurd or horrifying. His work is deliberate satire, except in the case of "The Whip-poor-will," which he admitted writing with an element of anger as a reaction to five eye operations. In other cases Freudian theory should not be applied to Thurber himself, for he was applying it to his characters, whose motivations, repressions, and releases he knew even though they may not have been aware of them. They are the ones who occasionally release repressed attitudes; and Thurber was in the position of the psychiatrist, not the patient. After seeing his drawings, many psychiatrists offered Thurber free treatment, but he had psychotherapy only after a nervous breakdown caused by the series of eye operations. Once he went to a lady psychiatrist, who told Mrs. Thurber: "Your husband doesn't need psychiatry any more than my dog does." Thurber recalled that the dog "was in fine fettle and feather."

For all of his awareness of the conflicts between spouses, Thurber was not cynical toward marriage. On the contrary, he appeared greatly concerned that the relation between men and women be a mature, rewarding one. The scintillating gibes and casual witticisms of the cynic merely entertain; but Thurber was an idealist, pained at seeing the reality so often fall short of its potential. Hence the intensity of his studies of corroding marriages.

IV *Thurber and the Genteel Tradition*

Mrs. Thurber observed that, when he first began writing, Thurber was, in fact, a good deal of a Puritan; and this remark is borne out by his "Credos and Curios" column of 1923 for the Columbus *Dispatch*. In it we find him denouncing the "sordid" treatment of sex in the writings of James Branch Cabell, Sinclair Lewis, Sherwood Anderson, D. H. Lawrence, and James Joyce, though he later came to admire their work. He complained that "Jurgen's endless, sly and sneaking philanderings become as tiresome as the double entendres in the Parisian Sans Gene. . . . Jurgen . . . is a sneaking, snickering whisperer behind doors." The young Thurber vastly preferred Zona Gale's *Faint Perfume* for "its note of idealistic love . . . flung like a fresh rose among the sordid sex stuff that prevails in present day novels," and he praised her book's "fine fragrance of a sensitive, clean love which permeates and changes everything." He wrote further that, like Carl Van Doren, he was "not interested in those aspects of woman which she shares with a rabbit, but in the aesthetic side of her finer self."

Considering the frumpy long gowns of his cartoon women, it is amusing to find a romantic young Thurber complaining of the short skirts of 1923: "There was no loveliness in them, no rhythmic music, nothing to suggest a lady in a garden or a girl on a river when it is summer and afternoon. They suggested, rather, stout ladies bowling duck pins. . . . The long dress breathes of muted harpsichord music, of old colonnades under the moon, of lilacs at twilight, of romance on wide shining stairways, of figures posed in tall palace windows, of lovers' heads against the blue night."

Looking over these early writings a few years before his death, Thurber was surprised and amused by some of his youthful views. We have already seen how *Is Sex Necessary?* turned against the genteel tradition; and, by 1933, he wrote of "the old-fashioned girl who yielded to a man's embraces as if she were slowly lowering herself into a tub of cold water." By the time he joined *The New Yorker,* he had shed any residual prudery and had become quite cosmopolitan (*cf.* his discussion of sex in Chapter IX of *The Years with Ross*). But always a gentleman, he criticized in his last years the excessive exploitation of sex in the literature of midcentury. "I'm tired of these people who make love a four-letter word," he told W. J. Weatherby in 1961. "The basis of development goes out of the human spirit. I'm a great Henry James man and his men and women were capable of friendship."[6] And in a posthumous essay, he wrote: "We talk too much about this damnable dehumanization, and the process shows up in too many of the dramas and novels of our day. Love has become a four-letter word, and sex is no longer creative but destructive."

Thurber considered love too important for the trivial, shallow treatment it receives in popular culture. "My pet antipathy," he told a *Life* interviewer, "is the bright detergent voice of the average American singer, male and female, yelling or crooning in cheap yammer songs of the day about 'love.' Americans are brought up without being able to tell love from sex, lust, Snow White or Ever After. We think it is a pushbutton solution, or instant cure for discontent and a sure road to happiness, whatever it is. By our sentimental ignorance we encourage marriage as a kind of tranquilizing drug. A lady of 47 who has been married 27 years and has six children knows what love really is and once described it for me like this: 'Love is what you've been through with somebody.'"[7]

Thurber was well aware that not all marriages are like those unfortunate ones in his stories and drawings; and he maintained not only that genuine love is possible but that it is the only solution for the human predicament. This is the theme of *The Last Flower, The White Deer,* and *The 13 Clocks;* and *The Thurber Album* shows a number of enduring marriages.

Since his own first marriage failed, Thurber knew personally the painful emotions attending divorce and the events leading up to it; and this knowledge gave an urgency to his stories. In 1922, he married Althea Adams, a Columbus girl, who was then a sophomore at Ohio State, where she had been picked as campus rosebud. Apparently she was quite ambitious for her husband and urged him to leave journalism in Columbus to try free-lancing in New York and later in France. Acquaintances said that she was too aggressive and domineering for Thurber; and, by 1929, they had separated. Later they were reunited long enough to have a daughter, Rosemary, born on October 7, 1931. Thurber said that his child made the reconciliation worth while; and, after his second marriage, he remained close to his daughter and later to his grandchildren.

But the first marriage continued to deteriorate; and on May 24, 1935, it was ended by divorce. In some newspaper articles of the time, his first wife was quoted as accusing him of getting into fights and coming home beaten up; but these statements were inaccurate. In reality, Thurber was not a brawler; he was never beaten up in his life, and many stories of his supposed wildness in the early days at *The New Yorker* are mere myths, such as the account of his ripping a phone booth off the wall and lying down in it as in a coffin. The day after the divorce, Thurber's first wife married a wealthy New Haven society man, but neither this nor a third marriage lasted. In June, 1935, Thurber married Helen Wismer, a clergyman's daughter from Nebraska, who had edited several minor magazines.

In Thurber's fiction marriage may become unendurable, as Charlie Deshler and Mr. Bidwell discovered; but its alternatives are even worse. When the nameless protagonist of "The Evening's at Seven" visits a former love as a relief from a routinely monotonous marriage, there is only loneliness and frustration in his abortive attempt at extra-marital romance. And so he returns to his hotel, where he finds some small measure of defiance in ordering consommé instead of his customary clam chowder.

When a marriage disintegrates to the point at which an affair is considered, it is only a short step to divorce. Yet divorce does not bring freedom, only isolation. This is seen most clearly in "One Is a Wanderer," a story written between Thurber's two marriages and autobiographical in mood and detail. It concerns Mr. Kirk, a forty-year-old divorced writer living alone in a hotel, where he fills his closet with soiled shirts rather than launder them, just as Thurber did at the time.

"Let's see, what have people living alone made?" asks Kirk, meditating upon his situation. "Not love, of course, but a great many other things; money, for example, and black marks on white paper." Alone in New York on a Sunday evening, Kirk desperately looks for something to do to ease his solitude. He thinks of calling upon various married friends, but he realizes that he would only take a damp blanket into their warmth. "It isn't because I'm so damned unhappy—I'm not so damned unhappy—It's because they're so damned happy, damn them. Why don't they know that? Why don't they do something about it?" he asks. As for Kirk, he goes to a night spot, drinks with some gaily intoxicated people he scarcely knows, and takes a cab home after three o'clock. It's all right to knock around a bit at joints and parties, Willie the cabman tells him: "But I got a home over in Brooklyn and a wife and a couple kids, and boy, I'm tellin' you that's the best place, you know what I mean?"

"You're right, Willie," Kirk replies. "You're absolutely right there. . . . A man wants to go home."

"Well, here we are, Mr. Kirk. Home it is," says Willie with unconscious irony, as he deposits Kirk at his lonely hotel.

At that time, Thurber would seem to agree with Dr. Johnson that, "Marriage has many pains, but celibacy has no pleasures." Mr. Kirk considers remarriage but realizes that it would not be easy, that one cannot simply become a new person by wishing it, and that his own faults were partly responsible for his divorce.

Thurber, at any rate, did marry again; and his second marriage was extremely successful. Friends wrote frequently about Helen Thurber's being a person of great charm and intelligence, and they observed that, though Thurber endured a good deal of suffering, he was spared at least the ordeal of marriage to a Thurber woman. After his blindness, Thurber called her his seeing-eye wife; and his English publisher, Hamish Hamilton, wrote that "For many years Helen took the place of his eyes. His writing was made possible by her infinite patience in copying, reading, and re-reading and helped by her critical comments. His burden was lightened by her stimulating company and her affectionate teasing. . . . Helen turned Jamie's night into day."

Fearing that a happy home life would make Thurber's work lose its bite, Harold Ross urged Robert Benchley to dissuade him from remarriage. Ross soon developed a warm admiration for Mrs. Thurber, and his fears proved groundless as Thurber continued to write harrowing accounts of domestic discord. However, after 1935, the shrews appear with less and less frequency in his stories and finally almost disappear. The second Mrs. Thurber, as she appears in his pages, is not a nagger but the voice of moderation and common sense; she is quite as witty as her husband; and, if she tops his last word, her perfect squelch seems appropriate. Beginning with *Let Your Mind Alone!* (1937), the studies of broken or breaking marriages are less frequent, though more skillfully done; and the man and woman are apt to be equally at fault. For the most part, the husbands are no longer dominated but are quite as strong as their wives and often, in fact, take the initiative.

Thurber later tended to show a single sharply etched scene in which a quarrel develops mainly through dialogue rather than incident and, igniting as a spark, is fanned into flames which are with difficulty suppressed or which, like a volcano, becomes momentarily quiescent but threatens future and more devastating eruptions. He showed himself a master of repartee, depending upon the flicking turn of a mood or phrase, as subtly dangerous as the feints and ripostes of a swordsman. Significantly, drawings of fencers or of sparring boxers accompany many of the matrimonial disputes. The stories are highly dramatic; and with their cutting repartee, they bear some resemblance to the comic drama of the Restoration in which the duel of the sexes was a dominant theme.

V *The Battle of the Sexes*

Because of the ungentle behavior of the gentle sex in Thurber's prose and the dowdy appearance of his cartoon women, some readers have concluded that he was a woman hater. "Why do you hate women, Mr. Thurberg?" a lady once asked him in Central Park. One correspondent suggested that he "quit harping on the imaginary flaws of the American Woman and start writing a novel about her true power and glory." Actually, Thurber was anything but a misogynist; and it becomes quite evident from a careful reading of his work that he had a particular appreciation of women. Those who come off badly are the intolerant and insensitive ones like Mrs. Mitty ("'I was thinking,' said Walter Mitty, 'Does it ever occur to you that I am sometimes thinking?'"); Mrs. Bidwell; and Mrs. Lockhorn, who wishes her novelist husband would give up writing and live comfortably on his income. Thurber complained in 1933 that women "lack the male's adventurousness, and their famed curiosity does not extend to the exploration of an after-world. . . . The female is inclined to adjust herself to her state, whatever it may be, whereas the male would like to adjust his state to himself. This last calls for violent and heroic action of one kind or another." But, while his domineering wives try to mold their men into conformists, his pages are also filled with exuberant and eccentric ladies, both in Columbus and in Connecticut, who display a raffish or radiant charm. Even many of his cartoon women have an immense vitality and *joie de vivre* and take up skiing, bullfighting, partying, or nudism with an uninhibited gleam in their eyes.

There was nothing Strindbergian about Thurber, whose portraits of Ohio aunts and colored maids were closer to Dickens and to Mark Twain. He wrote that "Men are more interesting than women, but women are indubitably more fascinating and possibly more amusing." He illustrated three books by women, wrote introductions to several others, encouraged promising women writers, and dedicated a number of his own volumes to women friends. In the Foreword to *The Thurber Album* he remarked that one of the most pleasant aspects of doing research for the book was his correspondence with Mrs. Dorothy Canfield Fisher. Elsewhere he commented that the only catty letters he got were from men; the only interesting ones were from women. Thus in spite of occasional annoyance with the fair sex, Thurber, like some of the exasperated men in his stories, ended up singing "Honey, Honey, Bless Your Heart."

Thurber admired intelligent women, though many of his favorite ones were not intellectuals. He told Eddy Gilmore that "when I get mad at women it's usually because they fall below my standard"; and he complained to Virginia Haufe that he didn't think the American girl cares much about knowledge: "She is interested only in her home town and her home state. She should show a wider interest than that." He said further that Russian women would not become less feminine from studying mathematics and physics, and neither should American ones. Wives should, in fact, be helpmates to their husbands: "My wife is a graduate of Mt. Holyoke. . . . She was an editor for ten years. Greatest proofreader and editor I know of. . . . She's a woman that helps her husband. Also runs the house. She handles all the accounts, the bank, income, proofs of manuscripts, servants, everything."[8]

When asked how her husband got started on the battle of the sexes, Mrs. Thurber said that it was a gimmick; and Thurber once remarked that he could not do without women, as his publishers well knew. Though marriage, in his work, settled into trench warfare (as Kenneth MacLean observed), Thurber told a *Life* reporter: "I like to do what I can to keep the American woman—my great mortal enemy—in excellent condition for the fight."[9] He did dislike arrogant women and would sometimes turn on those who cornered him and badgered him with questions all evening, but otherwise there is considerable good humor in much of the sexual combat, just as there is in the spats between Maggie and Jiggs or Blondie and Dagwood. One should read "What a Lovely Generalization!" as a counterbalance to the wild generalizations in "The Case Against Women," which ends with the patently absurd statement that Thurber hated women because they invariably lose one glove. "If there were no other reason in the world for hating women, that one would be enough."

There is, of course, a considerable literary tradition of anti-feminism but not among the authors Thurber particularly admired. Significantly, though, women are usually stronger (and often more admirable) than the men in the fiction of his favorite author, Henry James.

In the post-war years, Thurber's attitude toward the comparative strength of men and women took a new direction. More and more appalled at man's perverse politics in an age of atomic warfare, Thurber concluded that men seem "massively enamored of extinction." Accordingly, he came to see women as a force for preserving peace and continuing the cycles of life. Henry Adams also contrasted man's worship of force, symbolized by the dynamo, to the creative power of woman, symbolized by the Virgin; and, though the Thurber woman is a curious counterpart to the Virgin, she plays a somewhat analogous part in resisting man's destructive use of nuclear force. "The most frightening study of mankind is man," Thurber said. "I think he has failed to run the world, and that Woman must take over if the species is to survive." Men may dream of conquest or of utopias established by universal carnage, but women want a world in which they can raise their families peaceably and watch their gardens grow.

Since Jello will not set, and cakes will fall if men insist on tramping around and blowing things up, Thurber saw some hope in women's forming a conspiracy dedicated to not being blown to pieces by man's machines of destruction. As Oswald Spengler wrote, "Woman despises . . . man's politics—which she never comprehends, and of which all that she sees is that it takes her sons from her. What for her is a triumphant battle that annihilates the victories of a thousand childbeds? . . . There was and is and ever will be a secret politic of the woman . . . that seeks to draw away her male from his kind of history."[10] Likewise, Thurber predicted: "Almost any century now Woman may lose her patience with black politics and red war and let fly. I wish I could be on earth then to witness the saving of our self-destructive species by its greatest creative force. If I have sometimes seemed to make fun of Woman, I assure you it has only been for the purpose of egging her on." He once concluded that he would like to see a matriarchy. In fact, many of his sturdy Ohio women resemble Ma Joad, both in their salty realism and in their stubborn durability. And he asked Eddy Gilmore in 1961, "Wouldn't it be marvelous to see Mrs. Khrushchev take over from Mr. Khrushchev?"

Unfortunately, it appears that woman does need egging on. In

1958, Thurber observed: "I think it's one of the weaknesses of America, the great dominance of the American woman, not because of the fact in itself but because she . . . was the least interested in national and international affairs and the most ignorant. . . . The League of Women Voters, the last I heard, had only 127,000 members out of 88 million women in this country. . . . I was very much struck by the fact that the average American woman I know hated history in college—they just don't like history, they know nothing about it either."[11]

In the meantime, man "does not seem to know that he is doomed to go out like a light unless he abandons the weapons and blueprints of annihilation." If men continue to insist upon warfare, modern women, even more effectively than those in *Lysistrata,* can force them to their senses by boycotting sex or else dispensing with them altogether: "Nature, prefiguring the final disappearance of the male, has aided science in solving the problem of the continuation of the human being . . . by establishing the ingenious if stuffy technique of artificial insemination. It is only a question of time before the male factor in the perpetuation of the species becomes a matter of biological deep freeze, an everlasting laboratory culture, labelled, controlled, and supervised by women technicians."

Thurber did not intend such predictions to be taken literally, but behind his gallows humor was a serious concern. Throughout his work he opposed arrogance and aggression, whether on the domestic or the political scene. It is when they too closely resemble the aggressive male that his women become monstrous. If his anti-heroic protagonists are pathetic, the traditional concept of the hero is often that of a belligerent swashbuckler of the boudoir and battlefield. But Thurber found that the only answer to war—whether between nations or the sexes—was love.

Despite Walter Mitty's dreams of derring-do, Thurber challenged the worship of bellicose heroics. He wrote that none of his memoirs "is stained with blood or bright with danger, in the active, or Hemingway sense of the word. My experiences . . . have been distinguished by an average unremarkableness, touched with grotesquerie, discomfort, and humiliation, but definitely lacking in genuine .50 caliber peril." He recognized that the traditional heroism of the spectacular incident is superficial and merely a momentary display of good nerves and muscles, whereas a more genuine heroism is the quiet, modest confrontation of day by day problems. Echoing Thoreau, he found that "some of the most memorable adventures of any man's life are those that have had to be endured in a mood of quiet desperation." Thurber, who left shouting and posturing to the demagogues and the professional warriors, wrote that one of his favorite heroes in modern belles-lettres is the man who accepts a situation with calm and resignation. He found that "the gentle heart, thank God, is often armored in toughness, courage, and strength."

Thurber's most extended treatment of love versus false heroism is in his favorite fantasy, *The White Deer*. Here we find King Clode and his three sons Thag, Gallow, and Jorn, who lived in an enchanted forest. Clode, Thag, and Gallow were great hunters and warriors; but Jorn, while equally brave and skillful at war, preferred poetry and music; and, when he was persuaded to hunt, he cast his shafts wide of the quarry. Thag and Gallow bent irons and turned handsprings to show their strength, but Jorn merely watched them and played his lyre: "He sang that love, not might, would untie the magic knot, or open the mystic lock . . ."

One day the king and his sons went into the magical forest to hunt a legendary white deer which, when cornered, turned into a beautiful maiden. They took her back to the palace. In all things the lady was peerless except that she could not remember her name nor whence she came. Even so, all three princes were smitten with her beauty and desired to win her hand. The princess (for such she seemed) therefore gave each a commission, and he who best accomplished his was to win and wed her. She commissioned Thag to kill the great Blue Boar of Thedon Grove in the Forest of Jeopardy and bring back its tusks, and she ordered Gallow to overcome the Seven-headed Dragon of Dragore and bring back the sacred sword it guarded. When the princes complained of the danger of their tasks, in each of which a hundred knights already had lost their lives, the princess asked whether Thag and Gallow hunted nothing more perilous than white deer. Thus shamed, the princes set forth. Then the princess spoke to Jorn, whom she really loved, and commissioned him to vanquish the Mok-Mok and to bring back a chalice filled with a thousand cherries from the orchard which the Mok-Mok guarded. Jorn felt insulted, for the Mok-Mok was only a clay and sandalwood scarecrow on which a hundred children had carved their names. But the princess asked Jorn if he never hunted anything less perilous than white deer.

At half past hate or a quarter to fight, Thag rode along on his quest through a surrealistic landscape and a series of encounters vaguely reminiscent of Childe Roland's route to the Dark Tower. When he finally arrived at the boar's den, he found the beast asleep and killed him without difficulty. Gallow meanwhile found that the Seven-headed Dragon of Dragore was a mechanical wonder and that the sacred sword it guarded was won by tossing a ball into each of the seven moving heads. But the heads would stand still if a bribe were given the concessionaire. Gallow paid the bribe and won the sacred sword, which was only one of a hundred identical ones.

Thag and Gallow had to follow fantastic routes to accomplish their supposedly dangerous commissions. Jorn's path, however, was straight and smooth. He did not believe his assigned task worthy of his strength and courage, thinking it something any child could do. His pride hungered for "a difficult riddle, a terrible task, a valiant knight to overthrow." This task was granted him, for he found that the trees had rubies instead of cherries. These rubies could not be pulled off and would fall only when he counted to a thousand. Thus he must count to a million to get a thousand cherries—a terrible task to perform in a race against time. But he discovered at last that the cherry fell not when he said any number short of a thousand but only at his saying "one thousand." Thus by repeating "one thousand" a thousand times Jorn soon filled his chalice.

Just then a fearful-looking Black Knight all in armor appeared and challenged him. The knight, Duff of the Dolorous Doom, warned Jorn that he had magic on his side. "What's mightier than magic?"

"Miracle," Jorn replied.

"What's miracle?" asked the Black Knight.

"Love's miracle enough," answered Jorn.

Thereupon the two began to fight. Duff wielded his sword fiercely and valiantly, but Jorn overcame him at last. When the Black Knight's helm was removed, he appeared as an aged man of seventy years.

"I would not have fought so venerable a knight had I known," said Jorn.

"You fought the fearful thing I seemed to be, and that's the test and proof of valor," replied the knight.

Jorn however, was dismayed that the fact belied the appearance and asked in despair what there was to trust.

"Ah, trust your heart," the old man said. "Trust love. Fifty years ago I undertook a fearful labor for a lady's love. Armored all in pride and arrogance, I sought to meet the dreadful Mok-Mok face to face and came upon this harmless thing of wood and clay. 'Then love's a whim!' I cried, 'and man's a fool!' . . . The peril and the labor, Prince, lie not in dreadful monsters or in mighty deeds, but in the keeping of the heart a man has won."

This is the essential message Thurber presents, and it is in this light that his stories of marital disaster must be understood. It is not difficult to win love in courtship, but Thurber's stories begin in marriage, where most stories end, for the real test of love is in living happily ever after.

Thurber presented a similar message in *The Last Flower* (1939), a parable about the destruction of civilization by war. "Towns, cities, and villages disappeared from the earth, and human beings just sat around, doing nothing. Boys and girls grew up to stare at each other blankly, for love had passed from the earth." Not until love was relearned did civilization begin to recover. Then nature once more began to bloom, people learned to laugh, dogs came out of their exile, song returned to the world, and arts again flourished. Tragically, as civilization matured, hatred and aggression were reborn, war came again, and everything was destroyed once more. Even so there is still some hope in the end, for one man and one woman and one flower remain. If love is learned, there is yet a chance for rebirth. The real message of *The Last Flower*, therefore, is not simply the negative one that war is an evil, but is rather the positive command, "Love one another." This is not romantic love alone, but a sense of humanity; for as W. H. Auden, who reviewed Thurber's book, wrote in the same year, "We must love one another or die."[12]

CHAPTER 4

Less Alarming Creatures

IF MAN is going to the dogs, it might be just as well; for Thurber's dogs and other animals usually have a placid contentment and innocence that man might well envy. It is only when the hero of *The Male Animal* takes a lesson from the sea lions, penguins, and tigers that he is able to patch up his domestic troubles. Conversely the tiger who understood people and tried to live like them met with disaster. Except for those occasions when they take on human characteristics, most Thurber animals are inoffensive; as Dorothy Parker writes, "There is nowhere else existent an innocence like to that of Thurber animals. . . . Even that strange, square beast, beside which lie the neat hat, the cold pipe, the empty shoe, and in front of which stands the stern woman, her hands on her hips, demanding, 'What have you done with Dr. Millmoss?'"[1] In fact, Kenneth MacLean suspects that "Mr. Millmoss is much happier safely swallowed up with the rotund hippopotamus than he ever was outside with Mrs. Millmoss."[2]

I *Imaginary Animals*

This cartoon was created accidentally. Thurber had intended simply to draw a hippopotamus to amuse his small daughter. "Something about the creature's expression when he was completed convinced me that he had recently eaten a man. I added the hat and pipe and Mrs. Millmoss, and the caption followed easily enough." The Millmoss cartoon eventually led Thurber to create a group of imaginary "Prehistoric Animals of the Middle West" which were supposedly discovered by Dr. J. Wesley Millmoss prior to his being devoured by the piano-shaped hippo. Creating a Dr. Ponsonby to challenge Millmoss' claims, Thurber satirized the discourteous feuding between scholars jealous of each other's discoveries. At the same time he parodied scientific journals by presenting his fantastic creatures with the mock machinery of footnotes and illustrative plates.

Continuing to amuse himself with imaginary animals, Thurber created "A New Natural History" and a series of extinct animals of Bermuda. There is no purpose to these creatures; they are presented simply for their whimsical charm. "No labor of ingenuity could fit them into a continuable pattern," explained Thurber. "They emerged from the shameless breeding ground of the idle mind and they are not going anywhere in particular." The only pattern one can find is that "A New Natural History" combines Thurber's interest in drawing fancifully conceived animals with his grammarian's wit, resulting in a series of illustrated biological puns, such as a Hoodwink on a spray of Ragamuffin, the Stereopticon, the Hexameter, a female Volt with all her Ergs in one Gasket, the Troth (Plighted and Unplighted), and a group of flowers consisting of Baker's Dozen, Shepherd's Pie, Sailor's Horn-pipe, and Stepmother's Kiss. Here Thurber's imagination gave botanical dimension and zoological personality to the sounds of certain words and phrases. It is a pity that these animals and plants do not really exist. Thurber particularly missed the Woan, a creature the size of a small cream pitcher who built his nest of gum wrappers and violin bows and was capable of only one sound, a low, mournful "goodle-goodle."

Humorists have always been interested in animals, from the time of Aesop through Chaucer, Lewis Carroll, and Mark Twain down to the modern animated cartoon. Thurber's interest in them was more than a passing fancy. One of the most valued works in his library was Lydekker's *New Natural History*, to which he referred again and again. His most extended use of animals is in his two volumes of fables, a series of beast parables in which the animals are given human traits; and humans, by implication, have animal characteristics and appear as "just another of God's creatures." When asked why he chose to write fables, Thurber answered that they are the oldest form of literary expression. "And every writer, I think, is fascinated by the fable form; it's short, concise, and can say a great deal about human life; the little flaws and foibles and vanities of a man and his wife, or the larger political scene, or anything else."[3] Thus Thurber's animals serve as a counterpoint to his people. We have already seen how he preferred their common sense to man's excessive pride in his reason, and their instinct for survival to his destructiveness.

Likewise, his account of the courtship and mating of animals continues the war between men and women. Since Thurber's humans usually are already (and uncomfortably) married, he portrayed courtship mainly among the birds, bugs, and beasts, recounting "the sorrowful lengths to which all males must go to arouse the interest of a lady." He concluded that "Surely nothing in the astonishing scheme of life can have nonplussed Nature so much as the fact that none of the females of any of the species she created really cared very much for the male, as such." His espoused tigers, chipmunks, bears, and guinea pigs find matrimony at least as contentious as Chaunticleer's and Pertelote's marriage, and they often come to a violent end.

Outside of the fables, Thurber's menagerie usually has no overt political or social significance; his animals appear wholly for their unaffected charm. Yet numerous psychologists and theologians have commented on modern man's alienation from nature in an urban, industrialized society; and Thurber's creatures are a diverting though temporary refuge from the confinement of synthetic wall-to-wall living. As Whitman wrote:

> I think I could turn and live with animals, they are so placid and
> self-contained,
> I stand and look at them long and long,
> They do not sweat and whine about their condition . . .
> Not one is dissatisfied, not one is demented with the mania of
> owning things,
> Not one kneels to another, or to his kind that lived thousands of
> years ago,
> Not one is respectable or unhappy over the whole earth.

As one of Thurber's neurotic men explains, "I'm going to the Zoo and feed popcorn to the rhinoceros. That makes things seem right, for a little while anyway." And in one of his final pieces, a depressing dialogue about the spread of *Angst* and the morbidity of the modern personal and political world, Thurber and his friend found momentary relief by going to look at the peacocks.

Though an Islamic proverb calls nature and its animals the roots of heaven, some people feel that a man like Thurber must be a misanthrope who prefers animals to people, a defeatist who seeks sanctuary with anachronistic creatures that have no place in a technological age and whose haunts must give way to subdivisions, supermarts, parking lots, and progress. Thurber was fully aware of the savagery of some species and of the exasperating traits of others; but his animals more often represent a freedom from restraint, conformity, bureaucracy, and congestion. They seem, in a sense, his equivalent of Walden.

He did not, however, romanticize nature; and, if his affection for animals resembles Mark Twain's, so does his awareness of the sinister side of nature. If the insects or the steppe cat don't get man first, the claw of the sea puss will do so in the end. But while Twain, in his old age, reflected morbidly about disease germs and God's cruelty as argued from the design of the Darwinian

world, Thurber was not really concerned about this aspect of
nature and comically conceded only that "swallows at twilight
. . . scare the hell out of me."

Thurber felt that there is enough suffering in the animal world
without man's adding to it. He disliked vaudeville animal routines
and wrote in 1923 that "We can never think of the laboring animals
as other than sufferers of the most acute mental pain, and often of
considerable physical annoyance." Similarly he disliked hunting
and commented that he would never shoot a deer unless the deer
were armed to shoot back.

II *Thurber's Dogs*

Thurber's literary menagerie is quite comprehensive; it includes
poodles, penguins, seals, Sealyhams, dolphins, dinosaurs, moles,
fiddler crabs, pottos, polar bears, wombats, wogglebugs, bower-
birds, bandicoots, and even the bristle worm. But the most
celebrated of his animals and the one that appears most frequently
in his pages is the noble dog, whose sublime innocence provides a
foil to the folly or depravity of human beings. Thurber's first
published story, "Josephine Has Her Day," is about a bull terrier;
and over the years he wrote enough pieces about dogs to fill a
complete volume (*Thurber's Dogs*, published in 1955). But in the
case of dogs, his drawings are deservedly more famous than his
writing; for he created in his drawings a breed of his own. This
has come to be known as the Thurber dog or Thurberhound, and
Thurber's admirers wish he had found a way to breed such a
creature in the flesh.

The Thurber dog has the ponderous head and body of a bloodhound and the short legs of a basset. "He got his short legs by
accident," explained Thurber. "I drew him for the first time on the
cramped pages of a small memo pad in order to plague a busy
realtor friend of mine. . . . The hound I draw has a fairly accurate
pendulous ear, but his dot of an eye is vastly oversimplified, he
doesn't have enough transverse puckers, and he is all wrong in the
occipital region." Thurber recalled that the dog first appeared in
his cartoons merely for symmetrical composition. "When I had a
couch and two people on one side of a picture and a standing lamp
on the other, I'd put the dog in the space under the lamp for
balance. . . . Although at first he was a device, I gradually worked
him in as a sound creature in a crazy world."[4]

It is thus that the dog takes on significance. Noble, stoic, and
innocent, he looks with sympathetic detachment at harried humans
and thus makes a silent commentary on the proceedings. Ubiquitous

as he is, the cartoon hound rarely participates in whatever action is taking place. He functions rather as a silent chorus. His presence serves as a criticism for the silly, vain, cruel, or selfish conduct shown so often by his masters. The dog, said Thurber, "has been privileged to live with and study at close range the only creature with reason, the most unreasonable of creatures,"—man. "The dog has got more fun out of Man than Man has got out of the dog, for the clearly demonstrable reason that Man is the more laughable of the two animals."

However, the dog found that life with man was not all laughter. "His sensitive nose . . . has caught at one and the same time the bewildering smells of the hospitals and the munitions factory. He has seeen men raise up great cities to heaven and then blow them to hell." So it is no wonder in *The Last Flower* that when man, having destroyed civilization by war, descends to a level lower than the beasts, the dogs desert their fallen masters. Their departure is the final blow in man's degradation. Only when he rediscovers love and begins to reconstruct a civilization from the ruins, do the dogs return. Their reappearance is hailed with great joy, for without them a vital part of life is missing. "Man on this planet has reached the point where really he needs all the friendship he can find, and in his loneliness he has need of all the elephants, all the dogs and all the birds," says Morel (in the novel *The Roots of Heaven*) who is fighting to save African wildlife as a means of preserving human freedom and dignity.[5]

Thurber even thought it conceivable "that the primordial male held the female, as mate or mother, in no aspect of esteem whatsoever, and that the introduction of the dog into the family circle first infected him with the benign disease known as love." Whether this be so or not, the dog usually is allied with the men rather than the women in Thurber's duel of the sexes, just as Rip Van Winkle and his hound were fugitives together from the wife's wrath. When one little man hitches a Thurber dog to his sled, a woman skating by mocks him with Swinburne's "The hounds of spring are on winter's traces." An irate housewife demands of her sad-looking bloodhound, "For Heaven's sake, why don't you go outdoors and trace something?" In another cartoon, a woman says to her husband and dog, who are waltzing in the living room, "Will you be good enough to dance this outside?" Yet another drawing shows a hound and man comforting each other in mutual sadness. In "The Hound and the Hat" it is the man's turn to defend the dog from feminine wrath. In this piece a husband, discovering his hound playfully chewing on the wife's hat just as she returns home, quickly takes the hat himself. When the wife enters, she finds her husband

with a guilty expression chewing on the hat, while their hound
reposes innocently on the floor.

This partisanship, when it occurs, is not chosen by the dog but
is thrust upon him. Thurber's women occasionally berate their
dogs, but the animals avoid any bickering or resentment. More
often than not, there is mutual fondness between the dog and both
sexes. The hound, however, has problems of his own and remains
somewhat aloof from man's seemingly silly activities. When the
master tries to supervise affairs in the canine world, he usually
finds that his sagacity is not appreciated by the beast, who relies
on animal instinct to do things in his own way. Man fixes up a
bassinet for his expectant bitch, who prefers to whelp in the barn,
the closet, or a hollow log.

Thurber knew that man can never fully comprehend the canine
outlook. He did not attempt to invest his hounds with a human
point of view nor to write animal adventure and career stories.
Dogs may have influential roles, but people are the chief actors
in Thurber's prose. Except in the fables, his dogs do not talk, have
romances, or think in human fashion as some do in Kipling, James
Oliver Curwood, and Albert Payson Terhune. In fact, there is no
mythical quality to his hounds, who lack the athleticism and intelligence of Lassie and Rin-Tin-Tin. As Kenneth MacLean
observed, "His dogs don't do a thing; they don't save men in
Alpine passes, they are not the seeing eye, they don't bring the
paper home from the drugstore. They are just dogs . . . lazy, hungry,
sleepy, standing and lying down, torpid, dull, dumb, flap-eared."[6]

Thurber avoided the pathetic fallacy of giving his dogs human
standards and emotions. A common mistake of judgment, he wrote,
is to say that a dog gets whatever conscience it has from its
master and that "the whole pattern of a dog's behavior, even its
familiar rituals and duties, have to be inculcated in the beast by
the Great God Man." Although Thurber was aware that the con-
templative sadness and seeming compassion of the dog could be
romanticized and exaggerated, he still felt that the dog does sometimes sympathize with its masters. (Michael Swan found in
Thurber's dogs—as in Chaplin's little man in the baggy pants—a
"strange pathetic quality which endears the comedian to the
public . . .") His poodle Medve could "take part in your gaiety
and your sorrow; she trembled to your uncertainties and lifted
her head at your assurances. There were times when she seemed
to come close to a pitying comprehension of the whole troubled
scene and what lies behind it. If poodles, who walk so easily upon
their hind legs, ever do learn the little tricks of speech and reason,
I should not be surprised if they made a better job of it than

Man, who would seem to be surely but not slowly slipping back to all fours." This conclusion recalls Swift's Houyhnhnms or Clarence's suggestion to Mark Twain's Connecticut Yankee that a race of cats to rule us would be best.

Thurber felt that in many ways dogs are superior to man. They do not, of course, have man's potentiality for achievement, but neither do they perpetrate the crimes of which man is guilty and then praise themselves as rational, wise, and good. There is a genuineness about them that makes them incapable of deceit, hypocrisy, and affectations; but "Man has practiced for such a long time to mask his feelings and to regiment his emotions that some basic quality of naturalness has gone out of both his gaiety and his solemnity." Admiring the "whither-thou-goest tradition" of the canine kingdom, Thurber stated that the example of dogs can serve to remind men, "infirm of purpose, weak of heart," of "the miracle which can be wrought by courage, loyalty, and resolution." He praised the integrity of Rex, the bull terrier he had had as a boy, that did the most difficult tasks "with a great wagging satisfaction" and never gave up in a fight or a job he undertook, no matter how impossible. Thurber admired the dog's "keen zest for living" and his devotion to the astonishing things of life and wished that man had these qualities to a greater extent.

III *The Innocent Beasts*

In his affection for dogs and other animals, Thurber reminds one of Mark Twain with his cats, bluejays, and various creatures. Edward Wagenknecht has observed that "There is something very touching about Mark Twain's attitude towards animals at the end of his life: as his pessimism grew upon him, as he became more and more disgusted with the damned human race, he turned to them for comfort."[7] Thurber's birds and beasts serve a similar function, though his view of the human race was not so bitter as Twain's. When one of the boys in Twain's *The Mysterious Stranger* speaks of an execution as a brutal thing, Satan (an angelic cousin of Lucifer) replies: "No, it was a human thing. You should not insult the brutes by such a misuse of that word; they have not deserved it. . . . It is like your paltry race—always lying, always claiming virtues which it hasn't got, always denying them to the higher animals, which alone possess them."[8] Similarly, Dostoevsky observed: "People talk sometimes of bestial cruelty, but that's a great injustice and insult to the beasts; a beast can never be so cruel as a man, so artistically cruel. The tiger only tears and gnaws, that's all he can do. He would never think of nailing people by the ears, even if he were able to do it."[9]

Thurber observed that, even so, "For nearly three thousand years, or since the time of Aesop, he [man] has blamed his frailties and defects on the birds, the beasts, and the insects. It is an immemorial convention of the writer of fables to invest the lower animals with the darker traits of human beings. . . . The English and American vocabularies have been vastly enlarged and, I suppose, enriched by the multitudinous figures of speech that slander and libel the lower animals, but the result has been the further inflation of the already inflated human ego by easy denigration of the other species."

Man often uses "dog" as a highly unfavorable epithet; but Thurber suggested that this contempt may contain a streak of envy and that man may have the Dog Wish, "a strange and involved compulsion to be as happy and carefree as a dog." A reviewer of *The Middle-Aged Man on the Flying Trapeze* bore this out when he wrote that reading Thurber made him "long for the carefree life of a dog." Still, man frequently calumniates the animal. Thurber observed that even Shakespeare, "knowing full well that it is men who are solely responsible for wars . . . wrote, 'Cry havoc, and let loose [slip] the dogs of war!'"

Most frequently libeled is Thurber's old friend the bloodhound, a peaceful beast with what Thurber called a Gothic cathedral of a head. The bloodhound, "One of the gentlest of all species—probably, indeed the gentlest—has been more maligned through the centuries than any other great Englishman with the exception of King Richard III." (Thurber was a member of Friends of Richard III, Inc., a group of amateur historians—including Tallulah Bankhead, Dorothy Kilgallen, and Helen Hayes—dedicated to clear Richard's reputation of the defamations raised against him.) An anonymous writer in *The Outline of Science* slandered the bloodhound as one of the few dogs that repel affection: "'True, Man has made him what he is. Terrible to look at and terrible to encounter, Man has raised him to hunt down his fellowman.' Accompanying the article was a picture of a dignified and melancholy English bloodhound." Thurber commented: "It pleases me no end that this passage, in its careless use of English, accidentally indicts the human being: 'Terrible to look at and terrible to encounter, Man . . .'" Man may slander the bloodhound and stain his name as that of a cruel and vicious beast, but the criminals the bloodhound hunts are humans. In a pro-and-con dog controversey in which Thurber was engaged years ago, his antagonist, a Mr. Walker, wrote, "'The history of the dog is one of greed, double-crossing, and unspeakable lechery.' I submitted then and I resubmit," stated Thurber, "that if you stopped ten persons on the street and asked them, 'The history of what species is one of greed, double-crossing, and unspeakable lechery,' six would promptly reply, 'Man,' three would walk on hastily without a word, and one would call the police." In 1935 Thurber asserted: "If I have any beliefs at all about immortality, it is that certain dogs I have known will go to heaven, and very, very few persons will be there. I am pretty sure that heaven will be densely populated with bloodhounds, for one thing."

Thurber maintained that "The gentle, good-tempered, well-balanced bloodhound is actually about as fierce as Little Eva, and you simply cannot discover one provable instance of a bloodhound's attacking a child or adult, including a cornered criminal." He did a good deal of research on bloodhounds and concluded that they have "done more for humanity than all other canines and most men." Not only do they track down criminals, but they are invaluable in finding lost children and missing persons, being more successful than Homo sapiens, who often wastes vital time following wrong scents.

Man, however, has not repaid the dog well for his services; for, according to Thurber, "The dog has seldom been successful in pulling Man up to its level of sagacity, but Man has frequently dragged the dog down to his.* He has instructed it in sloth, gluttony, pride, and envy; he has made it, in some instances, neurotic; he has even taught it to drink." This situation can be disastrous for the dog, just as it was to the tiger in the fable, who learned too late that, "If you do as humans do, it will be the end of you." Thus it is not surprising that a female chow from New York City, finding that she could not put up with the ways of man, decided to leave home and strike out on her own. " 'Just imagine,' said Mrs. Black to Mrs. Gray, 'a dog not wanting to live with people.' 'The very idea,' said Mrs. Gray." But Thurber asked, "Who is there to prove that there was not a sudden clarity in her mind, rather than a sudden cloudiness?"

---

*As Romain Gary wrote in *The Roots of Heaven*, "Dogs aren't enough any more. . . . You see, up to now, dogs were enough for a good many people. They consoled themselves in their company. But the way things have been going, people have been seized by such a need for friendship and company that the dogs can't manage it. We've been asking too much of them. The job has broken them down—they've had it. Just think how long they've been doing their damnedest for us, wagging their tails and holding out their paws—they've had enough . . . they've seen too much. And the people feel lonely and deserted, and they need something bigger that can really take the strain. Dogs aren't enough any more; men need elephants."[10]

But the chow is an exception; civilization has not yet reached the state of decay shown in *The Last Flower* when dogs leave their masters, and so most dogs are reasonably content to lead a dog's life at man's bidding. Even so there are difficulties. Admiring the Thurber hound, Hendrik Van Loon tried to domesticate a bloodhound only to find that it is easier to housebreak a moose than to fit a real bloodhound into a living room. Unfortunately the hound of Thurber's drawings does not exist in real life—a pity, since his temperament is admirable. "He may not be as keen as a genuine bloodhound, but his heart is just as gentle; he does not want to hurt anybody or anything; and he loves serenity and heavy dinners, and wishes they would go on forever, like the brook."

Thurber was aware that real dogs are not always so estimable and that they sometimes ate first editions and lace curtains, gnawed on spinets, or chewed up his glasses. Even worse, dogs can become jealous of new babies and have been known to attack them, sometimes disfiguring or even killing them. Consequently, Thurber formulated the law: "Never bring the baby to the dog, always bring the dog to the baby." So a reviewer of *Thurber's Dogs* was hardly justified in writing that Thurber fawned over dogs and groveled to them in a masochistic fashion. Indeed, the dogs in his stories often contribute to the dilemma if they participate in the action.

Certainly Thurber was sometimes sentimental when writing about dogs, but he recognized this fact and usually managed to be sufficiently restrained. He admired the absence of sentimentality in the family life of dogs, and he was frequently sarcastic at the maudlin behavior of dog owners and the "distortion of values in the relation of human beings with their pets." He shuddered at the coy people who give their dogs such syrupy names as Bubbles and Lovums and Betsy-Bye-Bye and Sugarkins, commenting that he passed these dog owners at a dog-trot, wearing a horrible, fixed grin. Even more foolish to Thurber was the leaving of legacies to dogs. For all his fondness for them, he did not put them ahead of people in the final run; and in "The Departure of Emma Inch," Emma's slavish devotion to the slightest whim, real or imaginary, of Feely, her seventeen-year-old bull terrier, appears grotesquely absurd.

Nevertheless Thurber became so identified with dogs by the public that he was sometimes misrepresented as the successor to Albert Payson Terhune. (Thurber's own references to Terhune are usually not very favorable to the master of Sunnybank, and in "Collie in the Driveway" he gave an unflattering report of Terhune's fanatical behavior when some visitors accidentally drove into a prize collie.) Thurber was bombarded with letters from dog owners, many of whom requested him to furnish a name for their pet; and to these Thurber replied that names of dogs end up in 176th place in the list of things that amaze and fascinate him. Inadvertently, though, he has named a number of dogs. Iowa author Phil Stong called his spaniel "Thurber," and in addition Thurber knew of a dozen basset hounds named Thurber, a New-foundland called Little Bears Thurber, and a bloodhound named Tiffany's Thurber.

Interviewing Thurber in 1961, W. J. Weatherby reported that "Thurber himself feels as though he is dogged by his dogs. People who meet him gush about how much they love his 'charming dogs' and his 'lovely cartoons,' while the gloomy social critic, the superb prose writer, fumes behind his glasses, behind the little moustache that seems to bristle with indignation." Thurber complained to him: "People seem to think I'm just a funny man, a dog man. I haven't done any drawings since I went blind but they still ask me how my dogs are coming along. Some people even think I make jokes about dogs. For God's sake anybody who looks at my drawings with enough intelligence should be able to see the dogs play the part of intelligence and repose."[11]

Thurber called himself a dog man and not a dog-lover, which implied to him a dog in love with another dog. His own favorites were poodles, and he had owned twenty-five of them by 1955. "Theirs is the most charming of species, including the human," he wrote, "and they happily lack Man's aggression, irritability, quick temper, and wild aim." But he was not always a poodle man. During his boyhood the household had a variety of spaniels, terriers, and an Airedale, the one breed he disliked. In his thirties he began raising Scotch terriers, notably Black Watch III and Jeannie. Not until the early 1930's did he switch to poodles, but thereafter they were the dominant breed in the Thurber menage. He continued to keep them after his blindness but never used a seeing-eye dog.

But the bloodhound-basset of Thurber's drawings has held first place in the affections of his public. This is not the only dog Thurber drew; his pages also contain pictures of Airedales, Scotties, pugs, poodles, police dogs, setters, cast-iron lawn dogs, and nondescript mongrels. Whatever their breed and appearance, they usually have a dignified serenity often lacking in their masters; and their friendly innocence makes the humiliation, greed, and cruelty of mankind all the more poignant and pathetic.

CHAPTER 5

Columbus, Cocktails and Conformity

SATIRISTS often are accused of being cynics who take a perverse pleasure in attacking with their facile wit everything that others hold sacred. For criticizing aspects of their society, the Athenians tried to deprive Aristophanes of his citizenship, Swift was labeled a venomous misanthrope, and Voltaire was driven into exile. Actually, no one can write satire effectively unless he has a standard of values; for satire is the product of a conflict between high ideals and a corrupt world. Its mordant wit is that of a disillusionment often mistaken for cynicism.

I *Thurber's Columbus*

What then are Thurber's values and where are they found? Those who see only his portraits of the middle-aged man on the flying trapeze might consider him a pretty thorough pessimist who viewed contemporary life as a spiritless wasteland. Walter Blair wrote in 1943 that in Thurber "frustration is inevitable and struggle futile. . . . These modern humorists make fun of all mankind and of all its opinions except one—the opinion that no ideas are very sound."[1] But such a reaction robs Thurber's satire of its significance. If this is Thurber's world—and welcome to it—there must be another from which his social criticism can be seen in perspective. His fairy tales show the healing power of love and laughter, but their landscape is that of dreams. For his real world we must turn to Columbus, Ohio. For all of his literary success in the East, Thurber—like William Dean Howells, Sinclair Lewis, and F. Scott Fitzgerald—was a partially unreconstructed Midwesterner; and *The Thurber Album* and other pieces written in his later years show a nostalgia for the simpler life of the Ohio he knew in his youth.

There are at least two Columbuses in Thurber's work. During the 1930's he portrayed the city as a community of madmen, wild eccentrics, bizarre and berserk events—a sort of Buckeye Bedlam. In his accounts of Aunt Ida, Mrs. Phelps, Jad Peters, and the night the ghost got in, Columbus is a haunt of Midwestern

Gothicism and comic horror, with preternatural visitations, morbid musings, and psychic premonitions of doom. There is an extra dimension of dementia. Uncle Zenas dies of the elm tree blight, a servant mistakes Mr. Thurber for Antichrist, Grandfather Fisher thinks he is still fighting the Civil War, and twenty-one-year-old musclemen with moustaches attend Thurber's grammar school.

Turning from *My Life and Hard Times* to *The Thurber Album,* we enter a different world. The latter has as many strange events and eccentric characters, but the tone is quite different and has a sort of idealistic reverence. Here we have a hesternalgic hymn to the stability and restraint of an earlier era. *The Thurber Album* celebrates the pioneering and vigorous spirit of Thurber's ancestors and associates; and, in so doing, it gives a cavalcade of life in Ohio from the days of the early republic to the 1920's. Here are people of honor, kindness, family pride, and irrepressible individuality.

To begin with there was Stacy Taylor, the stepfather of Thurber's maternal grandmother. As a young man Taylor went pioneering into Ohio to trade with the Indians. He became the first mayor of St. Mary's, Ohio; and during his long career he made and lost fortunes, receiving success or failure alike with a placid imperturbability. Thurber reported that in Stacy Taylor's memoirs, "There is no grief or gloom . . . for it is a tale of pioneer action in a period when men had little time for tears." This portrait is certainly quite different from the stories of Mr. Monroe. Taylor was not an intellectual, but he took volumes of Burns and Shakespeare with him to the frontier and at night after going to bed read by the light of a candle whose stick was balanced on his chest. (Insatiably curious, Thurber tried this himself and found that he had either too short a neck or too little chest.) When Stacy Taylor died at eighty-seven, having in his old age "honor, love, obedience, troops of friends," he had lived all but thirteen years of the nineteenth century.

Following the accounts of Stacy Taylor, Thurber gave admiring reminiscences of his great-grandmother's cousins: Dr. Beall, a homeopath, who lived to be almost ninety; and Mary Van York, who "smoked chawin' tabacca in her pipe, a chawin' tabacca strong enough to knock a dog off a gut wagon." Thurber appreciated the pluck and daring of this lady who once slid down a rope from the third floor of a burning building in St. Louis. She took this and other remarkable incidents in her stride and lived to be ninety-three in spite of smoking an estimated 200,000 pipefuls of Star Plug tobacco.

In the portrait of his great-grandfather Jake Fisher, Thurber gives an acount of frontier days along the Ohio Canal. Jake was a fighter of epic strength, and it is reported that when he was in a rage he could throw a six-foot grown man twenty-five feet. Even in his seventies he could lift two hundred pounds over his head. But he exerted his strength only in a good cause such as thrashing a gang of canalmen who were lashing his ducks around the neck and hauling the hapless birds into their barge, or in disarming a maddened neighbor who attempted to murder Jake's son. Thurber commented that "He had a clean conscience, a good appetite, and sound common sense. . . ." There were giants in the earth in those days, and Thurber wrote that "A far lesser breed of men has succeeded."

Thus it is when the modern hollow man, the middle-aged man on the flying trapeze, is seen through the perspective of the past, that his weakness is fully and dramatically apparent. David McCord wrote that when he tried to review *The Thurber Album*, he found that it was reviewing him. Another reviewer concluded that *The Thurber Album* "fondly evokes a life style whose simplicity and generosity differ from the virtues which we may claim today. . . . Perhaps what made 'The Thurber Album' so effective was its fond but unsentimental perception of family life—and the implicit sorrow that much of what that phrase meant has gone."[2]

It is in the light of this latter statement that Thurber's stories of marital quarreling and divorce must be seen. That is not the sort of life he was used to, and E. B. White reports that Thurber was appalled at the "grave thrumming of sex" in metropolitan New York. There is a world of difference between the promiscuity of Mr. Monroe and the note Mary Fisher recorded in her diary in 1888: "I can truthfully say I never kissed a fellow in all my life but once, and that was Charlie Thurber at the depot a few years ago." There was courtesy and chivalry in their courtship, and marriage was made to last. Hence Thurber lamented the passing of "a nineteenth century spirit of family solidarity that has not survived the women of my grandmother's generation."

We have already met Thurber's maternal grandfather, William Fisher, founder of the fruit and produce store. His grandson stated that his word of honor was inviolable. He always maintained that a Fisher never should be disheartened by any circumstances, and the last picture ever taken of him shows him holding a two-year-old great-granddaughter, who was frightened by a flashbulb and to whom he was probably saying: "Show your Fisher, girl, show your Fisher." Married at the outbreak of the Civil War, William Fisher died at seventy-eight in the year World War I ended. His widow survived him and lived to be eighty; and Thurber said that her death in 1925 "marked the close of a way of family life in the Middle West."

A frequent visitor to the Thurbers and Fishers was Aunt Margery Albright, an elderly lady who had dizzy spells from lack of sleep or overwork but never from the vapors. Thurber wrote that she had the secret of vitality and that there was nothing artificial about her. Mrs. Albright always maintained stoutly that a man should be able to tell a sow from a sawbuck and a jaybird from a bootjack. She listened to the complaints of others but never complained herself, though she was partially crippled; and Thurber called her one of "that noble breed of women the French call *brave et travailleuse*." He wrote that her generation was "a time of stout-hearted and self-reliant women," and indeed *The Thurber Album* contains none of the satire on women that appears elsewhere in his work.

Many of Thurber's characteristics were inherited from his father, also a disillusioned idealist. As a boy Charles Thurber cheered in his sleep for the white plume of Henry of Navarre. As a man, he entered politics and moved in political circles "not as an integral part of the noisy and smoky scene but as a keenly interested onlooker at a spectacle." This is quite like the position his son had among the people of light reverence and sharp tongue in the party and cocktail circle which he often satirized. By contrast to the conversationalists of that society, Charles Thurber "was never guilty of that glibbest of human faults, the habit of quick and automatic refutation." Though closer experience with political campaigns left him "exhausted and disillusioned of the hope he once had that the American Way was destined to produce a breed of men selflessly devoted to the ideal and practice of good government," he maintained his own integrity and encouraged others—so well that he was regarded as the best-beloved man in the Columbus City Hall. "He was sorrowfully aware, from twilight to twilight, that most men, and all children, are continuously caught in one predicament or another. . . ." Some of the more amusing predicaments into which he fell were caused by bafflement with the mechanical and the manufactured, which plagued father and son alike.

Thurber's mother was much more high-spirited and created ludicrous situations to enliven the domestic scene. The hour when she impersonated an old idiot woman with false, soda-cracker teeth, first gave Thurber's mind "a sense of confusion that has never left it." Too busy enjoying life to be dismayed by it, Mrs. Thurber took life in her erratic stride and preserved her vitality through almost ninety years. Her portrait in the *Album* is quite different from the quarrelsome, irritable wives of Thurber's stories and cartoons, though she may have inspired some of his more exuberant females.

Besides members of the family, *The Thurber Album* presents a number of Columbus citizens. One of the more colorful was [Benjamin] Frank[lin] James. After commanding the Blind Asylum baseball team for years, he went blind himself but bore his affliction with the same good spirits he displayed when playing a winning game. Another memorable figure was Julius Ziegfeld, a carpenter and marathon coffee drinker. Thurber wrote him this tribute: "Julius Ziegfeld had honest and workmanlike hands and mind. He lived a good, long life, full of stimulating arguments, and the incomparable pleasure of building things, and fixing things, so that they looked right and functioned properly."

The Thurber Album concludes with portraits of three of Thurber's professors of literature at Ohio State and of three Columbus newspaper men. Joseph Russell Taylor introduced Thurber to the works of Henry James and Joseph Conrad and encouraged him in "the literature of living." Another favorite teacher, William Graves, forever young in heart, was liked by his students for being "a mere visitor in the intellectual world, like themselves, and not one of its awesome, withdrawn first citizens." He was not one of the "eminent men" in literary scholarship, but he became a legend among students and alumni. The third professor is Joseph Villiers Denny, "distinguished scholar and administrator, lecturer and wit," whom we shall meet in connection with *The Male Animal*. At the Columbus *Dispatch,* the city (and later the managing) editor and Thurber's first boss in the publishing world was Norman Kuehner, a large, aggressive, and sardonic newshound with a passion for police reporting. Kuehner was a terror to some of his subordinates; but he was a good family man and friend, genuinely affectionate beneath his gruff exterior. A colleague was Billy Ireland, the beloved cartoonist of the *Dispatch,* a man of rare skill and charm, who possessed the gift of friendship and a love of his native region. The concluding portrait is of Robert Ryder, the quietly competent and greatly admired editor and paragrapher of *The Ohio State Journal.*

Here, then, are some of the people Thurber particularly respected and admired. They were people of courage, kindness, sound sense, and integrity; and T. E. Cassidy aptly described them as having "a very special kind of simple grandeur."[3] Thus they form a significant commentary on the abject and supine characters of Thurber's fiction. He remarked that Charles Dickens would have found the Columbus people entertaining and memorable if he had encountered them in his visit to Ohio; but, in the age of *The Organization Man* and mass production, Thurber found such individuality declining. Perhaps for this reason so many characters in his art bear considerable resemblance to each other, so that one often finds them referred to as "Thurber men" or "Thurber women." In Thurber's words, "Group civilization . . . has come. . . . I suppose the individual has taken on the gray color of the mass. But there were individuals about during the first decade of the century, each possessed of his own bright and separate values."

In our own age, a dominant literary theme is the fragmentation of personality, the difficulty or impossibility of achieving individual wholeness. Through the *Album,* Thurber showed that he did not subscribe to the futilitarian cult of despair. He had compared himself already to Lord Jim; and Conrad's description of the parentage of Jim's sort might well be applied to the people of the *Album*: men and women "whose very existence is based upon honest faith, and upon the instinct of courage. I don't mean military courage, or civil courage, or any special kind of courage. I mean just that inborn ability to look temptations straight in the face—a readiness unintellectual enough, goodness knows, but without pose—a power of resistance . . . an unthinking and blessed stiffness . . ."[4]

Though Thurber showed this stiffness, he was guilty of sentimentality also; occasionally the *Album* reminds one of Norman Rockwell's covers for *The Saturday Evening Post.* The Ohio of the *Album* is too undilutedly wholesome, and the nostalgia is a bit too reverent. Thurber later seemed aware of this, for he commented that *My Life and Hard Times* is a better book. His nostalgia can partly be accounted for by his blindness; when a man cannot see the world around him, he spends more time with his memories. In one of his last essays, Thurber has a fictional psychologist accuse him of "clinging to the somnolent and sentimental past," and there is a certain amount of truth in the charge.

Actually, Thurber did not always find life in Columbus so idyllic. Mrs. Thurber says that the accounts of his being a nervous, disheveled, and lonely teen-ager and undergraduate were not exaggerated. Despite his frequent tributes to his mother, he was not very close to her as a child and only later came to appreciate her unusual qualities. While his mother was an extreme extrovert, Thurber was a shy, self-conscious boy. He wrote that "in the case of my own family, it was the mother and not the father that dominated the scene"; and, though her *joie de vivre* was poles apart from Mrs. Mitty's damp disapproval, she no doubt influenced his portrayal of the dominance of the American woman. For a number of years Thurber did not even live at home; his mother found rearing three boys too strenuous; James was not her favorite, and, since he caused the least trouble, she sent him to live with Mrs. Albright, whom he adored. He lived at home again when he attended Ohio State, but he, therefore, had less chance to become intimate with his fellow students, most of whom ignored the gawky, unglamorous youth.

Elliott Nugent recalls that Thurber used to wander around campus on cold winter days, "dressed in an old pair of pants, an old coat, no vest, no overcoat and no hat." During his first three years at Ohio State, Thurber avoided student activities. The only record of him in the yearbooks for 1914-16 is a picture of him in military drill Company I, wearing a visored cap, high-collared military jacket, sagging belt, and striped uniform pants, looking like an unhappy motorman. Eventually he became so discouraged that he dropped out of school for a year, which he spent reading at the university library, so that his parents wouldn't know he was not attending classes. He made another try in 1916 but had trouble in botany because he could not see through a microscope.

The ludicrous accounts of university life in *My Life and Hard Times* are pretty close to the truth. Thurber had no aptitude for military drill; and in gymnasium, where he was required to remove his glasses, he kept bumping helplessly into instructors, equipment, and fellow students. Frequently he cut military drill, which he considered a waste of time, and told his superior officers he would rather quit school than march around with a gun every afternoon. He was, in fact, dismissed from the university for having too many demerits in military drill but was reinstated by President William Oxley Thompson. Only his English courses were rewarding, and he held a lifelong affection for the professors who inspired and encouraged him. It was in Joseph Russell Taylor's class that he met Elliott Nugent, who was so impressed by Thurber's writing that he sought out his friendship. Under Nugent's aegis, Thurber became active and reasonably popular for his remaining year and a half on campus. Phi Kappa Psi pledged him only because Nugent threatened to quit.

In his speech dedicating Denney Hall in May, 1960, Thurber said, "I have faith in Ohio State University and the great work it is accomplishing, not only in spite of, but because of odds and opposition"; but he usually showed no great fondness for his alma mater, which he sometimes criticized as a giant trade school minimizing the liberal arts. In his folder at the alumni office, several letters from John B. Fullen, alumni director, chide him for standing off from Ohio State and throwing brickbats. A letter to Thurber on

November 21, 1950, reprimands him for never having joined the Alumni Association nor contributed to the Fund. Mr. Fullen cited Ohio State's building campaign and urged Thurber to be a "good guy" and join the team. "P.S. Mr. Fullen," wailed the secretary in a note, "there isn't one completely sensible item in his over-stuffed folder."

When he was a journalist for the *Dispatch,* friends urged Thurber to go to New York if he wanted a career; and Mrs. Thurber comments that he would never have gotten anywhere as a writer had he stayed in Columbus. As a successful freelance, he could have returned to live in Columbus; but, despite his nostalgia, he never wanted to do so. The Columbus that he wrote of was always the early Columbus. When he portrayed it later, as in *The Male Animal,* it was not so idyllic; and in much of his publicized praise of the city he was merely going along with the Chamber of Commerce. In 1959, for instance, when Columbus was named an All-American city, Thurber wrote to the mayor: "I have always waved banners and blown horns for Good Old Columbus Town, in America as well as abroad, and such readers as I have collected through the years are all aware of where I was born and brought up, and they know that half of my books could not have been written if it had not been for the city of my birth." Columbus and Ohio replied with like tribute: Mayor W. Ralston Westlake gave Thurber the city's first citation in honor of a Distinguished Son; he received the Good Luck medal of the Ohio State Society; and Governor DiSalle proclaimed a James Thurber week in January, 1960. Columbus has almost become Thurbertown, and a recent suburb and shopping center is called Thurber Village.

There are several Columbuses, and the town takes a place in Thurber's work similar to Hannibal in Mark Twain's, where it appears alternately as a haven of innocence and serenity—an ideal place for boys—and a muddy village whose dullness is broken by occasional episodes of violence and terror. But while Hannibal evolved from St. Petersburg to Bricksville to Dawson's Landing to Eseldorf of the despairing *The Mysterious Stranger,* Columbus appears increasingly as a symbol of the Great Good Place. As such, it forms a dramatic contrast to Thurber's tales of Manhattan, which often seems to be the Unreal City, a denatured place with empty voices and a sequence of pointless parties where Thurber's hollow men and women go round the prickly pear. Thurber once called New York a jungle, a state of mind. His New York neurotics are not located very specifically on the map; the city and suburbs or exurbs appear as a colorless habitat and are seldom described in any detail except in "The Talk of the Town." Society is cold and repellent, and there is individualism only in Ross and among the *New Yorker* crew. By contrast, Columbus has a warm if eccentric vitality. But this Columbus is a state of mind too, and it and New York are almost mythical polarities in Thurber's work.

Of course not all of Thurber's comic Prufrocks are in New York; Tommy Trinway and Mr. Pendly are Columbians. The others, though city dwellers, are not used to the big city; the antithesis of both the stereotyped brash New Yorker and of *New Yorker* urbanity and restraint, they are really wild Ohioans incongruously adrift in the metropolis and its environs, which disconcert and baffle them.

Thurber's Columbus is located in time rather than place, despite the detailed geography of *The Thurber Album*. As the twentieth century entered an uneasy middle age, Thurber looked increasingly to the past as a symbol of stability. In a review of the posthumous *Credos and Curios*, John Updike called Thurber merely cranky in his old age, an "indignant senior citizen penning complaints about the universal decay of virtue. . . . The only oasis, in the dreadful world of post-midnight forebodings into which he had been plunged is the Columbus, Ohio, of his boyhood, which he continued to remember 'as fondly and sharply as a man on a sinking ship might remember his prairie home.'" [5] But his backward glances should not be casually dismissed as mere escapism. In a time of vertiginous change, when the cold war and McCarthy were upsetting national sanity and integrity, he wrote *The Thurber Album* and other period pieces as a means of redefining American values. Like Fitzgerald's Charlie Wales in "Babylon Revisited," "He believed in character; he wanted to jump back a whole generation and trust in character again as the eternally valuable element. Everything else wore out." [6]

Columbus thus becomes an answer to "the neurotic personality of our time" that "is rapidly becoming psychopathic." Thurber claimed that in the post-World War II years, "Too many of our writers seem to be interested only in creatures that crawl out of the woodwork or from under the rock." There has been considerable criticism that too much contemporary American writing gives a debased and repulsive image of our society, so that foreigners acquainted with us only through our literature might consider us largely a nation of sex addicts, perverts, criminals, demagogues, and delinquents. In view of this complaint, it is particularly interesting to read a British reviewer's reaction to *The Thurber Album*:

> Mr. Thurber is the most versatile of American writers. . . . He writes with a calmness, an unbrutal maturity, which removes him by a century from the American generation with which his date of

birth associates him, and makes him, almost alone among living American writers , , , as comprehensible and as lovable to the European mind as he is to the mind of his countrymen. . . . At least for the time that it takes to read *The Thurber Album,* Columbus, Ohio, is the real America; the posturing of politicians can be forgotten and the banalities of Hollywood ignored.[7]

In returning to the people of the *Album,* Thurber was formulating, in effect, a code of integrity and courage. In this sense the book has a kinship with the work of Willa Cather, Hemingway, and Faulkner, as well as with that of Conrad. Its resemblance is most obvious to the work of Miss Cather, both in chronology and characterization. Its people are the sort she admired, and Thurber cited three of her novels—*My Antonia, My Mortal Enemy,* and *A Lost Lady*—as among his favorite fiction. Hemingway, like Thurber, seemed to prefer traditional societies; and he often used old men—Count Greffi, Anselmo, the old man of "A Clean, Well-Lighted Place," and Santiago—to represent the principle of dignity, honor, independence, and survival. Faulkner also, seeing the modern world taken over too much by the Popeyes and Snopeses, looked back to the gentlemanly code of the Old South, tainted though it was by slavery; and he declared at Stockholm that man must relearn "the old verities and truths of the heart, the old universal truths lacking which any story is ephemeral and doomed —love and honor and pity and pride and compassion and sacrifice."[8] Seen in this light, *The Thurber Album* has more substance than sentimentality, though as literature it remains a minor work. For Thurber, Henry James was probably the author most influential in dramatizing the issues of integrity. Thurber, in fact, connected his reminiscences in the *Album* with the James revival; he wrote of the early Columbus: "Those were indeed the days . . . all the graceful things I remember are gone, like presenting your calling card to the maid. Most people long for these things deep down." In Yeats's words, "Many ingenious lovely things are gone."

Walter Lord calls the period chronicled in the *Album, The Good Years* and Thurber saw them as the time "when tranquillity did not come in bottles but was simply an anodyne of nature." He recalled it as an era of innocence and repose and wrote that "Columbus and the world can never recapture the serene spirit of those years. This is known as Progress." Yet even Lord shows that not all was then sweetness and light: there was wage slavery, child labor, and wide-spread poverty. In response to the *Album,* Professor James Fullerton of the Ohio State English Department wrote Thurber in 1952: "I suspect that as a true picture it offers a bit from the same idealization which I make of my own happy years. We of the middle class lived in something very fine indeed. I am not at all sure that the majority who were not in the middle class lived in anything very happy to contemplate at all."

Undoubtedly Thurber's memories of the Midwest are too idealistic. Winesburg is also in Ohio; and other authors have portrayed this same Midwest as a narrow-minded, materialistic, frustrated, and intolerant region—the home of the George F. Babbitts. Both views contain a partial truth; the whole answer seems to lie between the extremes of *The Thurber Album* and the writings of Edgar Watson Howe, Sherwood Anderson, and Sinclair Lewis.

By contrast to Ohio, Thurber's picture of New York society, with its alcoholic and acid parties, carries some of the same denunciation that Fitzgerald put into his fiction. Many of Thurber's pieces in the late 1920's and early 1930's are humorous counterparts to *The Great Gatsby* and *Tales of the Jazz Age;* they might aptly be entitled *All the Sad Middle-Aged Men.* Fitzgerald too was a Midwesterner who never became wholly reconciled to his generation in Eastern high society but felt it had a tragic flaw— a deficiency in honor, courtesy, and courage. After Gatsby is corrupted and destroyed by the glittering world of the Buchanans, Nick Carraway returns to Minnesota, observing that this is a story of the West after all: "perhaps we possessed some deficiency in common which made us subtly unadaptable to Eastern life. Even when the East excited me most, even when I was most keenly aware of its superiority to the bored, sprawling, swollen towns beyond the Ohio, with their interminable inquisitions which spared only the children and the very old—even then it had always for me a quality of distortion."[9]

II *Thurber's New York*

Thurber did not move to New York until he was thirty-one years old. "He loathed New York at first, with its roar, its dirt, its jostle, and the brash ways of its citizenry," reports one critic.[10] One of his earliest stories, "Menaces in May" (1928), gives a sinister, sordid impression of the city at night—lurching stragglers, sprawling drunks, cursing cops beating a bloody and leering young man, the thunder of ashcans, the shrieks and groans of taxis, dreary laughter and shouted oaths. While writing for *The New Yorker's* "Talk of the Town" department from 1927 to 1935, Thurber observed the big city with a keen eye for revealing detail. For all of its population, the city appears to have a cold impersonality, and this quality is reinforced by Thurber's use of the editorial "we" for his "Talk" sketches. These are largely a record of folly, frivolity, mob stupidity, and the intense value placed upon such trivia as autographs, marathon bridge, and the adulation of insignificant celebrities. Everyone seems impressed by size, sensation, and novelty. People are injured and trampled underfoot by mobs at bargain sales. With insensitive callousness, crowds endanger the landing of a crippled dirigible and mock police requests that they be quiet, stop smoking, and observe safety rules. Thousands come to gape at the burned-out *Morro Castle*, and souvenir vendors try to make it into a sightseeing museum. "Of course it was a terrible tragedy, but it was a godsend to us," remarks one vendor. The big and costly, the spectacular, the vulgarly flamboyant are worshiped. Glamor and junk, elegant hotels and slatternly shops are neighbors. Famous people are harassed by mobs of rude autograph hunters. To attract business, a peddler of mechanical dogs embarrasses a gentleman walking his Scotties. Thurber described these details of big-city democracy with an ironic tone implying that its values are too often found in bargain basements.

The city could be exciting and amusing as well, as Thurber showed in *The Years with Ross*. But there was always a lack of communication; and, despite his many literary and theatrical friends, he commented at some length on the ungregariousness of *The New Yorker*. Several of his serious stories—notably "The Evening's at Seven" and "One Is a Wanderer"—dramatize the city's loneliness.

Thurber was so prominent in setting the tone of *The New Yorker* during the 1930's that he was sometimes taken as the typical cosmopolite. Actually, as Kenneth MacLean pointed out, "The common impression that he is sophisticated is not correct. He deals continually with the folk mind."[11] Charles Brady also noted that Thurber mixed the urbane tradition of Benjamin Franklin, Washington Irving, and Oliver Wendell Holmes with a "folksy, home-spun vernacular tradition."[12] Despite the magazine's manifesto that "The *New Yorker* will be the magazine which is not edited for the old lady in Dubuque," Thurber did write for her as well as for sophisticates, and many of his Columbus women resemble her. The rest of the staff and contributors, from Ross to McNulty, were not invariably sophisticates or "typical" New Yorkers either. Thurber noted that "They drifted in from advertising agencies, from cow colleges, from anonymity on other magazines, from obscure jobs on newspapers, and from Paris, where they had not known Fitzgerald or Hemingway or Gertrude Stein."

Many self-styled sophisticates, in fact, were not the sort *The New Yorker* admires, and Thurber often portrayed them quite unfavorably. Many of his satires are comedies of manners criticizing literary society and the cocktail set. Often his accounts of the polite and witty savagery of intellectuals at a social gathering are rather caustic. The parties he or his characters attend are usually charged with tension; beneath the surface politeness there is a good deal of venom in the personality clashes and verbal warfare. Thurber frequently used the dramatic method in these comedies of manners; the stories often are almost pure dialogue connected by bits of narrative that serve as stage directions. This dialogue is keenly sharpened repartee, verbal dueling; and Thurber often presented it with rapier and fencing imagery.

Funny as it may be, repartee is a form of combat in which the participants try to break down their adversaries' guard and run them through with a thrust of wit. The very word comes from the French verb to return a blow. George Meredith observed that the comedy of manners is warlike: "In the neatest hands it is like the sword of the cavalier in the Mall, quick to flash out upon slight provocation, and for a similar offence—to wound."[13] Speakers try to assert their superiority over others, to eclipse their companions with their brilliance and make them seem stupid, gauche, or naïve. Thurber could show vividly this politely barbarous world; and, though he wrote superb repartee, he did so not in order to display his own brilliance and virtuosity but to cast a light upon this mannered milieu and to reveal the defects of its artificiality. Thus he was more akin to Molière than to Oscar Wilde. By the adverbs he used, Thurber made his criticisms of wit combats quite clear; the speakers are described as sneering, snarling, speaking nastily, or coldly, or chilly, or sharply, or snappily, or irritably, or with annoyance, or warily. One must always be on his guard. For instance, since the appearance of T. S. Eliot's *The Cocktail Party,* Thurber said he had been cornered at parties by people who seemed intent on making him say what he thought the play means, so they could cry, "Great God, how naïve!" He had to parry and riposte with a question of his own, "Do you believe in the innocence of the innocents in 'The Innocents'?"

A number of Thurber's stories illustrate the theme of social aggression and artifice. In one of the best, "Am Not I Your Rosalind?", George Thorne, the host at a dinner party, deliberately gets his wife and their guest Lydia Stanton tipsy and induces them to recite Rosalind's speeches (both had acted the part in school productions) from *As You Like It* over a tape recorder in order to make them appear ridiculous and critical of each other.

Mocking and grinning, Thorne deliberately calculates, thrusts, feints, parries, and subtly campaigns. Before the wives perform, he plays embarrassing recordings made by previous guests, whom he ridicules before the present company. After the Stantons depart, each couple drops the pretense of friendship and insults the other in absentia. All of the people involved are double-dealers, and in its indictment of hypocrisy the story has some of the intensity of Wycherley's dramas. At the end there is, significantly, a drawing of two duelists with crossed swords. (Though its indignation is genuine, this story has an autobiographical origin. Thurber had just gotten a tape recorder; and, since both of his wives had played Rosalind, he worked up the story from what might have happened if they got together. Thorne's imitating Jeeter Lester, W. C. Fields, Ed Wynn and others is a reflection of Thurber himself; but otherwise Thorne is an imaginary creation, and the characterization of his wife is totally different from Helen Thurber.)

III *Aggression and Alcohol*

Alcohol plays a large part in this sarcastic society depicted in Thurber's pages. Its members drink too heavily, developing either an obnoxious excess of aggressive extroversion—"atta boy, have another"—or a beginning of arrogant introversion. Drinkers of the first class tend to wave their glasses; those of the latter, to twirl them. In either case, Thurber's stories have many episodes of the difficult host or guest starting trouble and "making something out of it."

In the early 1930's, Thurber's cartoons were often aimed at the then daring practice of ladies' frequenting bars and engaging in public drinking bouts. "And this is the little woman," says a man casually introducing a friend to his wife, who has passed out on a table at a party. In another cartoon a gaily intoxicated woman squeals, "Look out! Here they come again," as she envisages two harpy-like creatures fluttering over the table. She is unperturbed at the disapproval and embarrassment of those around her. Another woman, sprawled on her back clutching a bunch of daisies, grins foolishly up at a passing clergyman and says, "There's no use you trying to save me, my good man." "Here's to the Old-time Saloon, Stranger!" says a dissipated-looking woman drinking at a bar rail. In another cartoon, a woman at a bar is about to engage in fisticuffs with the man next to her. The bar, after all, is traditionally man's domain, as one slightly inebriated male asserts; surveying the Sapphire Bar, filled entirely with women, he snarls, "You gah dam pussy cats!"

In the 1930's Thurber frequently satirized the ritualized in-
stitution of parties that carried over from the Jazz Age orgies of
the previous decade. Though no longer bootleg, the cocktail party
was the baby of Prohibition, when people got together for the
purpose of drinking rather than serving drinks as incidental re-
freshment. Thus "The Case of the Laughing Butler" is concerned
with how to persuade dinner guests to leave off cocktails and
begin the meal. Thurber commented that in France the problem
does not arise because the French look on before-dinner cocktails
as an invention of the devil that spoils the taste for food. But many
Americans, he objected, instead of giving up cocktails are giving
up dinner. The guests appear rude and inconsiderate, bullying
their hostess. "I happen to be an old-fashion host who does not
believe in the abandonment of dinner after cocktails," Thurber
wrote, concluding somewhat despondently that there is no simple
method to induce cocktail drinkers to file gaily out to dinner.
Instead the host is likely to be sent out for more ice and to be
laughed at if he has trouble procuring it. In another essay, Thurber
told of yachtsmen's using cocktail flags to signal people aboard for
drinks. To this he commented, "The advent of the cocktail flag,
with its strange device, seems likely to lead to a deplorable de-
basing of the dignity of yachts and yachting—and yachtsmen."

Thurber's fictional parties are full of hecklers, whoopers, arguers,
and quibblers; and they provide a ready outlet for aggression. The
pseudo-intellectual bully can be overheard saying such things as,
"What! You don't know André Simon's 'The Art of Good Living'?
But one cannot—" The cocktail party can be bad enough, as a
Thurber drawing captioned "Cocktail Party, 1937" shows. In it
people are standing around laughing artificially, a semi-comatose
husband is slumped on a sofa while his wife glares at him, people
are paired off in exclusive conversations except one solitary woman
who looks forlorn and lonely, and the picture seems to exude a
pungent odor of mingled smoke and alcohol. Significantly, this is
an illustration for the story "The Breaking Up of the Winships."
For many of Thurber's stories of dissolving marriages take place
either during or on the way home from cocktail parties, which seem
to act as a catalyst for the harsh words and irritating behavior
that chip away the edges of compatibility. And the overt act in
"The War Between Men and Women" takes place at a cocktail
party when a man throws his highball into a woman's face.

Thurber was no prohibitionist; James E. Pollard noted that,
"Socially he drinks scotch and soda steadily, with no side effects."[14]
(He said of martinis, "One is all right, two is too many, three is
not enough.") What he criticized is the ritualistic aspect of social

drinking and the rudeness, raucous play, or rasping irritability engendered by excessive alcohol.

Quite as bad as cocktail parties are those at which games are played. The party games which Thurber described resemble a state of war, for someone is always taking a beating and being subjected to the smug mockery of others. Parlor games have the facility of bringing out people's hidden nature; Thurber wrote that, as a result of playing them, his friends have "dropped their masks, spoken in unfamiliar tones, stood out sharply in strange and new postures."

One of Thurber's particular dislikes was the party-goer of exhibitionist tendencies who forces his rough-shod humor on the other guests, whether they are interested or not. Unfortunately, many of them are all too appreciative. Jack Klohman, for instance, was the funniest man in the world to everyone but Thurber and a few equally sensitive people. His humor included such feats as ripping a chancel rail out of a church and coming into a party with it, saying, "I've either lost a church or found a chancel rail." "Sounds like a swell guy to have around," Thurber said wryly. Yet Klohman was worshiped by his party-going friends; his devotees, for whom he could do nothing wrong, sounded his praises to everyone. " 'Does he do imitations?' I asked. Joe Mayer kicked my shins under the table. " 'Does he do imitations?' bellowed Potter. 'Wait'll I tell you—' "

"Six for the Road" tells of another kind of rude guest—people like the Spencers who will not leave at a considerate hour. The Spencers ad-lib, perform pantomime and apache dances that play havoc with the furniture, and they are magnificent together while practically unaware of the existence of their hosts, who have to get up early. In addition, they are eager controversialists, ready to enter into a tooth-and-fang intellectual debate at the slightest opening. Thurber said that Emily Post's etiquette is completely inadequate to get rid of such boors. Just as annoying as those who will not leave at a decent hour, are people who come barging drunk into one's house in the middle of the night, like the belligerent literati in "Here Come the Tigers," who rouse the protagonist from bed to harangue him on a new literary dimension they think they have discovered.

Thurber's drawings reinforce his prose satires about the excesses of party-going society. "Ooooo, *Guesties!*" squeals an exuberantly coy woman to a group of scowling cocktail drinkers in one cartoon. Occasionally people release their inhibitions. One cartoon shows a woman with her highball raised on high as she toasts a bearded gentleman "With a hey-nonny-nonny and a nuts to you." Another cartoon shows a belligerent man shouting imprecations at his fellow guests at a cocktail party, while one woman explains to another, "He hates people." *The Seal in the Bedroom* (1932) has an entire section of drawings entitled "Parties." These include "First Husband Down," "Love" (which shows a husband flirting with a woman in front of his scowling wife), "When I Wore a Tulip" (in which a group of maudlin drunks are singing around a piano while half a dozen others who have passed out lie around on the floor), "The Brawl" (in which two men, their drinks spilled on the floor, are restrained by their friends from tearing into each other), "Berserk" (the picture of an uncontrollable drunk running amok in the house), "The Bawling Out," "The Fog" (in which a blear-eyed man has a delirium of being surrounded by laughing, singing, raucous, accusing faces), and "Four o'clock in the Morning" (which shows half a dozen people sleeping in an alcoholic coma on a sofa, surrounded by stale and spilled drinks and by smoldering ash trays). Whether there is an intentional irony or not, this group of pictures is followed by another series entitled "The Collapse of Civilization."

Perhaps the worst social gatherings in Thurber's stories are those made up of arrogant literary intellectuals, who can have a veritable genius for belligerently asserting their views and theories, snarling contemptuously or sneering superciliously at those whose conversation is intellectually uncongenial to them and who fail to appreciate properly their genius. They are like the spider in Swift's *The Battle of the Books,* who "having swelled himself into the size and posture of a disputant, began his argument in the true spirit of controversy, with a resolution to be heartily scurrilous and angry, to urge on his own reasons, without the least regard to the answers or objections of his opposite, and fully predetermined in his mind against all conviction."

Thurber commented that it is almost impossible to keep writers from fighting and quarreling whenever they get together socially. Malcolm Cowley recalls that a writer once compared the literary game to a boys' game of buckeyes. "Two authors bump their heads together, or their reputations, until one of them cracks. The victor moves on to crack another reputation or be cracked in turn." In addition, there are all sorts of gradations among writers. "X can make offensive true remarks to Y, who can make them to Z, but Z can't make them to X."[15]

This sort of thing is devastatingly shown in a story of Thurber's about the discussion of T. S. Eliot's *The Cocktail Party* at a cocktail party. (Here Thurber is, as he once put it, caught in a trap within a trap.) "I presume you're talking about the *play,*" said Charles

Endless, waving his empty highball glass. "Endless is forever repeating the critical judgments of his psychiatrist, Dr. Karl Wix, and embroidering them with the skeins of his own prejudices. 'There is no such thing as the power of conscious selection in the creative writer,' Charles went on." Grace Sheldon replied that she simply wanted to know what Thurber thought *The Cocktail Party* is about. "Great God!" cried Charles. "The woman seeks narrative sense in the sheerest mechanism of expiation."

Such arrogant literary controversialists often resort to jargon (frequently of a pseudo-psychoanalytical kind) and to esoteric and sometimes spurious interpretations in order to assert their superiority and to exclude people not in the select circle of initiates. Malcolm Cowley remarks that "This loose professional [literary] world is in some ways as snobbish as the Faubourg Saint-Germain." So in "What Cocktail Party?" Tom Frayne contentiously asserted that any straightforward explanation of the play simply was not intellectually respectable.

"For God's sake, Betty," Frayne was saying, gesturing with his cigarette, "say the Psychiatrist is Ambition, or Hope, or God, or Escapism, or Dedication, or the Father Image, or the Death Urge, or the Oedipus Complex, or a snatch of song you can't get out of your mind, but don't stand there and try to tell me he is an actual, carnate, human male psychiatrist."

"Eliot himself says—" began Thurber.

" 'I don't care what Eliot himself says,' snapped Tom. 'Eliot has missed a great many of the meanings in his play—wasn't that obvious to you when you saw it?' "

In desperate mockery, Thurber invented an imaginary theory to explain the play:

"The Catonian Trium," I said. " 'The Cocktail Party' is plainly a revaluation of the theory of Cato the Elder that two primary identities can sustain an unidentifiable third. That is, the *duum* differs from the *unum* in that it can absorb, without distortion of meaning, the introduction of an unknown, or mysterious, or debatable third."

"Naturally," said Tom with crisp impatience. "Everybody knows that. But it doesn't apply here. You are adding the Psychiatrist to Julia and Alex when, as a matter of fact, *they* are added to him. You don't seem to understand what identity is being concealed."

I found myself in the embarrassing position of being routed in an argument involving a theory I had made up.

Here is the very essence of the ridiculous, as Thurber showed with perceptive irony the absurdity of the intellectual so intent upon impressing others with his superior insight that his self-importance blinds him to the fact that he is being spoofed. Exasperated, Thurber slipped away from the party and walked twelve blocks home rather than endure more literary dissection from the cab driver.

He wrote in 1959: "it isn't easy to entertain writers and have any fun. . . . Nobody can ever remember exactly what happened at any drinking party invaded and taken over by writers, because, as the bowl continues to flow, their eloquence and invention take on the sharp edge of temper and cussedness." Apparently Thurber himself was not immune; one critic wrote that "As a brilliant if somewhat domineering conversationalist, Thurber was apt to be the life of a party, and sometimes too lively. He had a gusty temper and, a born ham, he was not averse to throwing glasses when lit."[16] If so, he was an amusing self-critic; his cartoon "Thurber and His Circle" shows him, highball in hand, haranguing a stupefied audience who are holding their ears or who have passed out. On the other hand, he said that he was often at drinking parties in body only: his mind, accustomed to "many years of writing news stories in city rooms, with 20 typewriters banging around me," was busy writing and rewriting.

Thurber frequently assumed various roles in his stories, and in "The Ordeal of Mr. Matthews" he took the guise of an ebullient writer intent upon expounding at great length upon his own genius to anyone he could trap as an audience. (This, of course, was no more the real Thurber than the Thurber who appears as an esoteric critic dedicated to unraveling the weird writings of Chanda Bell.) Totally inconsiderate of others and indifferent to whatever they try to say, his only concern is to elaborate upon his own presumed talents and depreciate his rivals. He manages to corner a Mr. Matthews at a cocktail party and to browbeat him with an uncalled-for *apologia pro vita sua,* rudely brushing aside any attempt by Matthews to enter the conversation. Matthews has to seek sanctuary in a cigar and bottles of ale, while Thurber, as a bully duelist of wit, practices the great retort, "the slash supreme, the stab sublime." Although Thurber told the story about himself, he made it quite clear that his sympathies were for Matthews. There is a touch of grotesquerie in the complete lack of self-criticism by the Thurber who appears in the story, while the author was evidently critical of his fictional self, who exercises a rather lame wit by snarling parries and ripostes in reply to anyone's remarks to him. "One of us ought to be a Boswell, taking all this down," one guest whispers sarcastically to another in a cartoon of a writer proclaiming his views with loud voice and extravagant gesture.

IV *The Literary Scene*

In spite of his satire, Thurber objected to sweeping condemnation of the contemporary literary scene. In "The Moribundant Life, or, Grow Old Along with Whom," he ridiculed irresponsible generalizations such as the statement that all American writers harry their wives, end up in divorce court, and drink themselves to death. But in various stories he showed the folly of some authors who do just this. "The Interview" and "The Case of Dimity Ann" both portray heavy-drinking writers harassing their wives toward impending divorce, though the wives are equally at fault in both cases. "We have been accused of making a career of sex, a hobby of drinking, a havoc of marriage, and a tradition of divorce," wrote Thurber. He refuted this as an all-inclusive statement, but his work dramatizes it in some particular cases.

In *The Literary Situation,* Malcolm Cowley draws similar conclusions. He reports that the divorce rate is quite high among young writers living in cities though rather low among older writers. He also states that while not all writers drink too much, a great many do, "and in fact the nondrinkers are regarded as a little eccentric. . . . One of the general reasons, often overlooked, is that the heavy drinkers in many professions form an inner group, almost like a Yale senior society, which people want to be considered worthy of joining."[17] Thurber knew that alcohol and art make a dangerous mixture. Fitzgerald, he wrote, "began to use liquor for posture and gesture, like almost any other writer of the 1920's. . . . But when Fitzgerald began to drink because he thought he had to, in order to write, he was lost."

"The American Literary Scene" is a piece of Thurberian irony satirizing an imaginary British critic who makes sweeping accusations against American writers without checking the facts. He makes patently absurd statements, such as: "Publishers all occupy sky-scraper penthouses, or 'random houses' and . . . dictate ideas for novels to the writers, supplying them with titles and, in some instances, writing the book themselves." However, in the last half of this essay Thurber also satirized the American literary scene at the same time that he defended it. For instance, the comment that nocturnal literary meetings are, in reality, "gloomily planned assemblages of separate lonelinesses" seems to have a touch of truth. Another statement that Thurber was not not saying (as Chanda Bell might put it) is that at literary social gatherings, "A controversy usually arises out of a fiercely stated prejudice, hatred, or admiration by the host or one of his guests. A novelist or essayist is likely to get to his feet, on his twentieth or twenty-first highball, and announce that he is 'the greatest goddam writer in the world' or that one of his friends is. This is instantly challenged by one or more candidates for the special distinction of greatest goddam writer in the world."

One such candidate is Elliott Vereker in "Something to Say." The literati in "What Cocktail Party?" at least observed the social amenities, but Vereker combined arrogant and phony estheticism with crude Bohemianism: "Vereker was a writer; he was gaunt and emaciated from sitting up all night talking. . . . At the most inopportune and inappropriate moments he would snap out frank four-letter words, such as when he was talking to a little child or the sister of a vicar. He had no reverence and no solicitude. . . . His was the true artistic fire, the rare gesture of genius."

The narrator making these statements is a burlesque of the hyper-sensitive Jamesean observer, awed by the "great man" and hoping to reflect some of his light. It was fortunate that Vereker proclaimed himself a genius, for he had produced no works to demonstrate his talent: "When I first met him, he was working on a novel entitled 'Sue You Have Seen.' He had worked it out, for some obscure reason, from the familiar expression, 'See you soon.' He never finished it, nor did he ever finish, or indeed get very far with, any writing, but he was nevertheless, we all felt, one of the great original minds of our generation. . . . 'Achievement,' he used to say, 'is the fool's gold of idiots.' He never believed in doing anything or in having anything done, either for the benefit of mankind or for individuals."

Often he attempted suicide but was deterred by his friends. " 'You have so many things yet to do', I said to him. 'Yes,' he said, 'and so many people yet to insult.' "

> He would call on people, drink up their rye, wrench light-brackets off the walls, hurl scintillating gibes at his friends and at the accepted literary masters of all time, through whose superficiality Vereker saw more clearly, I think, than anybody else I have ever known. He would end up by bursting into tears. "Here, but for the gracelessness of God," he would shout, "stands the greatest writer in the history of the world!" We felt that, despite Vereker's drunken exaggeration, there was more than a grain of truth in what he said; certainly nobody else we ever met had, so utterly, the fire of genius that blazed in Vereker, if outward manifestations meant anything.

While denouncing Vereker, Thurber satirized those who reverenced him and tolerated any amount of insulting, obscene behavior simply because he was a writer. As Malcolm Cowley says,

"The man of talent is invited to parties for a long time after it is known that he might get drunk and start breaking up the furniture, like Hart Crane. One should add that the talented writer is likely to be more interesting and less objectionable than the untalented."[18] Thurber apparently did not believe that an artist is above the common decencies and can do no wrong, and he ridiculed the fawning of those whose pampering of supposed geniuses simply encourages insolent egomania. Vereker is one of the untalented, and fortunately most writers are not like him; nevertheless, Thurber's comments on the general literary scene are often far from flattering, though he wrote with respect and affection of individual authors with whom he worked.

V *Art, Affectation, and Conformity*

Though they may inhabit Manhattan or Connecticut, the aggressive and exhibitionistic characters of Thurber's art are the antithesis of the *New Yorker* ideal. Commending gentlemanly restraint and control, *The New Yorker* dislikes poseurs in the arts, pretentious performers, and intolerant dogmatists. Its various departments are advocates of urbanity, which includes moderation, nonchalance, intelligent rationality, and discriminating taste. Eustace Tilley would be appalled at Jack Klohman, Birdey Doggett, Elliott Vereker, the Spencers, and Thurber's antagonistic controversialists. Sometimes the magazine may be supercilious, but even its snobbery is often tongue-in-cheek.

A modest man himself, Thurber admired people who are inoffensive, unassuming, and considerate of others. He and his favorite characters were strong individualists, but their eccentricities were inherent and not cultivated and affected. Thus Thurber found that he could not arouse much sympathetic admiration for the behavior of Salvador Dali, who as an *enfant terrible* attempted to escape from the commonplace by biting bats, kissing dead horses, kicking tiny playmates off bridges, breaking the family doctor's glasses with a leather-thonged mattress-beater, throwing himself from high rocks (a favorite pastime), and hanging by his feet with his head immersed in a pail of water. As a young lover, Dali covered himself with goat dung and aspic in order to give off the noble odor of the ram. When a doctor was seized of a fit and attempted to beat Dali up, the contention that the doctor was out of his senses at the time was Dali's, not Thurber's. Thurber did not join with the townspeople of Figueras in worshiping Dali; instead he objected to Dali's conduct as a "desperate little rebellion against the clean, the conventional, and the comfortable."

And it is the clean, the comfortable, and in part the conventional that Thurber defended. He preferred the world of Willa Cather to Henry Miller's tropics, Nelson Algren's wild side, or the hipsters' beat generation. (He commented that the latter go in more for sin nudism than for Zen Buddhism.) As for Dali, "He put perfume on his hair (which would have cost him his life in, say, Bayonne, N. J., or Youngstown, Ohio), he owned a lizard with two tails, he wore silver buttons on his shoes, and he knew, or imagined he knew, little girls named Galuchka and Dullita. Thus he was born halfway along the road to paranoia, the soft Poictesme of his prayers, the melting Oz of his oblations. . . . Or so, anyway, it must seem to a native of Columbus, Ohio, who as a youngster, bought his twelve-dollar suits at the F. & R. Lazarus Co., had his hair washed out with Ivory soap, owned a bull terrier with only one tail, and played (nicely and a bit diffidently) with little girls named Irma and Betty and Ruby."

Thurber dismissed the conceited exhibitionism of artiness (as distinct from art) as precious affectation. He recalled that the adult world in which he was brought up consisted mainly of "eleven maternal great-aunts, all Methodists, who were staunch believers in physic, mustard plasters, and Scripture, and it was part of their dogma that artistic tendencies should be treated in the same way as hiccups or hysterics. . . . It never occurred to me to bite a bat in my aunt's presence or to throw stones at them."

Of course conformity is not the answer either. Thurber himself was an artist; and, though he washed his hair with Ivory soap and owned a bull terrier, he shared with Dali the imagination of a surrealist. Though objecting to the irresponsible extremes of Dali's youthful conduct, he could hardly be in complete sympathy with his great-aunts, whose outlook requires a dull conformity to the norm—and a turn-of-the-century norm at that. He too had to escape, he explained, through his secret world of idiom; and the "Ah there, Salvador," with which he concluded his essay seems as much a greeting as a reproach. This conflict between romantic individuality and unimaginative conventionality is at the crux of much of Thurber's art.

Thurber explained that the difference between Dali and himself is partly one of environment. "Salvador was brought up in Spain, a country colored by the legends of Hannibal, El Greco, and Cervantes. I was brought up in Ohio, a region steeped in the tradition of Coxey's Army, the Anti-Saloon League, and William Howard Taft." Francis Hackett points out that early Ohio had a strong romantic streak that appears in town names like Canton, Toledo, Cincinnati, Antioch, Columbus, Jerusalem, Ravenna, Illyria, and others but that this early romanticism was replaced toward the end of the nineteenth century by commercialized industrialism. He observes further that many of the women in Thurber's stories and cartoons are not New York sophisticates but are instead frustrated latter-day Ohio romantics. "It is for the feminine, soulful grandchild of the Ohio Illyrians that Mr. Thurber reserves his attention. She is not a siren. She is a frump. She hasn't the suspicion of a [*New Yorker*] Profile. What he sees in her is her blithe domesticity, her comic afflatus, her bookishness, her suburbanity. Under her dominion is a faithful spouse. She is a worm-tamer. He is a worm."[20] She is the counterbalance to the cocktail party hostess, and she is no less defective. The Ohio Illyrian now finds romance in the soap operas that Thurber criticized or in best-sellers; her own life is commonplace, and her husband is not a great lover but a henpecked mate.

Thus the romantic imagination is distorted to destroy itself. The result is a suspicion and antagonism to anything different from the mass mind. Emotional and artistic sensitivity brands one as a high-brow or a sissy. Like Thurber's great-aunts, the guardians of middle-class morality have a disposition to suppress or ostracize artistic tendencies. Thurber complained that the legislators for Ohio State University were frequently trying to ban the teaching of Shelley because of his un-Ohioan love life. Similarly the police who investigate the Thurber household on the night the ghost got in stare with hostile suspicion at Thurber's irregular behavior, and efficient mechanics glare with resentment at his or his characters' ignorance and daydreaming inefficiency with automobiles. "He wasn't so goddam sensitive when we were both with the Cleveland Telephone Company," protests a character in "The Cane in the Corridor." "He wasn't so goddam sensitive then. No, he was practically a regular guy." We can see this attitude (which is by no means confined to the Midwest) become potentially tragic in Robert Anderson's *Tea and Sympathy*, in which a student is falsely accused of homosexuality and driven to attempted suicide merely because he is sensitive (hence, not a he-man) and prefers the arts and "long-haired" music to extroverted horseplay.

Hackett asserts that Thurber meets this sort of subjugation to the mass mind "not by rejecting the mass, but by affirming its preposterousness." "Conformity," observes Hackett, "is a card of introduction, a proof of good will among strangers, a kind of re-assurance and nose-rubbing, and if we think of the Flying Trapeze as the symbol of individual withdrawal and secret fantasy, Mr. Thurber is highly conscious that the Trapeze may throw the Don Quixote. Hence one of his mocking titles, *The Middle-Aged Man on the Flying Trapeze.*"[21] He concludes: "Mr. Thurber's comedy is to contrast gentle, feeble flights of fantasy with, first of all, his acknowledged timidity and commonplaceness," and he calls the kidding of genius, irregularity, and sensitivity, a sort of conformity to the mass. Hackett interprets Thurber's account of his failure to be an inscrutable Conradian wanderer as "a mocking deference to the Columbus norm."[22]

Although Thurber claimed that "Nobody from Columbus has ever made a first rate wanderer in the Conradian tradition," his romantic instinct was genuine. He would have liked to find a real Lord Jim, just as the husband in the fable believes in the unicorn in the garden. In "Casuals of the Keys" Thurber pretended to have wandered as far as the Florida Keys, where he met Captain Darrell Darke: "Tall, dark, melancholy, his white shirt open at the throat, he reminded me instantly of that other solitary wanderer among forgotten islands, the doomed Lord Jim." Thurber listened eagerly to Darke's tales, only to be frustrated. Among other incidents, Darke recalled that in 1931 an aged, white-bearded man swam over fifty miles from the mainland; he was apparently too stupid, said Darke, to take the boat. " 'He was as dull about everything as about that. Used to recite short stories word for word—said he wrote them himself. He was a writer like you, but he didn't seem to have met any interesting people. Talked only about himself, where he'd come from, what he'd done. I didn't pay any attention to him. I was glad when, one night, he disappeared. His name was. . . . His name was Bierce. Ambrose Bierce. . . . That's the kind of beings you meet with down here,' he said. 'Stupid, dullish, lacking in common sense, fiddling along aimlessly.' " Here there is an ironic twist: the captain, who resembles a Conradian wanderer, has a commonplace mind that rejects the real thing; Thurber, with his horn-rimmed glasses and Ohio accent, is excited by what Darke finds boring and senseless. The tables are turned.

Thurber employed an ambivalence in his treatment of society's norms. While he deflated Romanticism, spoofed the Civil War, and ridiculed such poems as "Barbara Frietchie," "Excelsior," and "Curfew Must Not Ring Tonight," he and his heroes have incurably romantic instincts, which manifest themselves in frustrated ways. Society finds Mr. Bidwell absurd for deviating into his private life, where he finds an escape by holding his breath, multiplying numbers in his head, or seeing how many steps he can take without opening his eyes. In a disenchanted society these pitiful outlets are Bidwell's only remnant of the romantic vision. His conduct seems ridiculous, both to his wife and to the reader; yet there is something about him with which we sympathize, while we are antagonized by the aggressive normality of Mrs. Bidwell. Except in the fairy tales, there is no genuine outlet for the romantic urge, and Hackett observes that Thurber, a post-Romantic Ohioan, develops fantasy "against the dead weight of the bourgeois community." He notes that Thurber deflates deviations from the norm; "yet to be inflated, to be enchanted, to admit magic, to be carried away, is still native to him, and comes to him in blasts of fantasy that are touched with nightmare and fear and horror. He does not want to be differentiated lest he be too much so. He may be from Columbus, but he may also be brother to Salvador Dali under his skin."[23]

It is lonely to be different, and Thurber's characters actually want to conform in order to be accepted. Mr. Monroe weeps when he is unable to manage the moving men. Walter Mitty thinks of wearing his arm in a sling so he will not be embarrassed at having a garage man take chains off his car; and Mr. Pendly, a sensitive man who is in awe of automobile experts, dreams both of swooping down upon his wife in an autogyro and of being such a casually brilliant repair man as to win the admiration of a baffled mechanic. In the autogyro dream the sensitive man relieves his frustration by romantic non-conformity; in the second dream, he does so by demonstrating his ability to beat the average conformist and regular guy at his own game. But it is significant that both these solutions lie in the secret world of dreams. "For nonconformity, the world whips you with its displeasure," so Thurber's protagonists keep their deviations invisible. His little men have an intense desire to be average and unnoticed. They do not want to be different, but they cannot achieve the unruffled routine of ordinary lives. Some defect—their inability to cope with machines or shopping lists, or even the accident of a shoe-shaped scar—throws them off the track, makes them self-conscious, drives them for refuge into fantasy, which in turn takes them increasingly away from the norm, until at last the quite ordinary Mr. Bruhl, mistaken for a gangster because of his appearance, makes a mental transference and becomes Shoescar Clinigan, finding a peaceful fulfillment in being shot by gunmen and snarling at the police who try to help him.

But there is one more twist. While characters like Mitty and Pendly do want to be normal, they resent the normal for its insolent self-satisfaction and do not really admire it. They are not really interested in cars, shopping, or business but feel they should be, while their deeper instincts are romantic. Both the concept of normal Ohio life and of the romantic adventurer are stereotyped patterns into which Thurber's individuals do not fit. They want the best of both worlds but get neither.

CHAPTER 6

The Male Animal and the
Political Animal

THURBER always had a lively interest in the theater. Both his parents had wanted to make a career of acting; and they passed on to their sons a talent for mimicry and an enthusiasm for the stage. Before her marriage, Thurber's mother had starred in amateur play productions and wanted to become a professional; but, in the late 1880's, her parents considered this too improper and discouraged her theatrical aspirations. Thurber's father, too, abandoned reluctantly his youthful ambitions for the stage. During his Columbus boyhood, Thurber found vicarious adventure on the stage in such shows as *Custer's Last Fight* and *The Flaming Arrow* at the High Street Theatre, *The Round Up* with Maclyn Arbuckle at the Southern Theatre, *King Lear* with Mantell and the Get-Ready Man at the Colonial, and the Empire Stock Company's repertory of such Civil War melodramas as *Secret Service* and *Barbara Frietchie*. Later, until his eyesight failed, he was a great movie fan, especially of the better "Westerns."

I *Ohio Theatricals*

At Ohio State, his best friend Elliott Nugent induced him to go out for The Strollers, a dramatic club of which Nugent was a student director. In a production of Arnold Bennett's one-act farce *A Question of Sex,* Nugent played George Gower, the leading role, while Thurber acted the part of Francis Gower, "his well preserved bachelor uncle." He also played a vengeful temple priest in Dunsany's *A Night at the Inn*.

In June, 1918, Thurber left Ohio State without taking a degree, having failed to qualify in biology, which he neglected for literature and the arts. Ineligible for the draft because of his eyesight (he had tried to enlist), he became a code clerk for the State Department, first for five months in Washington, D.C., and then, after the Armistice, at the American Embassy in Paris. Returning to

Columbus in the summer of 1920, he handled the city hall beat as a reporter for the Columbus *Dispatch*. During his spare time in the next five years, he wrote the book and some of the lyrics for five musical comedies for Ohio State's Scarlet Mask Club. He directed some of these and occasionally substituted in the cast. Once, with Ralph McCombs and Ray Jackson, he made a two-reel movie, *Twenty-five Minutes from Broad and High*, using a local cast. These early productions are the work of a promising amateur, and it was only to be expected that Thurber should some day try his hand at professional playwriting. He waited fourteen years after leaving Columbus, but it was Ohio State that finally furnished the necessary impetus and inspiration.

Elliott Nugent had gone on to become a successful actor and playwright. Almost six years younger than Thurber, Nugent was born into a theatrical family in Dover, Ohio, on September 20, 1900. His parents were on the Keith-Orpheum vaudeville circuit, and Elliott first appeared on stage in Los Angeles when he was four years old. After leaving Ohio State, he began his own stage career under the auspices of his father, J. C. Nugent; performed with him; and collaborated with him in writing several plays. In 1921, before Thurber had even started writing scripts for The Scarlet Mask, Nugent made his Broadway debut as the advertising man in Kaufman's and Connelly's *Dulcy*. Among his later more notable stage roles were the male lead in the original Broadway productions of John Van Druten's *The Voice of the Turtle* and Philip Barry's *Without Love*, in which he played opposite Margaret Sullivan and Katherine Hepburn, respectively. For his work in *The Voice of the Turtle*, Nugent was voted the best male performer of the season by the New York drama critics. Philip Barry said of him, "No other actor can bring such skill and sincerity to the presentation of a sensitive nature, a troubled spirit, or an embattled intellect." A versatile man, Nugent also worked for Hollywood, acting with such stars as Lon Chaney and Greta Garbo and directing innumerable films, including such hits as *The Cat and the Canary, Up in Arms,* and *My Favorite Brunette*. He portrayed Hollywood somewhat caustically in his first novel, *Of Cheat and Charmer* (1962).

II The Male Animal

Meanwhile, Thurber and Nugent maintained their friendship (Thurber was best man at Nugent's wedding), and naturally enough they reminisced about their college days. Amusing themselves by imagining what might have happened if they had stayed on at Ohio State, they recognized the seeds of a play. Inspiration struck Thurber first; he recalled that he thought of the first scene when he had climbed to the garage roof for some purpose which slipped his mind. Climbing down again, he wired Nugent in Hollywood: "You and I are going to write a play." Nugent wired back, "No, we're not." "So," Thurber said, "I went to Hollywood, showed him the scene. He sighed, sat down and began cutting it out. The collaboration was on."

In a note to Nelson Budd of Ohio State, Thurber explained the creation of *The Male Animal*:

> I asked E. to do the play with me in Oct. '38. We outlined it here in Jan. '39. I wrote the first two scenes—of which only a few lines remain. I went to H'wood in June & we wrote it there till September when I came East for 2 weeks & did "The Last Flower." Returned to see the play tried out in San Diego, Santa Barbara, and Los Angeles (12 performances in all). It was well received & enthusiastically reviewed. It was seen there by Walt Disney, Groucho Marx, Marc Connelly, Myrna Loy, Sam & Bella Spewack, Harold Lloyd, King Vidor, Bob Montgomery, Jas. Cagney.
>
> Arthur Beckhard produced it on the coast. We closed it for 3 weeks of rewriting.[1]

The play then moved east for a Broadway run. Everything was satisfactory except the second act curtain, which still was not right when the play was showing in Baltimore three days before the New York opening. As it was, the act ended with general bedlam on the set. Watching this, Thurber commented to the director, Herman Shumlin, that it seemed phony to him. Shumlin was delighted; he had misunderstood Thurber and thought he had suggested ringing the phone at the height of all the uproar on stage. This was tried and turned out to be an effective ending for the scene, though the noise on stage was so great that four phones had to be rung off-stage at once in order to be heard above the tumult.

With all the kinks ironed out, *The Male Animal* opened in New York on January 9, 1940, at the Cort Theatre. In a distinguished season of comedy, notable for the opening of *Life with Father* and *The Man Who Came to Dinner, The Male Animal* was a smash hit. Part of the play's success was due to its excellent cast, headed by co-author Elliott Nugent in the leading role of Tommy Turner and supported by Ruth Matteson as Ellen Turner, Gene Tierney as Patricia Stanley, Leon Ames as Joe Ferguson, and Don DeFore as Wally Myers.

The Male Animal deals with and combines most of the main themes in Thurber's work. Here again is the war between men and women, the development of marital discord, the conflict between the sensitive introvert and the coarsely aggressive extrovert, and the need for the ordinary citizen to respond with quiet courage when his liberties are threatened. In its affirmation of traditional American liberalism *The Male Animal* is an effective reply to those who have asserted that Thurber's work verges on lunacy and is replete with eccentricity and the uncontrolled symbolism of the unconscious. Joseph Wood Krutch wrote that he expected a play by Thurber to resemble the fantasies of Strindberg and was considerably surprised by *The Male Animal,* which he called "one-fourth recognizable Thurberian madness and one-fourth mild social protest," the remainder being "skillful domestic farce of a thoroughly American kind."[2] Thurber's fantasy and his war between men and women have only a remote resemblance to Strindberg's bitter dramas, and his manner is completely unlike the Swedish playwright's. There is considerable method in Thurber's seeming madness, but there was a genuine madness, as well as genius, in Strindberg. Thurber's ability to see things humorously enabled him to keep a sane view of life and *The Male Animal* rather than *The Ghost Sonata* is the sort of play one might logically have expected from his pen.

The Male Animal has two interacting plots. One is a study of domestic discord in the vein of Thurber's stories of marital squabbles and misunderstandings. The other is a defense of academic freedom and is one of Thurber's few ventures into political satire. As usual, he avoided any entanglement with party politics and did not propose any political program. He simply spoke out against an abuse and showed that each man must take a stand to resist oppression.

The play's protagonist is Tommy Turner, a young professor of English at Midwestern University. Since the idea behind the play was what might have happened if Thurber and Nugent had remained at Ohio State, it might be assumed that Thurber is a compound of the authors. (Nugent's play *The Poor Nut* also deals with Ohio State, and Nugent says that its title character was at least partially based on Thurber.) In his appearance and personality, Turner is quite like Thurber (who had once considered becoming an English professor): sensitive and intelligent, adept at irony, physically awkward and unathletic and slightly disheveled. Turner resembles Thurber more than Nugent, who was an athletic star and big man about campus; but Nugent played the role on stage, possibly modeling his performance on Thurber's personality. Nugent was reluctant to take the role, having been away from the stage for a while. At Thurber's insistence he assumed the part and gave an outstanding performance.

Tommy Turner is a mild, unaggressive, and unassuming person; but, when he plans to read to his class a letter by Vanzetti as an example of ungrammatical eloquence, he finds himself faced with unexpected trouble. Under the leadership of Ed Keller, a boorish and dictatorial trustee, Midwestern University has been conducting an inquisition into the politics of its faculty, from which it purged supposed Communists. Keller is described as "a Neanderthal man who rolls like a juggernaut over the careers of young professors," and he does not tolerate free expression of any opinions divergent from his own. In whipping up a Red scare, he has not discovered any genuine Communists but has libeled and fired several perfectly loyal professors who are liberals but in no way subversive.

Such is the situation at Midwestern University. Professor Turner has no Communist leanings and has managed to stay aloof from the controversy; but Michael Barnes, a radical young student, writes an editorial for the campus paper in which he calls the trustees Fascists and praises Turner's courage for planning to read Vanzetti's letter. Learning of this, Keller demands that Turner not read the letter and that he issue a statement denying Barnes's editorial. Turner intended only to demonstrate the eloquence of Vanzetti's broken English. "I'm not standing up to anyone," he explains to Barnes. "I'm not challenging anyone. This is just an innocent little piece I wanted to read." But he finds that a larger issue has been forced upon him and that he must either make a stand or yield to Keller's bullying. "Free should the scholar be,—free and brave," wrote Emerson. There is no freedom when one must always pretend submission; and, though Turner wants to keep quiet, he has to speak up to defend a friend whom Keller calls "a damn Red" and who Turner says is a humanist.

"We don't want anything Red—or even Pink—taught here," says Ed Keller. "But who's to decide what is Red and what is Pink?" asks Turner. Keller replies that the trustees are to be the judges and that the faculty is too wishy-washy: too prone to weigh all the evidence, they are accordingly unfit to decide what should be taught. A university, he says, should teach nothing but Americanism. Keller cannot define Americanism but maintains that everybody knows what it is. "What do you believe in?" he asks Turner, who replies, "I believe that a college should be concerned with ideas. Not just your ideas or my ideas, but all ideas."

But Turner finds that, if he stands up for academic freedom, he will lose his job and possibly his wife as well, for she fears losing her security and wants him to avoid facing the issue. Dean Damon, head of the English department, would also like to avoid trouble but is not sure that trouble can or should be evaded, despite the importance of public relations and "academic calm."

Ellen. There must be some way—some compromise—that wouldn't be too humiliating.

Damon. The policy of appeasement? Yes, it has its merits, and I'm afraid it's all I have to offer. . . . Tell him that if he decides not to read the letter, I shall feel easier in my mind. Much easier. And—slightly disappointed.

Tommy finds that he cannot disappoint Damon or himself; he must stand up for his rights. He does not wish to be a martyr, but he realizes that each man is responsible for what goes on; there is no innocence in letting evil win by default. "I think you'll have to take a stand too," Tommy says to Dean Damon.

Damon. I hope not.

Tommy. So did I hope not. I didn't start out to lead a crusade.

But he must take a stand somewhere if he is not to lose his integrity altogether.

Tommy. Don't you see this isn't about Vanzetti. This is about us! If I can't read this letter today, tomorrow none of us will be able to teach anything except what Mr. Keller here and the legislature permit us to teach. . . . We're holding the last fortress of free thought, and if we surrender to prejudice and dictation, we're cowards.

Dean Damon agrees, decides to back Turner, and promises Keller a fight.

Ed. Do you think Bryson and Kressinger and I are afraid of a few dissatisfied book-worms who work for twenty-five hundred a year?

Damon. These men are not malcontents! Some of them are distinguished scholars who have made this University what it is!

Ed. They've made it what it is! What about me? Who's getting this new stadium?

Joe. He means that this thing is bigger than stadiums and coaches.

Ed. Nothing's bigger than the new stadium.

Thus in Keller, Thurber presented a prime specimen of anti-intellectual arrogance. Contrasted to him, Turner's integrity is an example of the sort of unspectacular courage that Thurber so greatly admired. He has "the calm in adversity, the self-command and humor and hard victory without bugles. . . ."[3] When the crisis comes, he resists Keller and loses his job; but, in so doing, he inspires others to take a stand.

Dean Damon, the wise and witty head of the English department who opposes Ed Keller, is clearly modeled on one of Thurber's old professors, Joseph Villiers Denney, the subject of a chapter in *The Thurber Album*. Like Dean Damon, Dean Denney was professor of Shakespeare and Dean of the College of Arts. (The Damon was taken from Dr. Virgil G. Damon, a classmate and fraternity brother of the authors, who delivered Nugent's three daughters.) Denny was one of Thurber's favorite professors, a faculty member of Thurber's and Nugent's fraternity, an authority on Burke, and a distinguished scholar. "He resisted, during his long career, a hundred alien restrictions on the freedom of teaching at Ohio State, and his reputation as a firm and courageous crusader for teachers' rights became widely known in academic circles and resulted in his election as president of the professors' association. In his inaugural address to his colleagues, who had gathered from all over America, he boldly named their potential enemies: state legislatures, ecclesiastical bodies, and 'powerful influence operating through trustees.'" So it was natural that Thurber and Nugent should think of Dean Denney as the model for the distinguished older professor opposing the restriction of academic freedom. During the attacks on academic freedom at Ohio State in 1951, twelve years after the appearance of *The Male Animal*, Thurber wrote that Denney "must have turned restlessly in his grave. Ohio State, trapped somewhere between Armageddon and Waterloo, needed him and his strategy of reason and his tactics of friendliness, and all the armament of his intellect and his humor."

Prompted by the counterparts of stadium-obsessed Ed Keller, Ohio State became, according to Thurber, "one of the chief fortresses of the academic army opposed to liberal education and in favor of the practical and empirical training in the useful modern sciences, crafts, business, and trades. . . . A 'campus leader' is reported to have said, 'Do they think Shakespeare is going to get me a job with U. S. Steel?' There is one man whose answer to that question I would love to hear, but he is, God help us all, no longer living." This man is Denney, described by Thurber as the last of the old-fashioned apostles of the classics and humanities at Ohio State. Unfortunately Dean Denney had died before the appearance of *The Male Animal* and the most dangerous attack on academic freedom at Ohio State.

The events in the play anticipate this development but are not, according to the authors, based on any specific people or happenings at Ohio State. (There was, however, as early as 1937, a hysterical witch-hunt for "radicals" on the Ohio State campus.) But though the university in the drama is called Midwestern, details clearly reveal that it represents Ohio State: it has the same colors (scarlet and gray); a band off-stage is heard playing Ohio State's pep song, "Fight the Team"; and as at Columbus there is a Neil Avenue gate, a place called Hennicks across the street from the campus, and a popular Granville Inn a few miles from the university.

While Tommy Turner faces troubles in the academic world, he also has to overcome problems in his own household, for the interminable war between men and women flares up. Tommy's wife, Ellen Turner, is described as completely feminine, acting always from an emotional, not an intellectual stimulus. Her husband, on the other hand, tries always to act rationally, though he fails signally to do so. Ellen at any rate feels intellectually inferior to her husband, and she cannot see why he must make a fuss over reading the Vanzetti letter. At this crucial point an old beau of Ellen's comes to Midwestern for a big football weekend. This beau, Joe Ferguson, is another foil to Tommy Turner: Tommy is shy, introverted and unathletic; Joe is a back-slapping, extroverted, and slightly stupid football star. The situation is ripe for marital fireworks, since Ellen and Tommy are quarreling over the Vanzetti letter and Joe is preparing to divorce his wife.

The Male Animal is Thurber's most thorough analysis of marriage; and in it he shows clearly that his views on matrimony are realistic rather than cynical. For, though Tommy and Ellen seem for the time being to be incompatible, the real butt of Thurber's satire is Joe Ferguson, who advocates "the modern way of doing things" in marriage. Joe jokes about divorce, says it is just one of those things, and thinks it sophisticated to take his wife and her new boy friend out to dinner. But though many of Thurber's stories deal with the break-up of marriages, they always show divorce as a wretched though sometimes inevitable affair.

However, Ellen finds Joe's hearty good humor a relief from Tommy's irritability over the academic situation; and she allows herself an idle flirtation with him, trying to recapture the romantic atmosphere of her student days. She thus initiates a quarrel with Tommy; but he aggravates it needlessly; will not be pacified; and, by heaping faggots on a mere spark of domestic discord, works up a fiery battle with his wife. In his jealousy Tommy insists that Ellen wants to leave him for Joe, and he almost succeeds in persuading her that she does. Thurber was always brilliant at depicting the growth of quarrels through tart dialogue, ironic innuendo, and subtle sarcasms of speech and mannerism that rise upon a crescendo of trivial annoyances to a climax of angry mis-understanding. *The Male Animal* is a prime example of his skill.

In a parallel subplot we find another sensitive intellectual, Michael Barnes, the radical student editor. He is in love with Ellen's younger sister Patricia Stanley, but she seems at the moment to favor a husky, amiably oafish football star named Wally Myers. Michael, who is jealous of Wally, contemplates socking him with a ball bat. "No," Tommy tells him. "You are a civilized man, Michael. If the male animal in you doesn't like the full implications of that, he must nevertheless be swayed by reason. . . . Nowadays, the man and his wife and the other man talk it over. Quietly and calmly. They all go out to dinner together."

Tommy therefore tries to talk rationally and unemotionally to Joe about his going off with Ellen, but for all his modernity Joe is embarrassed and distressed by Tommy's attitude. At first Tommy lets Joe and Ellen push him around; he will play the innocent victim, the unaggressive man of reason, getting some perverse pleasure from his self-denying martyrdom. Furthermore, Joe, with all of his experience, has a highly unrealistic attitude towards marriage. He thinks that love is all glamor and romance and is perturbed when Tommy explains to him the humdrum details that are part of daily domesticity with Ellen. He tells Joe how to fix a hot-water bottle for Ellen, how to make her hot coffee for cold afternoon football games, how to find her nail file, how to do all the little things that seem quite unromantic but are essential to a lasting marriage and are part of the calm and unassuming life that Thurber admired.

For the moment, however, Tommy's love does not exhibit quiet fortitude. He has tried to be modern, intellectual, and sophisticated; and he finds that this behavior will not hold his home together. He must fight to defend his marriage as well as academic freedom. If he allows himself to be pushed around in either case, the cause is lost. And so he feels the stirrings of resistance against Joe's aggressive self-assurance. "I know I'm not a tiger," Tommy says, "but I don't like to be thought of as a pussy-cat either."

Thurber, who was even more emphatic on this point, told a *Life* reporter in 1960: "One thing let's get straight—I'm not mild and gentle. Let the meek inherit the earth—they have it coming to them. When *Life* called me 'mild' in 1945 my old friend Nunnally Johnson said, 'It must be a misprint for "wild."' Boris Karloff is mild but I am not. Other mild guys are James Cagney and Peter

Lorre unless backed into a corner. I am in a corner without being backed there and often come out fighting."[4]

Deciding he must do the same, Tommy gets drunk with Michael in the most hilarious scene of the play, and he lectures him on the duty of the male animal to defend his home:

> Tommy. Let us say that the tiger wakes up one morning and finds that the wolf has come down on the fold. What does he—? Before I tell you what he does, I will tell you what he does not do. . . . . He does not expose everyone to a humiliating intellectual analysis. He comes out of his corner like this—(Assumes awkward fighting pose, fists up—rises—sits quickly.) The bull elephant in him is aroused.

> Michael. Can't you stick to one animal?

> Tommy. No, that's my point. All the animals are the same including the human being. We are male animals too. . . . Even the penguin. He stands for no monkey-business where his mate is concerned. Swans have been known to drown Scotties who threatened their nests. . . . A woman likes a man who does something. All the male animals fight for the female, from the land crab to the bird of paradise. They don't just sit and talk. They act.

Tommy does act; he punches Joe in the nose and is knocked cold in the ensuing brawl. Though he loses the fist fight, he regains Ellen's sympathy; and he wins back her respect and admiration when he finally defies Keller and insists upon his right to read the Vanzetti letter. Ellen finally stops quarreling and understands her husband's position.

Thus it can be seen that *The Male Animal* combines most of the basic ideas in Thurber's work. The most memorable scene, in which Tommy expounds on the male animal, says that man's rationalism is inadequate and inferior to instinctive animal wisdom. Intellectual analysis is merely humiliating. Tommy's speech says in a humorous way what Thurber elsewhere says seriously of man: his pride in himself as a rational being is unjustified; he is not superior to the other animals, and "he will not get anywhere until he realizes, in all humility, that he is just another of God's creatures. . . ." Therefore Tommy "evokes the image of those sad, monolithic creatures that haunt the Thurber page: the long-eared, piteous mastiffs, the sea-lions, massive but gentle, the nameless, primordial creatures rising laboriously from the ooze, the beasts and birds who are our friends and forbears."[5]

"I rather liked you as a sea lion," Ellen tells Tommy; for the male sea lion rules and defends his mate and home. As in the illustrations of "The War Between Men and Women," the husband must win to maintain his integrity. Tommy says that there is no defeat that can be quite so complete as the story of the defeated male. "The important thing about dancing is that the man has got to lead," explains Joe in the final scene as he yields Ellen to Tommy as a dancing partner and returns to his own wife.

In *The Male Animal* Thurber also gave his most extended treatment of the conflict between sensitivity and arrogant extroversion, for Turner, Dean Damon and Michael Barnes are ranged against Ed Keller, Joe Ferguson, and Wally Myers. Thurber sided as usual with the unaggressive, thoughtful people; but, aside from Keller, who is the only thoroughgoing Thurber villain outside the fairy tales, he did not paint his characters in monochrome. The undiluted cerebral temperament is shown to be insufficient; it is not enough to be unaggressive, for the aggressors will win by default. Besides, Joe Ferguson and Wally Myers are basically sound, and Midwestern's football stars sign a petition in Turner's defense.

Since a number of his reminiscences of school days portray moronic athletes, while his stories and cartoons often match mild little men with heavy-handed women, Thurber was sometimes mislabeled as a timid type who pitted brain against brawn. It is true that he disliked competitive coarseness and that his heroes are anything but Mike Finks or Earthquake McGoons, but he admired athletic skill and had an encyclopedic knowledge of sports. He liked to listen to ball games, wrote several pieces about baseball, and had total recall for players and scores. Though his poor eyesight kept him from childhood sports and helped make him studious and introspective, he became (before his blindness) an excellent bowler, croquet player, horseshoe pitcher, ping-pong player, and tennis partner. His writings are full of allusions to athletic figures and events, most notably the Red Barber metaphors in "The Catbird Seat." Among his lifelong admirations was Chic Harley ("The Only One"), Ohio State's legendary halfback, who turns up persistently in Thurber's reminiscences. As for football, Thurber wrote that it "has more beauty in it than any other competitive game in the world, when played by college athletes."

On the other hand, his 1923 *Credoes and Curios* halfpage protested Ohio State's poor support of the literary magazine when $40,000 a week was spent for football. " 'Millions,' say Ohio State students, alumni and downtown fans, 'for football programs, but not one cent for literature.' " With its stadium-building and athletic dominance Thurber diagnosed Ohio State as "a cockeyed and a lop-sided school," where, "Out of the 8000 students, not more than 150 actually know or care anything about lyrics or short stories or the novel. . . ." He wrote that, while he liked football, "we refuse to join that rapidly swelling throng which is making football not an institution but the institution. . . . Almost every lover of literature that we know among university students or alumni also loves football. As much cannot be said for the other side. The enmity, started by the virile American parent, is kept up only by the bull-headed idiocy of the fellow who is never anything but a football player. And the public is siding in with that type. The public would vote today to keep football and kill off everything else in the university, if a choice had to be made." Perhaps the most pernicious aspect was the idea that an interest in the arts was a sign of effeminacy. "It is as much as your reputation is worth to be caught carrying a concealed Shelley at this virile school," observed Thurber thirty years earlier than *Tea and Sympathy*. It was better to be a belligerent Babbitt with your eye on the main chance, in the approved American fashion; and Thurber complained that most students were brainwashed by "the American parent, who secretly thinks it is smart for his son to club the neighbor kid in the eye because he saw him reading a 'girl's book' (viz. any book of verse except Robert W. Service, Berton Braley or the Princeton Limericks)."

III   *"Teacher's Pet"*

These 1923 remarks not only anticipate *The Male Animal* but also a highly effective story called "Teacher's Pet." The protagonist is Willber Kelby, a middle-aged scholar, who had been abused all his life by noisy, aggressive bullies. As a child in grade school, he had been the smartest boy in his classes; and his teachers, with no attempt at tact, made him their official and unwilling pet. Kelby hated the two "l's" in Willber, and he resented both his own frail physique and the swaggering athleticism of the class bullies. One of the latter, Zeke Leonard, "who had the brains of a pole vaulter, had hated Willber from the time they were seven for his intelligence, his name, his frail body, and his inability, according to Zeke, to do anything except study." Kelby could never forget Zeke's bullying, especially the time when Zeke pursued him after school and slapped and kicked him around while Kelby impotently and ineffectually tried to defend himself and the other boys jeered at him. At a cocktail party thirty-seven years later, he was reminiscing on that incident when a woman asked him what *was* he thinking about. Provoked, Kelby replied truthfully that he was thinking out the time Zeke Leonard beat him up because he was a teacher's pet.

"What in the world for?" exclaimed the woman. "What had you done?"

"A teacher's pet doesn't have to do anything," Kelby said. "It is the mere fact of his existence that makes the stupid and the strong want to beat him up. There is a type of man that wants to destroy the weaker, the more sensitive, the more intelligent."

The woman replied that her son Elbert had that sort of trouble and was always being tormented by his more arrogant classmates, especially Bob Stevenson, the bullying son of their host at the party. Kelby was bitter; he hated the bullies, but he also had contempt for the weakness of their victims.

"But they are not cowards," the woman interrupted. "At least I know Elbert is not a coward."

"There are a lot of comforting euphemisms," Kelby replied. "Hypersensitive, nonaggressive, peace-loving, introverted—take your choice."

Two days later, while out for a walk, Kelby encountered Bob Stevenson and Elbert Reynolds. The scene was a repetition of Zeke's bullying of Kelby; for Bob was tormenting Elbert, ridiculing him and insolently roughing him up. Kelby interrupted and furiously ordered Bob to leave the other boy alone. Elbert, meanwhile, stood sniffling and whimpering. Angry both at the aggression and at the impotent cowering of the victim (too much like himself as a child), Kelby turned on the boy he rescued, slapped him, and called him a coward and crybaby. Ironically Elbert's father appeared at this point, in time to see only the end of the incident. The conclusion of the story is a masterpiece of irony. "'I've seen some bullies in my time,' Mr. Reynolds told the elder Stevenson later, 'but I never saw anything to match that.'" Robert Stevenson, Sr., replied that his son had been threatened by Kelby too. "'You never know about a man, Reynolds,' he said. 'You just never know.'"

This is an intramural story based upon an episode involving one of Thurber's associates but to a certain extent it may reflect Thurber's own schooldays. He was then thin, awkward, nervous, and wore thick-lensed, steel-rimmed glasses. He reported with humorous exaggeration that the grade school he attended was one of the toughest anywhere and that he probably would not have gotten through it alive if one of the strongest and toughest boys, a pupil named Floyd, had not appointed himself Thurber's protector. In 1926, he observed sarcastically that the fist fight "has even attained the dignity of an art in Anglo-Saxon countries. In our own no schoolboy's youthful mettle can be properly tempered without recourse to it; it is an honorable tradition at West Point; it is part of the bulwark of American civilization." He recalled threatening to fight his friend and boss Harold Ross when the latter once called his concern for dogs the attitude of a "sis." And in a story about that time called "The Thin Red Leash," Thurber told of being insulted by a bunch of burly laborers because he had a Scottie instead of a pug-ugly pooch until they learned that Scotties were tough enough to rip the tonsils out of Airedales.

However, Kelby should not be identified emotionally with Thurber. Kelby is emotionally unbalanced, whereas Thurber wrote the story with artistic control. In seeing the weak as cowardly, Kelby has come to accept the values of the bullies he hates. Thus he is angry with himself and attacks Elbert in contempt even as he rescues him from Bob Stevenson. His anger is directed as much at the fact that he was on the receiving end as it is against the principle of aggression. Elbert and Kelby fail not because they are poor fighters but because they lack emotional fortitude; they break down and snivel when attacked. Their defeat is not that they lose the fight with others but that they lose it with themselves. In *The Male Animal*, the fact that Tommy does win this fight is more important than his ludicrous attempt to "KO" Joe Ferguson. It is not his pugilism but his Quixotic gallantry that wins Ellen back.

IV   Dramatic Shortcomings

For all of its popularity, *The Male Animal* is not without faults as a play. The picture of university life as a menage of cheer leaders and sprightly young coeds is an artificial stereotype in which the students are too forcedly pert or flashy to be quite convincing. At times Patricia, Michael, Wally, and "Nutsy" Miller are annoyingly like characters in a high school play. Michael Barnes, the radical student editor, is supposed to be a brilliant senior and student of literature; but his romancing with Patricia has little more maturity than that of Henry Aldrich and Corliss Archer. These students "pal around" on terms of casual intimacy with the faculty and use them as confessors for their adolescent romances; as a result, the picture of student-faculty relations resembles that between a group of campers and their counselor. Whether this is desirable or not, it is hardly realistic. Moreover, the play's picture of university life makes it hard to conceive of any serious academic program at Midwestern.

The major characters have their implausibilities too. For one thing, they are too young. Turner is only thirty-three, yet he is about to be promoted to full professor because he has published some articles in *Harper's* and in *The Atlantic*. Actually some departments consider this sort of publication trivial and pressure their faculty to write for the learned journals and academic scholarly presses, and it is unusual to find a full professor of English under forty-five. Ellen is still in her late twenties, Joe is thirty-five, and even Trustee Ed Keller is only thirty-eight. It would be more reasonable to have Turner and Joe pushing forty, Ellen toward her middle thirties, and Keller about fifty; and this change in age would also make the momentary marital fatigue and nostalgia for youthful romance more plausible. Actually, the characters sound and act older, and it would be simply a matter of changing their assigned ages and casting them accordingly.

There has been some speculation as to who wrote what parts of the play. Joseph Wood Krutch assigned Nugent the major credit; Rosamund Gilder said it is Thurber's play done with Nugent's assistance. George Jean Nathan suggested that Nugent was responsible for the conventional plot devices. Mrs. Thurber says that her husband furnished most of the comic dialogue but that he relied on Nugent for play construction. Thurber explained that he did not bother to diagram his work. "Elliott Nugent, on the other hand, was a careful constructor. When we were working on *The Male Animal* together, he was constantly concerned with plotting the play. He could plot the thing from back to front—what was going to happen here, what sort of situation would end the first act curtain, and so forth. I can't work that way. Nugent would say: 'Well, Thurber, we've got our problem, we've got all these people in the living room. Now what are we going to do with them?' I'd say that I didn't know and couldn't tell him until I'd sat down at the typewriter and found out."[6]

Nugent recalls that when Thurber first suggested the collaboration, "He had the *main* story idea clearly in mind and just three characters at first. The notion of weaving into the 'triangle story' a theme about academic freedom was I believe mine. All the other characters were invented jointly during long talks when I returned to New York for two weeks about February 1939." Mrs. Thurber credits Nugent with writing the scene in which the Vanzetti letter is read, but academic freedom is a theme that long concerned Thurber too. As early as his student days during World War I, he was disturbed by Ohio State's German-baiting and accusing innocent people of being German spies. Recalling that the teaching of German was then banned at Ohio State and that at various times the legislators tried to prohibit the teaching of Shelley because of his "un-Ohioan" love life, he concluded: "It was a period of muddy thought and marked, I believe, the decline of higher education in the Middle West."

Nugent also has been very attentive to the state of the world during his dramatic career. He directed the Broadway production of *Tomorrow the World* (a play about the reconstruction of a Nazi youth); and in 1945, he expressed some of his political and social views in a play of his called *A Place of Our Own*. But as John Gassner observed, "his long suit as a playwright is light and fast comedy; and if *The Male Animal*, in which the liberal attitude was leavened by laughter is any indication, he has no reason to slight his talent in favor of sober evangelism."[7]

The two plots—marital bickering and academic freedom—fit smoothly; the struggle for the latter implements the former; and both are neatly resolved together. However, the play lacks unity of mood. Both plots are well written; but, after the wild comedy in the Turner household, it is difficult for the reader or spectator to feel quite serious about the grim, even sinister, academic situation. He may agree with the arguments, but he finds it hard to regain a sufficiently sober mood to give the academic freedom issue the thoughtful attention it deserves. The change from broad comedy and farce to problem play is too abrupt, and sometimes the former intrudes even in the midst of the latter. Thurber recognized this difficulty, admitting that the soundest criticism of the play came from Groucho Marx, who said in Hollywood, "'You got too many laughs in it. Take some of them out.' He meant we should take out irrelevant gags and stick to the laughter of character and situation, and he was, of course, right."

Praising *My Fair Lady* in 1956, Thurber complained that too often, "Comedy has ceased to be a challenge to the mental processes. It has become a therapy of relaxation, a kind of tranquillizing drug." While *The Male Animal* is often provocative, it falls short of the highest place that Thurber said is attained "only when the heart and mind are lifted, equally and at once, by the creative union of perception and grace."

Ever since its first run, *The Male Animal* has been popular with college and community theaters. There is opportunity for much amusing stage business; there are a number of good roles for talented performers; and, with skillful direction and cast, it makes a highly successful production. Ohio State presented it in arena style for two weeks in July, 1950. Then in 1952, it was revived in New York at the City Center, with Elliott Nugent again playing the lead, supported by Martha Scott and Robert Preston as Ellen Turner and Joe Ferguson, respectively. Though scheduled for only a two-week run, it had such a favorable reception that it was moved on May 15 to the Music Box for a prolonged showing. In fact the revival played for more performances than the first production, running for 301 performances to the original 244.

V Academic Freedom and the Red Decade

The success of this revival has a particular interest, for it was at this time that the House Committee on Un-American Activities was probing into presumed Communist activities on campuses and creating a Red scare similar to that in the play. Most ironically, Thurber's own Ohio State began to suppress academic freedom. Thurber described this situation regretfully in *The Thurber Album*, reporting that, in the fall of 1951, the university's trustees, consisting largely of "aggressively patriotic gentlemen always ready and eager to save America from the perils of academic freedom . . . decided that nobody could speak on campus until he had been intellectually seized and searched to see if his political opinions contained anything that might corrupt the minds of the students, such as Communism, or anything else modern or liberal or radical enough to warrant suspicion." This situation is essentially what happened twelve years earlier in *The Male Animal*. Furthermore, "While the trustees were qualifying freedom of speech at the university, they decided it was a matter of good old plain common sense, or good old-fashioned Americanism, to qualify freedom of research too." In reaction, scholars boycotted Ohio State, and protests poured in from all quarters, forcing the trustees and administration to loosen their restrictions.

Thurber observed that for years before this, legislative interference at Ohio State had been a thorn in the side of academic freedom. But he maintained that, "a communist speaker could not possibly sway an Ohio State audience and that in refusing to let communists talk, the university deprives itself of a wonderful chance to heckle and confound such speakers. If we cannot be strong enough Americans to withstand such arguments, if we are in such danger of being politically debauched, then all we have in the Western conference is the greatest football area in the world. . . ."[8] Accordingly, Thurber refused an honorary degree from Ohio State University in protest against the 1951 gag rule.

If *The Male Animal* was daringly outspoken in 1940, it was doubly so in 1952 when the late Senator McCarthy and his associates were at the height of their power. The very real danger to academic freedom no doubt gave the revival of the play an immediacy that contributed to its success, and its reception shows that a large segment of the theater-going public endorsed Thurber's and Nugent's indictment of inquisitorial practices. But inquisitors are a touchy lot, and they reply to criticism by attempting to smear the character of their critics and to label them as agents of the devil's party. When the Laguna Beach Playhouse in California performed *The Male Animal* in 1952, the South Coast *News* denounced it with the headline, "Americans attacked at Playhouse!" and its anonymous drama critic went on to accuse the play of ridiculing sincere Americanism like Ed Keller's. "One gets the impression," he wrote, "of being told that, as a group, college trustees, administrators, and even realistic faculty wives are lacking in ideals, toady to the ogre of big business, and are unappreciative of the teaching profession." Like Ed Keller, this critic also said that the play has no business to include a speech of Vanzetti's.[9]

Like Cyrano, Thurber replied sarcastically that the critic was not adequate in his insults; he forgot to add Thurber's other subversions, such as "my effort to prevent the building of college football stadia, my special pleading on behalf of extramarital relations, and my attack on the competence of Republican presidents, which shows up in the line, 'Hoover can't write as well as Vanzetti.'" Apparently, even before this attack, Thurber had been accused of un-Americanism. In 1948, he referred ironically to *The Male Animal* as "a subversive play" of 1940. "But," he added sarcastically, "I have promised to submit any plays I may write in the future to either Congressman Thomas or Mrs. Lela Rogers, the eminent authorities on the Drama . . ." "People ask why there isn't a comedy like *The Male Animal* anymore—something that's free and exuberant," said Thurber in 1952. "It isn't possible to write a comedy like that any more because we're living in the most frightened century in the world."[10] He claimed that McCarthy's Congressional probes—"more of a political device than a patriotic endeavor"—made the Broadway theater "moribund and demoralized"; and he recalled that, during the 1952 revival of his play, the audience was tense rather than relaxed.

Certainly it is apparent to any clear-minded reader that the play does not have any leanings towards communism. It does not champion Communist professors; its point is that the discharged faculty members have been accused unjustly. Even Michael Barnes, the radical student who started the furor, is not a Communist but "an unconfused liberal." Turner himself is not actively interested in politics until they are thrust upon him. As one critic commented, "Professor Turner really hasn't any potential pinkness. He just happens to think that a man called Vanzetti once wrote a very well expressed letter, and happened to say so much to a boyfriend of his sister-in-law's who exploited it in a student editorial."

Thurber, too, was no insurrectionist; he wrote in 1960 that "It is comforting, in a vaguely uneasy way, to realize that American students do not engage in political demonstrations, but reserve their passions for panty raids, jazz festivals, and the hanging of football coaches in effigy."

In fact, Thurber always showed hostility toward communism, even in the 1930's, when it was fashionable for some writers and intellectuals to dabble in it. Though the Red Decade is no doubt a misleading label for that period, Marxist criticism was militant and influential, and proletarian literature was prominent. Writers suspicious of communism were attacked as intolerant and accused of kicking the underdog. In the midst of the Depression, it required particularly acute thinkers to perceive—through all the defiant slogans—that though capitalism was indeed sick and in need of surgery, the Communist alternative might prove fatal. When such able writers as Clifford Odets, John Dos Passos, Ernest Hemingway, Malcolm Cowley, and Granville Hicks were not yet disenchanted with the Soviet "experiment," liberal but unsympathetic critics like Thurber and E. E. Cummings, both irreverent humorists and ardent advocates of individual liberty against any dogmatic restraints, were viewed by the left with resentment and dismay. Traditionalists like Willa Cather and Thornton Wilder were condemned as cowards. The *New Yorker* writers who stayed aloof from didactic proletarian prose were dismissed by Mike Gold as a bunch of "college punks."

Incensed, Thurber wrote Malcolm Cowley of *The New Republic* a fifteen-page letter assailing literary communism. Cowley replied by inviting Thurber to review Granville Hicks's edition of *Proletarian Literature in the United States* (1936). In an unbiased critique, based on literary merit, Thurber praised some selections but complained that too many degenerated into invective and irrelevant insult against "bourgeois" writers. He was particularly irritated by Joseph Freeman's "sweeping insinuation" that the middle class consisted of lechers and Narcissists and that love is confined to the proletariat. On artistic grounds, he objected not to the subject matter but to the too-often slipshod prose: "I grant the importance of the scenes on which all these stories are based, but they cannot have reality, they cannot be literature, if they are slovenly done. . . . Art does not rush to the barricades." Thurber advised the proletarian authors to study the work of such *New Yorker* writers as Robert Coates and St. Clair McKelway, whose "writing is hard, painstaking and long." And a final and fatal defect was the anthology's total lack of humor. "The nature of humor is anti-communistic just as the nature of Communism is anti-humor," wrote Thurber seventeen years later during the Red scare.

Objecting to the dogmatism of Marxist critics, Thurber devoted two essays to them in *Let Your Mind Alone!* (1937), ridiculing their dialectic ("the process of discriminating one's own truth from another person's error") and factionalism ("that process of disputation by means of which the main point of issue is lost sight of"). A fastidious stylist, he disliked their addiction to jargon and the pretentious and calculated quality of their elaborate autobiographical correspondence. Since it seemed that the main purpose of leftist literary meetings was to unmask everybody else's ideology, Marxist criticism struck Thurber as being very similar to psychoanalysis: "Ideology-unmasking is a great deal like dream interpretation and leads to just as many mystic results."

Art cannot be regimented, and Thurber concluded that he was "opposed to every restriction, mould, pattern, and commandment for literature that is set up by the Marxist literary critics." Three years earlier, in "Notes for a Proletarian Novel," he had ridiculed Granville Hicks for believing "that Emily Dickinson failed miserably in her lyrics about bees because she didn't give any serious attention to the problem of the workers." Thus he challenged Malcolm Cowley, "If these men, who write such attacks, should ever get in control, do you think there wouldn't be a commissar of literature who would be appointed and commissioned to stop it, who would set us at work writing either poems in praise of the American Lenin or getting up time tables for work trains? If you do, you're missing a low, faint, distant rumbling."[11] Actually, Thurber didn't think there was any chance of such a revolution. "I believe the only menace is the growing menace of fascism," he wrote to Cowley. "I also firmly believe that it is the clumsy and whining and arrogant attitude of the proletarian writers which is making the menace bigger every day."[12]

In his zeal to oppose fascism, Thurber was among four hundred signers of the Open Letter denouncing—just before the Nazi-Soviet pact—"the fantastic falsehood that the USSR and the totalitarian states are basically alike" and criticizing the Committee for Cultural Freedom that had included the USSR among totalitarian states. But Eugene Lyons, author of *The Red Decade,* concedes that the signers, "prominent people from all sections of the country," wanted to attack Nazism, not defend the Soviets, and that these mostly reputable citizens were duped by the double talk of the form letter, which he calls "a masterpiece of political jugglery."[13]

Ed Keller's ghost was not laid to rest, for in the post World War II years, Thurber was alarmed by the internal peril to the

American scene from the investigations and inquisitorial techniques practiced by some government committees and self-righteous civic groups of the extreme right, whose irresponsible accusations of disloyalty, he felt, created an era of fear and uncertainty. He lamented the decline of political satire at this time, when all writers were suspect. Thurber said sarcastically that he himself might appear guilty to the three-man inquisitions run by the State Department in 1947: "I believed then, and still do, that generals of the Southern Confederacy were, in the main, superior to generals of the Northern armies; I suspected there were flaws in the American political system; I doubted the virgin birth of United States senators; I thought that German cameras and English bicycles were better than ours; and I denied the existence of actual proof that God was exclusively a citizen of the United States."

It appears that Thurber and other perfectly loyal writers had some reason for apprehension; for Malcolm Cowley, in his study of the current literary situation, revealed that in practice—though not in theory—the restrictions on travel abroad were more heavily imposed on the writing profession than on any other; the investigators seemed to have an instinctive hostility to writers, who might criticize the political scene. "As for positions with the government," Cowley observed, "very few writers applied for them after 1950, word having gotten around that anyone who had published a book was likely to get into trouble with Congress. Roy M. Cohn, chief counsel for Senator McCarthy's subcommittee, might have been speaking for many Congressmen when he was asked about the choice of speakers for a television program and said, 'Any author is out.' "[14] Thurber protested our taking the passport away from Arthur Miller, to whom a Congressman had asked, "Do you really believe that the artist is a special person?" Thurber replied in the New York *Times*: "A nation in which a Congressman can seriously ask: 'Do you think the artist is a special person?' is a nation living in cultural jeopardy." Coming to his colleagues' defense, Thurber stated that most writers he knew always hated communism, "but they have the curiosity of male spaniel puppies or female spotted deer. They get into things, but this can be defended on the sound ground that nothing can be intelligently accepted or rejected unless it has been examined and understood." "If we don't stop suspecting all writers," he said in 1952, "it will be a severe blow to our culture. I think all writers, even the innocent ones, are scared. There's guilt by association, guilt by excoriation, there's guilt by everything the politicians invent."[15]

There was, even for the acquitted, what Thurber called guilt by exoneration—a stigma attached to one for having been suspect at all. As early as 1948, Thurber complained of the atmosphere engendered by such finger-pointing and remarked that, "In the present Era of Suspicion, it is a wise citizen who disproves any dark rumors and reports of his secret thoughts and activities before they can be twisted into charges of disloyalty by the alert and skillful minds now dedicated to that high-minded and patriotic practice." He feared that such heresy-hunting repressed satire or any criticism of the political scene. If the expression of humor was stifled, he felt that the danger was as great of our being destroyed from within as from without because we were fighting the enemy with its own weapons. "As a matter of fact," he wrote in his reply to the Ohioana award, "comedy, in all its forms, including the rusty art of political satire, is used to surviving eras of stress and strain, even of fear and trembling, but it sickens in the weather of intimidation and suppression, and such a sickness could infect a whole nation. The only rules comedy should tolerate are those of taste and the only limitations those of libel."

VI *The Necessity of Satire*

Thurber liked to think of himself as a sharp-penned and sometimes savage satirist rather than as the harmless humorist some careless readers took him to be. On television ("Small World," March 22, 1959), he said that he preferred Mencken to Will Rogers for American political satire, since Rogers never said anything dangerous or daring. This statement does not mean that Thurber was indiscriminately iconoclastic; for he would doubtless have agreed with Swift that, "although some Things are too serious, solemn, or sacred to be turned into Ridicule, yet the Abuses of them are certainly not. . . ." Insofar as he distinguishes truth from hypocrisy, cant, and fraud, the satirist is a public servant. Believing that whatever is genuine can endure the test of laughter, Thurber insisted that "Our comedy should deal, in its own immemorial manner, with the American scene and the American people, without fear or favor, without guilt or grovelling."

Ordinarily apolitical in his work, Thurber wrote most of his political satire after the advent of McCarthy, who aroused rather than intimidated him, and whom he compared to an enormous caterpillar eating the vegetation of the Republic. In 1958, he told Henry Brandon that "The six or eight years that went by—those terrible years—when all the American Congress seemed to do was to investigate writers, artists and painters—to me were the dreadful years. All this time Russia was getting ahead of us, all this time we were fighting a new cold civil war—suspecting neighbors, suspecting the very nature of writing, of academic intellectualism, anything—that was a very bad moment in our history—perhaps the darkest we've ever had. But I think we're coming out of that."[16]

During the height of heresy-hunting, even Thurber needed some mental relief; and he confessed that he wrote *The Thurber Album* partly to return to the placid years of his parents' generation—"the age of innocence, when trust flowered as readily as suspicion does today. . . ." Thus, "The *Album* was a kind of escape—going back to the Middle West of the last century and the beginning of this, when there wasn't this fear and hysteria. I wanted to write the story of some solid American characters, more or less as an example of how Americans started out and what they should go back to. To sanity and soundness and away from this jumpiness. It's hard to write humor in the mental weather we've had, and that's likely to take you into reminiscence."[17] Actually, though Thurber stated that, "In 1918, Americans naively feared the enemy more than they feared one another," the Red Scare after World War I was in some ways more extreme than McCarthyism; and Attorney-General Palmer was even more high-handed in his suppression of civil liberties.

Ironically, many of the witch-hunters themselves also want to return to the simpler past, when "solid American characters" were supposedly more common. Hysterical reactionaries, labeling the entire contemporary scene as subversive, frequently clamor for the virtues of the Old Frontier and its lynch-law justice. Thus William S. Schlamm, writing in the ultra-conservative *Freeman* in 1952, took Thurber to task for not siding with McCarthy and insisted that Robert Ryder and all the characters in *The Thurber Album* would have supported the Wisconsin senator, since the "last refuge of honor and guts and cockeyed friendliness" was on his side.[18] But in the *Album*, Thurber praised as Robert Ryder's greatest paragraph: "A hardened reformer never seems able to make up his mind which is the most beautiful word in the language, 'compulsory' or 'forbidden.'" McCarthy is the perfect example of such a reformer, and it is unlikely that Ryder or any of the other individualists in the *Album* would submit to the bullying of a humorless demagogue.

Schlamm wanted to enlist Thurber as an ally; but some "super-patriots," apparently using the logic that, since he opposed witch-hunting, he must be a witch, labeled him as subversive. Thurber said that he was always, in fact, "a vehement anti-communist, a fact that could be proved in a few hours of research, but I have no doubts that, like almost all writers, I will one day be named as a

Red."[19] Since he dared write *The Male Animal* and was one of the bitterest critics of Senator McCarthy and the more recent rabble rousers of the radical right, we find that the pamphlet, "Red Stars— No. 3," issued in 1960 by the Cinema Educational Guild, Inc., includes Thurber among the "best known of the REDS and FELLOW-TRAVELERS who made our SCREEN Communism's most effective 'Pied Piper,'" with "films that sanctify MARXISM— ONE-WORLDISM—DESEGREGATION." This hysterical document accuses a long list of artists of "brainwashing and poisoning your children right under your very eyes" and urges each individual to boycott their work and to drive them from the theater. Along with a few acknowledged Communists, the list includes such "subversive" figures as Thurber, Danny Kaye, Sir Douglas Fairbanks, Jr., Bennett Cerf, Edward R. Murrow, Chet Huntley, Gypsy Rose Lee, Groucho Marx, Burgess Meredith, Leonard Bernstein, Aaron Copland, Agnes DeMille, Sidney Poitier, Oscar Hammerstein II, Moss Hart, George S. Kaufman, Archibald MacLeish, Dorothy Parker, and dozens of other perfectly innocent people. The pamphlet provides no evidence (because there is none) but relies upon mere slander and libel.

But, wrote Thurber, "Guilt is not a matter of guesswork or conjecture, but of proof." Thus from the fable of "The Very Proper Gander" (1940) to that of "The Peacelike Mongoose" (1956), he attacked those who would, on the basis of hearsay or other insufficient evidence, denounce their neighbors as traitors, with the result that, "if the enemy doesn't get you your own folks may." Lamenting the decline of "the old abandoned American assumption of innocence" until one is proven guilty, Thurber invented several holidays to remedy the situation. These include Fact Day, when "only the proved is tolerated"; Liability Day, when senators and congressmen "would be deprived of immunity and could be sued for libellous remarks"; and (to balance the scales) Immunity Day, when anyone could freely criticize anybody. "Many persons, in our era of fear and hysteria," he wrote in 1955, "are afraid to say what they think about public figures and national affairs, and have become neurotic victims of ingrown reticence, no longer able to tell discretion from timidity, or conviction from guilt." Even the comic strips were under attack: some papers censored *Pogo,* and Al Capp was pressured to remove the Schmoo from *Li'l Abner* and to tone down the strip generally because it seemed to some "superpatriots" to be suspect in its satire of military and business interests. Despite Mike Gold's leftist attack upon it, *The New Yorker* was now denounced as "Red from top to bottom," and was sufficiently intimidated in 1956 that it refused to print some of Thurber's political fables—the very ones that won him the American Library Association's Liberty and Justice Award.

"Humor should never take the form of penance or of penitence," Thurber insisted, for a free society decays in an atmosphere of humorlessly grim self-righteousness that proscribes healthy self-criticism. The methods of Ed Keller and McCarthy are too similar to those of the Soviets, and it is impossible to retain freedom by employing the tactics of its enemies. "Well, there isn't a trace of humor in communism, is there? I think any political system that vehemently attacks humor reveals a great weakness," Thurber told Harvey Breit.[20] In 1960, he charged that comedy had been beaten by both the intellectual left and the political right. "Humor, as Lord Boothby has said, is the only solvent of terror and tension, and terror and tension are among the chief ideological weapons of Communism." Besides, tyrants and bigots have always feared laughter because it shows them up "in a clear and honest light and drives away the big distorted shadows in which they love to lurk." Hence Thurber opposed demagogues of any sort, whether of the extreme right or left. Enemies to laughter, both would strangle freedom of expression; and it was for this freedom rather than for any specific political program that Thurber fought. In *The Male Animal,* Keller says that he would not allow the Vanzetti letter to be read under any circumstances. "I wouldn't care if that letter were by Alexander Hamilton." "Neither would I," replies Turner; "the principle is exactly the same."

CHAPTER 7

Thurber and Thespis

THE SUCCESS of *The Male Animal*, ranked as one of the best plays of 1940, and included by John Gassner in a volume of the best plays of the modern American theater, seemed to herald a new career for Thurber as a popular dramatist. However, he failed to develop along this line and to follow up his lead successfully. Twenty years later, *A Thurber Carnival* was a smash hit; but, aside from one new piece, this was a series of adaptations from his work in *The New Yorker*. For years he and Nugent planned to do another play together but never got around to it. They did collaborate once again but only on a sketch written for the all-star radio show opening the Fourth War Loan drive in Franklin County, Ohio, on January 18, 1944. In 1943, it was announced that Thurber was working on a play about *The New Yorker*.

This project occupied his attention on and off for the rest of his life, but he never completed it to his satisfaction. He was in the habit of working on many pieces simultaneously and putting aside, sometimes for years, those which failed to sustain his interest. Though *The Years with Ross* revived his enthusiasm for The *New Yorker* play, *Make My Bed*, which he hoped would be ready for production by the fall of 1958, he never worked it into presentable shape. Mrs. Thurber says that her husband was not good at construction and did not have an adequate second act for the play. Elliott Nugent once read several hundred pages of it in manuscript and discussed with Thurber some of its problems but without much effect. Thurber could write superb dialogue; many of his later stories are almost straight conversation. They are extremely effective as fiction, but they lack dramatic action. "Am Not I Your Rosalind?", one of the best, was adapted for *A Thurber Carnival* but turned out to be too static for the stage.

A few years before his death, Thurber started another play, a triangle comedy about Bermuda, which was planned for production in the fall of 1957. It had a perfect title, *The Welcoming Arms*, but again a workable script failed to materialize. Under the pressures that led to his final illness, Thurber became obsessed with finishing these projects and once had Burgess Meredith read a hastily rewritten version of The *New Yorker* plays that Thurber himself knew was no good. In one of his last interviews, he told W. J. Weatherby that he was doing a play called *The Last Romantic*, but this project never got beyond his imagination.

I *Thurber on Film*

Others dramatized Thurber with varying degrees of success. Having paid $150,000 for the film rights, Warner Brothers produced a 1942 movie of *The Male Animal*, starring Henry Fonda, Olivia de Havilland, and Jack Carson. Allowing for the flexibility of the camera, the scenario by Julius J. and Philip G. Epstein did not confine the action to the Turner living room but included additional scenes on campus, a game rally, flashes of the game itself, and set the climax in the university auditorium. For authentic atmosphere the film was shot at Pomona College, Claremont, California. Elliott Nugent was again on hand, this time as director; and, under his skillful guidance, the picture was a hit. The climax, however, was weakened by a sentimentalized conclusion in which Keller repents and Turner is carried off in triumph by huzzahing students. Nugent explained that the Epsteins made these concessions toward a happier ending for a mass audience. Nugent also wrote a few new speeches to make the Vanzetti resolution as effective in the film as on stage. Later he directed a United States Organization overseas production of the show; and on January 12, 1947, he played Turner in a broadcast by "Theatre Guild on the Air."

Unfortunately, *The Male Animal* was so successful that Warners decided to remake it as a musical and in 1952 produced a meretricious adaptation called *She's Working Her Way Through College*. In this version we find Virginia Mayo as Hot Garters Gertie, a burlesque queen who has written a play and decides to enroll at Midwest State University in the playwriting course of Professor Johnny Palmer (read Tommy Turner), played uncomfortably by Ronald Reagan. To the annoyance of his wife Helen (read Ellen), Gertie also boards at his house. Though he is underpaid (only Coach Sprague has had a raise in five years), Palmer lives in an extensive mansion suitable for big musical numbers in the living room and up and down the staircase. This humble abode he rents from Copland (read Keller), chairman of the board of trustees, who had unsuccessfully propositioned Hot Garters during her burlesque days.

Adding "oomph" to Palmer's class, Gertie suggests that, for the annual play, the school should get away from the traditional Shakespearean production and give the students what they really want. Palmer lets the class select the program, and they vote to do Gertie's play as a musical. At this point the academic freedom issue raises its feeble head, for Trustee Copland, who thinks that *Oedipus Rex* is dirty, insists on the right to censor the production. Now football star Shep Slade (read Joe Ferguson), played by Don DeFore, returns to campus for no particular reason, since there is no big game. He makes some perfunctory passes at the professor's wife so that Palmer (Turner) can go through the famous drunk scene, and then Slade disappears. Though drastically altered and ineffectively rewritten, the drunk scene kept some of Thurber's lines and was the best bit in the film.

Meanwhile, Gertie's musical is progressing, with Virginia Mayo and Gene Nelson doing embarrassingly cute and implausible dance routines on the professor's desk during class sessions. Then disaster threatens, as an envious rival reveals Gertie's burlesque career. In a travesty of academic procedure, Copland insists that the entire student body gather for a special session in the auditorium, where Palmer (Turner) is to expel Gertie publicly if he wants to keep his job. Instead, he defends academic freedom with a tepid tirade about the right of burlesque queens to have a college education. Gertie tames Copland by threatening to reveal his off-campus lechery, and the film ends in glorious technicolor.

Seeing the screen credits, one wonders how Warner Brothers had the gall to give Thurber and Nugent the blame for this film. They were appalled, but they had no control over the remake since they had sold the movie rights ten years before. It is perhaps significant that this film, reducing the academic freedom issue to a farce, was produced at the height of McCarthyism.

Most of Thurber's experiences with Hollywood were unhappy. In 1942, the movies released an unrecognizable adaptation of *My Life and Hard Times*—retitled *Rise and Shine*—which featured Jack Oakie in a plot about a stupid football player. This film passed unnoticed into oblivion, but the screen treatment of "The Secret Life of Walter Mitty" left Thurber exasperated and disappointed. Shortly after the story's appearance Hollywood started to bid for it, but Thurber held off for a while. In 1942, Metro-Goldwyn-Mayer offered to buy it and "The Catbird Seat." Thurber demurred, however, hoping to sell it to Rogers and Hammerstein as the story for a musical. Perhaps those gentlemen could have done it justice, but they were too busy with *Oklahoma!* Meanwhile, the demand for "Mitty" continued. In 1944, Moss Hart announced that he would like to dramatize it. Robert Benchley played it on the radio in a performance that Mrs. Thurber considers the best Mitty ever done. Both Nunnally Johnson and 20th Century Fox wanted to buy it as a vehicle for Jack Benny, but Thurber finally sold it to Samuel Goldwyn.

"Walter Mitty" proved difficult to adapt satisfactorily to the screen. The story is about four thousand words long, with five daydreaming sequences which contrast to Mitty's humdrum life with his nagging wife. The problem, of course, was how to expand this material into a feature-length film. It took Goldwyn three years to complete the motion picture, which appeared in the summer of 1947, directed by Norman McLeod, with Danny Kaye in the title role. Mr. Kaye is a talented performer, and Goldwyn made the mistake of turning the movie into a vehicle for him, violating Thurber's story in the process. The screenplay by Ken Englund and Everett Freeman substituted a nagging mother (played by Fay Bainter) for Mrs. Mitty, thus leaving Danny Kaye free for romance with Virginia Mayo. The dream sequences were well done, and three new ones were added showing Mitty as a cowboy (Slim Mitty, the Perth Amboy Kid); as Gaylord Mitty, a Southern riverboat gambler; and as Anatole Mitty of Paris, a designer of ladies' hats. Thurber said he wished he had thought of the riverboat sequence, but he muttered that no man would ever dream of being a milliner and that the scene was included simply for Sylvia Fine's song. When the script involved Mitty with Boris Karloff and a gangster plot about international art thieves, Thurber's story was reduced to just another mixture of suspense and musical comedy. The monotonous, commonplace realities of Mitty's waking life are essential as contrasts to the daydreams; otherwise they are pointless. "Did anyone catch the name of that picture?" Thurber asked after seeing Goldwyn's film. He was angry with the treatment his story received, and he objected to the slapstick and the "git-gat-gittle" of Kaye's gibberish songs. The story needs a light touch, but Goldwyn drenched it with the splashy Hollywood flamboyance Thurber so heartily disliked; Danny Kaye smothered in Goldwyn girls bore little resemblance to Thurber's character.

"The Secret Life of Walter Mitty" later fared better as an opera, written by Charles Hamm of the Cincinnati Conservatory of Music, whose version won Ohio University's 1953 opera workshop award. Thurber finally made his own adaptation for *A Thurber Carnival*, where Tom Ewell gave a memorable performance.

Several times Thurber turned down offers to become a movie scriptwriter. Otto Friedrich once accused him of writing trivia to meet "a constant need for money," but he rejected Goldwyn's lure of $2500 a week to come to Hollywood and write. He had seen enough of the film capital in 1939, while writing *The Male Animal,* and he hated its gaudy ostentation. Besides, he had too much independence and artistic integrity to contract himself to a studio's demands, and so he escaped the sort of frustration Fitzgerald and Faulkner experienced at Hollywood's treatment of their screenplays.

Thurber's definitive portrayal of Hollywood is "The Man Who Hated Moonbaum," a minor masterpiece that says as much in several concise pages as *What Makes Sammy Run.* Thurber's story catches perfectly the cadences and inflections of manic-depressive, slightly paranoid, aggressive vulgarity, as a screaming drunk producer ("Don't get me screaming! What are you trying to do to me?") explains to a visiting writer the exasperations of filming the story of "What's-His-Name" ("'Tristram,' said Tallman. 'Don't prompt me!' bellowed the little man") and Isolde. ("Name of God, man, you can't call a woman Isolde! . . . I want her called Dawn. . . . It's short, ain't it? It's sweet, ain't it? You can say it, can't you?") Here is Romanticism debased with a vengeance. ("Whozis writes her a message made out of twigs bent together to make words: 'I love you'—sends it floating down a stream past her window—they got her locked in—goddamnedest thing in the history of pictures.")

Along with "Mitty" Thurber sold the screen rights of "The Cat-bird Seat" to Goldwyn and even agreed to write a screenplay for it. For this he was given a $10,000 advance and was to receive $40,000 more when he turned in a fifteen thousand word scenario by the specified date. He began the job but was not satisfied with the result; and, fearing that his story might receive screen treatment like that given "Walter Mitty," he returned the $10,000 and destroyed his script. In 1948, he sold the screen rights of the story to Burt Lancaster's Norma Productions, that planned to film it at its proper length as one of four stories, including Ring Lardner's "The Love Nest." This time the producers defaulted. In July, 1952, a version of "The Catbird Seat" was presented on television. Finally, Monja Danischewsky wrote and produced an effective film. By switching the story's locale from New York to Edinburgh and transforming the unspecified F & S business to an antiquated Scottish woolens firm, she made it more a comedy of manners, working in a number of amusingly eccentric characterizations and heightening the contrast between the American Mrs. Ulgine Barrows and the stubborn traditions of her Scottish victims. The expanded plot had Mr. Martin furtively sabotage the new office gadgetry Mrs. Barrows introduced before he accomplished his unexpected *coup de grâce.* Released in 1959 as *The Battle of the Sexes,* with Peter Sellers and Robert Morley in memorable performances as Mr. Martin and his employer, "The Catbird Seat" was the most satisfactory feature film adapted from Thurber.

At one time there was an ambitious project for a full-length film, half animated cartoon and half live drama, tentatively entitled *The Thurber Carnival*, to be made from a number of short pieces; but the producers had to drop the plan because of insufficient funds. The cartoon company, United Productions of America (U.P.A.), producers of "Gerald McBoing-Boing" and the "Near-sighted Mr. Magoo" series) did, however, proceed to make a highly praised short of "The Unicorn in the Garden."

II *Adaptations for Theater, Ballet, and Television*

A number of dramatizations from Thurber have been staged more or less successfully. The most ambitious production was *Three by Thurber*, a trio of related one-act plays that Paul Ellwood and St. John Terrell created from the Monroe stories. Produced in the spring of 1955 at the Theatre de Lys on Christopher Street, it had a moderately favorable reception. Bertram Yarborough's direction and the performances of Edward Andrews and Roberta Jonay were pleasing, but critics felt the script failed to do complete justice to Thurber. As the title of Wolcott Gibbs's review, "In a Glass Darkly," suggests, the adaptation tended to dilute Thurber's wit and partly obscure his charm.

Thurber's fables and fantasies had better luck. In 1946, Charlotte Barrows Chorpenning turned *Many Moons* into a play that is popular for school and children's theater productions. The Barter Theatre of Virginia dramatized and produced *The 13 Clocks* in 1953, to the then largest audience in that theater's history; and a touring company did another version for the summer circuit of 1953, double-billed with Leonard Bernstein's *Trouble in Tahiti*. *The 13 Clocks* also has been made into a children's opera, with music by Mary Johnson and libretto by her with Maritza and Norman Morgan, which was premiered at Hunter College. On May 1, 1957, the Hartt College of Music at Hartford, Connecticut, premiered another Thurber opera, Russell Smith's one-act version of "The Unicorn in the Garden," given on a double bill with Gounod's *Philemon and Baucis*. In 1957, Jule Styne was planning a musical of Thurber's fantasy *The Wonderful O*, for which John McGiffert of television's "Camera Three" was making an adaptation, with lyrics by Carolyn Leigh and music by Cy Coleman. Mr. Styne wanted Peter Ustinov in the leading role of Black the pirate. Apparently this project was abortive, for nothing yet has come of it.

Some of Thurber's pieces have been successfully turned into ballet. Doris Humphrey did a ballet reconstruction of the picture parable "The Race of Life." Some of the fables also appealed to Charles Weidman, once Miss Humphrey's dancing partner. His troupe performed in 1950 and 1951, a program including "The Unicorn in the Garden," "The Owl Who Was God," and "The Courtship of Arthur and Al" to highly appreciative audiences. Weidman later presented a ballet of "The War Between Men and Women" at the YMHA's 1954 Summer Dance Festival. Finally, television's "Wonderful Town" did *The 13 Clocks* as ballet, with Faye Emerson narrating off camera.

Thurber had a number of other television offers. There were proposals at one time to televise *The Thurber Album* and *My Life and Hard Times,* but these plans came to naught. "There are always a lot of prospects," said Thurber, "but most of the time nothing happens." Robert Montgomery once produced a disappointing version of "The Greatest Man in the World." "Omnibus" did somewhat better with "The Remarkable Case of Mr. Bruhl" in 1954, adapted by Tad Mosel and starring Elliott Nugent; and it planned future productions of "Mr. Preble Gets Rid of His Wife," "Many Moons," and "Helpful Hints and the Hoveys."

In December of 1953, *The 13 Clocks* appeared in an hour-long dramatic version during the Christmas season. Starring Basil Rathbone as the Duke, Sir Cedric Hardwicke as the Golux, John Raitt as Prince Zorn, and Roberta Peters as Princess Saralinda, with music by Mark Bucci, it was, in the words of one critic, "one of television's finest achievements in make-believe." Selecting it as an outstanding production, *Life's* critic commented that "Audience and critics, feeling it was high time TV got this far, began looking with renewed hope to the new year for more Thurber, more fantasy and many repetitions of *The Thirteen Clocks.*

Another TV highlight was the "Camera Three" presentation of *The Last Flower* on October 12, 1958. On the other hand a "Playhouse 90" production of *The Male Animal* on March 13, 1958, was quite disappointing, despite a capable cast headed by Andy Griffith, Ann Rutherford, and Edmund O'Brien; for the adaptation by Don Mankiewicz retained little of the original dialogue and played fast and free with details of the plot. More successful was the "G. E. Theater" version on September 28 of the same year, of "One Is a Wanderer," starring Fred MacMurray. Finally a whole series, "The Secret Life of James Thurber," was planned; but only an uneven pilot film appeared on "Goodyear Theater" in June, 1959. Here Melville Shavelson's adaptation of "Christabel" presented Arthur O'Connell—thinly disguised as Thurber himself—in the role of John Monroe, writer and cartoonist for *The Manhattan* magazine. The drama was a conglomeration of Thurber, borrowing the protagonist's name from the Monroe stories, that of a hound named Muggs from the Airedale that bit people in *My Life and Hard Times,* and inserting "The Topaze Cufflinks Mystery" into the plot, which was climaxed by the death of the aged poodle Christabel and concluded by quoting Thurber's eulogy for his own dog of that name. Despite good performances, the show did not quite come off. Two years after Thurber's death, television did a "Children's Theater" color production of *The Great Quillow,* now retitled "Quillow and the Giant." Shown on November 3, 1963, it had songs by Ralph Blane and Wade Barnes and featured Win Stracke as the giant, with the other characters portrayed by the George Latshaw Puppets.

Ultimately, the most successful adapter of Thurber turned out to be Thurber himself, with his 1960 revue *A Thurber Carnival.* This may have grown out of an earlier project that was announced but never materialized; for several years before, Haila Stoddard, one of the producers of the revue, had obtained stage rights to twenty-five Thurber pieces to be produced as *Thurber Country.* It was reported that the first part of the program, based on *My Life and Hard Times,* would be about Thurber himself, while the second half was to be a series of connected sketches based on "My Own Ten Rules for a Happy Marriage." The once-planned *Thurber Carnival* film may also have been in the background.

Its was Burgess Meredith, an old crony of Thurber's, who was the catalyst for the *Carnival;* he suggested material and practical revisions and helped shape the show for the stage. Produced by Michael Davis, Helen Bonfils, and Haila Stoddard, and directed by Meredith, it had its premiere in Columbus on January 7, 1960. Reviews were favorable, but much work was still needed. The opening version had fourteen sketches and eight fables, a number of which—"The Departure of Emma Inch," "Memorial to a Dog," "The War between Men and Women," "The Owl Who Was God." "The Sea and the Shore," "The Godfather and His Godchild," and "The Tigress and Her Mate"—were cut or replaced during six weeks of revision before the revue reached Broadway. Thurber, who traveled with the show, rewrote *The Carnival* after performances at Detroit, Cleveland, St. Louis, Cincinnati, and Pittsburgh.

Thus road-tested, the revised production opened on February 26 at the ANTA Theatre to highly enthusiastic notices by Kenneth Tynan, Walter Kerr, Brooks Atkinson, John Chapman, and others. Tom Ewell, Paul Ford, and Peggy Cass performed memorably in a variety of roles, and Don Elliott's jazz score was an appropriate accompaniment. Opening and closing with a word-dance sequence, the program consisted of a narration of "The Night the Bed Foll" and "The Last Flower" and of dramatizations of familiar Thurber pieces—"The Wolf at the Door," "The Unicorn in the Garden," "The Little Girl and the Wolf," "If Grant Had Been Drinking at Appomattox," "Casuals of the Keys," "The Macbeth Murder Mystery," "The Pet Department," "File and Forget," "Mr. Preble Gets Rid of His Wife," "Take Her Up Tenderly," and "The Secret Life of Walter Mitty"—plus an entirely new sketch, "Gentleman Shoppers." (For the road production, starring Imogene Coca, Arthur Treacher, and King Donovan, "Take Her Up Tenderly" was replaced by the fable "The Clothes Moth and the Luna Moth.") The adaptation weakened a few pieces, notably "Mr. Preble," which sent the couple to bed in a happy ending; and "Walter Mitty," which dropped the trial and Royal Air Force episodes and ended differently though effectively with Mitty giving the last command to the firing squad and dismissing it from its post. Still, *A Thurber Carnival* was an outstanding hit of the season, and it won for its author the Antoinette Perry Award from the American Theatre Wing for distinguished writing.

III   *Thurber as a Performer*

Thurber had his final theatrical triumph when he appeared himself in the revue, fulfilling a lifelong desire to perform in a professional Broadway show. His agent, John G. Gude, protested, saying that Thurber was such "a ham at heart" that he might never write another sentence. Actually he wrote fifteen pieces in the remaining year of his life. But it is true enough that he was a ham. As a child, he used to act imaginary dramas for the family audience. Once he and his mother pretended to be shoplifters at a Columbus department store. Later, as we have seen, he joined the Ohio State University Strollers. "I act constantly, as my friends know," Thurber stated; "I've always wanted to act."[1] Once he threatened to replace Nugent for a one night performance in *The Male Animal* but was prevented by an eye operation.

The New Yorker's late drama critic, Wolcott Gibbs, said that he would like to see Thurber star in his own roles and that anyone who saw his interpretation of Jeeter Lester from *Tobacco Road* had seen great acting. Burgess Meredith was impressed with this living-room version of Erskine Caldwell and noted that Thurber liked to memorize favorite stage roles. Mrs. Thurber writes that "He did a wonderful W. C. Fields, an even better Ed Wynn, and a very funny Bing Crosby singing *White Christmas*." She adds that "He was a great late-evening singer, and while most famous for his rendition of *Who* and *Bye-Bye Blackbird,* he had scores of other numbers which he sang in private and public—some songs he wrote himself that were never put on paper. He played tunes and rhythms with his incredibly strong fingers on the arms of his chair—and even with his thumb and forefinger on his cheek until a gland swelled up once. No one ever sang the double verse of *People Will Say We're in Love* better than he and a girl in Bermuda."

W. J. Weatherby called Thurber "one of the greatest talkers in America," and Kenneth MacLean claimed that Thurber was not just a conversationalist but offered a complete show, "talking in every form of American dialect, now going through his nose in Brooklynese, now coming through his lips in good old labial Southern negro speech—now acting out scenes from the life of his Erskine Caldwell character . . . reciting now a high-school gradua-tion speech covering the history of the introduction of music into tuneless, tone-deaf New England! Or he may recite for you fifty completely original limericks, the fruits of idle hours when he can't think of anything better to write. Thurber's talk is as brilliant as his writing, and will remind one that all the literature of America is not in the printed word."[2] Frank Sullivan summed it up for the British Broadcasting Corporation: Thurber "told his stories with wit, with perfect timing and a great sense of dramatic climax. In short, he was a first rate actor."

Before joining the cast of *A Thurber Carnival,* Thurber made a number of TV appearances in England and Canada and on many Martha Dean, Mary Margaret McBride, and Dave Garroway day-time shows. In March of 1956 he appeared on "Omnibus" in con-versation with Alistair Cooke; on March 22 and 29, 1959, "Small World" presented him in a three-way trans-Atlantic telephone con-versation with Noel Coward and Siobban McKenna; and on June 1, 1959, he was a guest on the "Jack Paar Show." His last TV appear-ance, two months before his death, was on David Susskind's "Open End" in September, 1961.

Replacing Eddie Mayehoff in *A Thurber Carnival,* Thurber was perfectly cast as himself in "File and Forget," a twelve-minute sketch about his correspondence with his confused publishers. With his total recall, he had no trouble memorizing his lines. He had only two days of rehearsals with Burgess Meredith before making his debut on September 12, 1960. Louis Calta observed that Thurber had perfect timing and showed no nervousness; Thurber remarked that he was so relaxed that one of the cast whispered, "That guy isn't calm, he's stunned." Because of his blindness, he made his entrance seated in a white leather chair moved by a conveyor belt. He had the privilege of leaving on two weeks' notice but stayed with the show for eighty eight performances until its close and even considered touring with the road production. Mrs. Thurber writes that she saw many people do "File and Forget"—"pros, most of them—but nobody gave it the humor and exasperated charm that Jim did on stage, amateur that he was." It is perhaps appropriate that Thurber's last public appearance was at the theater for the opening of Noel Coward's *Sail Away.* Thurber addressed the cast after the show; the next day he collapsed with the stroke that brought on his final illness.

An attempt to follow up the success of *A Thurber Carnival* failed. James Costigan—author of *The Little Moon of Alban*—wrote another revue, with music by Don Elliott, based largely on the fables. Entitled *The Beast in Me*, it opened in New York on May 16, 1963, at the Plymouth Theatre. Reviewers found the show sensitively written and tastefully produced but too fragile for Broadway. Damned with faint praise, it closed after four performances.

There may yet be more Thurber and Thurbers in the theater. Plans have been made for a movie of *The 13 Clocks*, and there has been some discussion of a science-fiction film to be adapted from "The Greatest Man in the World." Thurber was pleased that his daughter is active in the theater. She showed considerable talent as an actress at the University of Pennsylvania, and now helps her husband operate a children's theater near Chicago, thus carrying on the Thurber thespian tradition.

CHAPTER 8

Thurber's Drawings

THURBER may have a wider reputation as a cartoonist and illustrator than as a writer, but he considered himself primarily an author whose drawings were to a large extent casual and incidental. He was a writer for some years before any of his drawings were published, and it was only through the initiative of E. B. White that his pictures were published at all. On the other hand, it is a mistake to dismiss the cartoons as unimportant. The attitude that gives them primacy over Thurber's prose is superficial; that which shrugs them aside, stuffy.

I *Thurber's Art*

Regardless of the relative merit of drawings and prose, the cartoons are essential to a thorough appreciation of Thurber. They complement and reinforce the themes contained in his stories and essays and add an extra dimension to his work. Besides, many of Thurber's most memorable lines (some included effectively as random "Word Dance" dialogue in the *Thurber Carnival* revue) are captions to his cartoons. The drawings of the middle-aged man and woman on the flying trapeze give increased vividness to their verbal portraits. In addition to the captioned cartoons, Thurber provided innumerable illustrations as a visual commentary to his prose. But these are hardly essential; except for "The Pet Department" (his first drawings to appear in *The New Yorker*) and the first collection of fables, Thurber's magazine pieces appeared originally without illustrations, and they were omitted for the stories and essays anthologized in *The Thurber Carnival* and *Alarms and Diversions*. Many of the pictures were done years earlier or later than the pieces they accompany in his other books; and his work of the last ten years was illustrated by old drawings used before in some other context. Though the prose is thus independent, Thurber's sketches add considerable spice to his books, just as Phiz's and Cruikshank's do to Dickens, and Tenniel's to Lewis Carroll. For, "What is the use of a book without pictures?" thought Alice.

Critics have compared Thurber's drawings to those of Edward Lear, Clarence Day, and William Blake, but their differences are greater than any similarity. He resembled these artists as well as Thackeray, W. S. Gilbert, and Sir Max Beerbohm in that all were both writers and illustrators, but otherwise their styles have little in common. Thurber's resemblance to Day was more in matter than in manner. As critic William Murrell put it, "Both author-artists, in spontaneous untaught draftsmanship, reveal subconscious perplexities of beings of subhuman appearance."[1] But any resemblance is coincidental, for Thurber said that he did not see Day's drawings until 1933, nor Lear's until 1937—long after his own appeared in print.

Some critics are repelled by the figures in Thurber's drawings; a greater number feel affection for them. One disturbed reviewer called them a subspecies, "a modern and hardly less bestial equivalent of Swift's Yahoos."[2] On the other hand, Dorothy Parker, while admitting that Thurber's people "have the outer semblance of unbaked cookies," writes that "There is about all these characters, even the angry ones, a touching quality. They expect so little of life; they remember the old discouragements and await the new. They are not shrewd people, nor even bright, and we must all be very patient with them. Lambs in a world of wolves, they are, and there is on them a protracted innocence."[3] Since she was chosen to write the introductions for his two collections of drawings, Mrs. Parker's attitude toward Thurber's pictures was probably close to his own. He himself explained: "I'm serious, and people either like me or hate me for it. Some love the ludicrous men and women I draw, think they are the funniest characters in the world. Others despise me for them. They insist that I must hate all human beings to draw such miserable people while I can draw such pleasant cats and dogs. All I can say to that, and say it with all seriousness, is that it is physically and mechanically impossible for me to draw a good-looking man or woman."

As a draftsman, Thurber was entirely self-taught. His parents expected brother William, who made careful copies of Charles Dana Gibson, to be the family artist and dismissed Thurber's efforts as mere scrawls. Thurber began drawing prolifically when he was seven; one of his pictures preserved from that time shows a panoramic scene of a Civil War battle, surprisingly well composed and carefully detailed, with crowds of soldiers blazing away at each other. The first to discover any promise in his work was his fourth-grade teacher, Miss Gallinger, who picked his rendition of a large white rabbit as one of the best in the class. During his editorship of the Ohio State *Sun-Dial*, when most of the staff were off to war,

Thurber managed to publish some of his drawings (including some fancy silhouettes) in the magazine until his colleagues suggested that he stick to writing and leave the art work to those who knew more about it. (When he wrote his Sunday halfpage for the Columbus *Dispatch*, it was illustrated by Ray Evans.) Unrepressed, Thurber continued scrawling for the fun of it, and some of his early efforts can be seen in the end papers of several books he owned as an undergraduate and reporter (now in the Thurber collection at the Ohio State University library).

Is Sex Necessary? introduced Thurber as a professional illustrator. Noticing that Thurber was filling the waste baskets with penciled drawings, co-author White became curious and discovered that they dealt with material in the book. White, who felt that they were too good to waste, rescued them from the trash, inked them in, and persuaded the reluctant publishers to accept them as illustrations for the text. He still insists that they are the best things in the book. Editor Harold Ross was still hesitant to accept Thurber's drawings for *The New Yorker* but was finally persuaded by his colleagues. Thurber illustrations soon became a hallmark of the magazine, and Ross became fond enough of them to suggest additional ones for famous poems or for Thurber's "A New Natural History." For a while Thurber also drew for Hearst's New York *American,* until Hearst ordered, "Stop running those dogs on your page. I wouldn't have them peeing on my cheapest rug."[4]

Thurber's style of drawing became more certain and skillful over the years. At first both the figures and situations tended to be more abstract and disembodied. In the earliest work, his men and women often do seem a subspecies, for they have no features and only a vague suggestion of a body. The figures are poorly proportioned and lack the distinct personality and lively expression of his later cartoon characters. Thurber still seemed to be sketching tentatively, working toward a style he had not yet mastered. The best drawings of his first two books are in "The Pet Department"; in it the animals are genuinely hilarious and more fully developed than the humans, who are still rather shapeless in form and vague in feature. The famed Thurber hound has not yet appeared, though there are several dogs of other breeds.

The Seal in the Bedroom (1932), Thurber's first complete book of drawings, shows the maturing of his style. The pictures in this volume were done over several years, and the transition in style is apparent in the uneven quality. Many of the pictures, including the cartoon of the title, show Thurber's art at its best. (The seal cartoon is not, as some people think, his first for *The New Yorker,* for it did not appear until January 30, 1932; his first cartoon was printed in the January 31, 1931, issue.) Others, done in the earlier manner, do not yet have his confident touch. Still merely suggested, the figures have not taken on personality. They do have character of a sort, but it is only a vague nervousness. The backgrounds are non-existent or have just the barest of properties. Much as the abstract and Freudian suggestiveness in the earliest work may have intrigued those who wanted to psychoanalyze Thurber, the later drawings are considerably more satisfying from a humorous and esthetic point of view. The preliminary ones display a groping talent; the later ones have the touch of erratic genius.

Beginning with the more advanced pictures in *The Seal in the Bedroom*, the cartoon people become more human. They are recognizably and amusingly proportioned, more individualized and expressive in features and appearance. They still resemble cookies, but the cookies now look baked or at least more substantial. They retain their boneless, plastic appearance; the outlines simply become more accurate and complete. They are less often nude, and their clothes are sketched in more eccentric detail. In addition, Thurber began to fill in background details, at least in his indoor scenes. His bars and doctor's offices were fully equipped. Where he had once drawn merely the suggestion of a sofa in an otherwise bare room, he now filled his cartoon settings with considerable bric-a-brac: pictures and wall ornaments, bookcases, stair railings, furniture, draperies, and baseboards. His interiors, in fact, began to have some resemblance to those of the Jiggs household in the late George McManus' "Bringing Up Father." He became especially fond of putting in lamps with elaborate shades, pull chains, and even cords winding their way to the wall socket. Thurber's art became so representational that, when he showed the interior of an office, he would even have the room number and the official's name and title neatly lettered backwards on the glass door pane.

This development apparently was due less to a change in outlook than to an improvement in draftsmanship, for there is not so much an alteration as a strengthening of mood. Thurber himself said that he saw no change in his style except "a certain tightening of my lack of technique over the eras, the inevitable and impure result of constant practice." The concentration of this lack of technique becomes the formulation of a style. Since Thurber was self-taught, it may be that the simplicity of his first drawings was partly a lack of skill. But recognizing the effectiveness of this simplicity, he perfected it into a controlled mastery, successful because of its unpretentiousness. He seemed to be having more fun with his drawings, since humor depends largely on selective detail. Thurber reported that he did experiment about 1930 with a more complex style, "laboring over cross-hatching and other subtleties of draughtsmanship beyond the reach of my fingers." Fortunately E. B. White prevented him from losing himself in such techniques: " 'Good God,' he said, 'don't do that! If you ever became good you'd be mediocre.' "

The uncertainty of line in some of Thurber's earliest drawings can to some extent be accounted for by the fact that he did most of them rather faintly in pencil, and E. B. White inked them in. Thus the strokes in these pictures appear less bold, less firmly executed. But Thurber could not forever go on having White ink in his drawings. By 1932, Dorothy Parker could report that "He draws with a pen, with no foundation of pencil, and so sure and great is his draughtsmanship that there is never a hesitating line, never a change."[5] Thurber maintained, however, that "My best stuff is in pencil on yellow paper and it has never been published, but at least thirty people . . . own from forty to fifty done with pencil while cockeyed."[6]

In *The Seal in the Bedroom*, Thurber's mature style is first revealed. This book also introduces the justly celebrated Thurber dog with its bloodhound head and body, sorrowful eyes, floppy ears, and short basset-like legs. One cartoon introduces a dozen and a half pups of this breed, with the caption, "The Father Belonged to Some People Who Were Driving Through in a Packard," and since then the pups have grown up and whelped a prodigious progeny. The inspiration for these dogs can be seen if one compares a picture on the wall, in which the heads of six hounds are framed (in the cartoon captioned, "I Yielded, Yes—but I Never Led Your Husband On, Mrs. Fisher!") with "an elaborately framed lithograph of six hunting dogs [named Calypso, Marcano, Sereno, Lantenor, Necanor, and Barbaro] with strong muzzles and melancholy eyes" which hung in Grandfather Fisher's house and is reproduced at the end of *The Thurber Album*. Thurber commented that the dogs of this lithograph "were to remain permanently in my memory for fond, if perhaps imprecise, reference later on, when I began to draw." After his grandfather's death, Thurber inherited this picture, which he hung above the widest fireplace in his country house. The Thurber-bred bloodhound does not appear to have gone through the maturing artistic process that Thurber's humans had, but appears fully developed in *The Seal in the Bedroom*, where two of the highlights are devoted to him—the captionless sequences "The Bloodhound and the Bug" and "The Bloodhound and the Hare."

A major section of *The Seal in the Bedroom* is the picture parable, "The Race of Life," in which a man, woman, and child journey nude and on foot through a barren terrain to arrive at last at a celestial city on a high hill. Along the way, they encounter and escape many dangers a water jump, an alluring stranger who tempts the man, an Enormous Rabbit, a spectral figure entitled "Menace," a blizzard, drought, a sun-baked skull, warlike Indians, and an angry-looking bear. This sequence seems ripe with symbolism and appears to lend itself to various subtle interpretations. However, Thurber mocked the attempt to explain the work symbolically; and it seems likely that he created it ironically to parody the stream-of-consciousness fad and the sometimes overloaded symbolic art of the 1920's. Thurber said of his parable that "Anything may be read into it, or left out of it, without making a great deal of difference. . . . It is better to skip pictures, or tear them out, rather than to begin over again and try to fit them in with some preconceived idea of what is going on." Elaborate analysis "mars the flow of the sequence by interrupting the increasing tempo of the action." Perhaps he meant to suggest that overly symbolic and cryptic works are deficient in dramatic movement and spontaneity. His own interpretations of the items in his sequence are anticlimactic and debunk symbolism: The Enormous Rabbit may be Chickens Counted Too Soon, or a ringing phone, or several other possibilities, but more than likely is an Unopened Telegram which contains no dreadful news but merely "some such innocuous query as: 'Did you find my silver-rimmed glasses in brown case after party Saturday?'"

However, a few scraps of analysis suggest themselves. The journey through a waste land beset with hazards, in quest of a towered city on a mountain peak is reminiscent of "Childe Roland to the Dark Tower Came," though Thurber's comic mood and mock-heroic treatment have nothing in common with Browning's poem. Throughout his works, Thurber refers more frequently to Browning than to any other poet except Shakespeare, and he makes several specific references to "Childe Roland." So it is quite possible that Browning's poem suggested the framework for Thurber's parable. T. S. Eliot also used Browning's image of the waste land; and it may be that "The Waste Land"—still a fairly recent sensation with its highly symbolic, allusive, and cryptic manner—was the immediate object of Thurber's satire.

The waste-land imagery of "The Race of Life" anticipates Thurber's later parable in pictures, *The Last Flower*, as does another section in *The Seal in the Bedroom* entitled "The Collapse of Civilization." Whether symbolic or not, "The Race of Life" has a graceful and flowing movement suggesting dance, so it is not surprising that Doris Humphrey choreographed it and presented it as a ballet. *The Last Flower* should be equally successful if translated into this medium.

This quality of fluid movement is one of the great achievements of Thurber's art. He was especially skilled at drawing dogs in action, whether they are ambling after a bug, pursuing rabbits, or participating in a full-dress hunting scene. The little pictorial dramas "The Bloodhound and the Bug," "The Hound and the Hat," and "The Bloodhound and the Hare" are almost like animated movie cartoons. A number of Thurber's captionless drawings show skaters, skiers, fencers, boxers, or dancers in action. Perhaps his most awesome example of suspended motion is "Mrs. Pritchard's Leap." Even when his figures are sitting or standing still, we expect them to move in a moment, to uncross their legs, wave their arms, or make some gesture. Thurber was also particularly good at drawing crowds of people and could handle them more skillfully than Cecil B. DeMille did his casts of thousands. He caught the rush and swirl of mobs, the frenzied activity of city pedestrians, and the melee of battle in such outstanding examples as the picture of "2000 people in full flight" when the Columbus dam was reported broken, the battle scenes in *The Last Flower,* and the fights in "The War Between Men and Women." And Harold Ross said of Thurber's illustrations of Leigh Hunt's "The Glove and the Lions," "It's the goddamdest lion fight ever put on paper."

For the most part Thurber's drawings have a linear structure, figures and objects being merely outlined, without the surface area's being filled in with cross-hatching, shading, or any of the devices used to give solidity. Consequently, his people are what Dorothy Parker calls "boneless, loppy beings," and what another critic described as "yawping protoplasmic creatures." There is a nebulous quality to them that has a vague affinity with Blake and with some of the work of Picasso. (Thurber, of course, used only black and white.) In 1930, the English art critic Paul Nash called Thurber "a master of impressionistic line," and compared his style to early Matisse.

Thurber himself disparaged such comparisons and made no grandiose claims for his pictures. He said that he drew largely for relaxation, as a relief from writing, and because he could whistle while drawing but not while he wrote. Many of his drawings are mere doodles, and others that evolved into cartoons began as idle sketches. He presented the doodles because, having been amused with them, he thought others might find them amusing. They are for the most part whimsical rather than philosophical or symbolic. Thurber said that "if the drawings have any merit, it was that they were—some of them—funny. And that's what they were intended to be. They weren't intended to be a special form of art over which I struggled."[7] In spite of Thurber's modest claims for his art, his drawings have been highly successful at professional exhibitions.

As for his views about other artists, Mrs. Thurber says that her husband admired the French impressionists (he had at home large reproductions of Seurat, Dufy, and Rousseau) and that among his contemporaries he was a great friend and admirer of Peter Blume, Paul Nash, and Ronald Searle, who said of Thurber's work that "The sloppy refinement of his drawing was, in fact, both the admiration and the despair of better draughtsmen." Thurber wrote in 1948 that his favorite cartoonists included Daumier, Nast, Beerbohm, H. B. Bateman, E. C. Bentley, Clarence Day, David Low, Helen Hokinson, Mary Petty, Peter Arno, Steig, O. Soglow, Milt Cross, H. T. Webster, and Clare Briggs.[8] He also liked the work of Charles Addams and Reginald Marsh. The newer artists, of course, he could not see.

In a review of *The Last Flower*, W. H. Auden attempted to place Thurber's art in historical perspective. According to Auden, there has always been in visual art a competition between iconography and portraiture, the symbolic and the unique. Until the middle of the sixteenth century (or during the period before Raphael), these two elements were maintained in harmonious equilibrium, with religious painting combining symbolism and realistic detail. Then occurred a separation of the two elements, akin to what T. S. Eliot calls the dissociation of sensibility in poetry. Portraiture, the concern with realistic detail, came to predominate art until recent years when iconography (represented by the interest in primitive art and the expression of the subconscious in doodles) has begun to receive more attention. This iconographic art is non-representational, with landscape and the human figure reduced to the barest outline. Auden says that Edward Lear fathered the tradition in comic art, and that Thurber is a modern representative of it. Thurber's icon, he says, is the average non-political man of an industrialized society.[9] Auden and others say that this art is conceived pessimistically, and they find that the human being it portrays is a subspecies, merely suggested in form, and lacking substance or dignity. This criticism is, however, not wholly applicable to Thurber and can be more accurately applied to his very early work than to his mature products. As his style became surer, toward the end of 1932, it approached an equilibrium between the abstract and the representational.

A few critics find the people of Thurber's art repellent and see only pessimism and cynicism, a sort of gallows humor, in his work. Winston Churchill once referred to him as "that insane and depraved artist."[10] But this is to miss Thurber's charm. Often, indeed, the situations of his drawings are precarious and disheartening, but the gloom is only in the matter, not in the manner of his art. Even the subject is as often playful as disillusioned. Thurber's pictures are not nearly so pessimistic nor his cartoon figures so non-human as those in some contemporary cartoons and greeting cards which are almost gleefully malevolent in portraying grotesquerie and neuroticism. There is a crabbed quality to them which is nowhere to be found in Thurber's graceful lines. In the words of Henry McBride of the New York *Sun*, "He is one of the two or three artists in our land who has evolved a style for himself. . . . But he is unlike anybody—his great charm."[11] His people, unbaked as they appear and foolish as they may behave, do have (as Dorothy Parker points out) a simple, innocent character; and the reader has a kindly feeling for them. Perhaps that is why Thurber sometimes got requests like, "Please send me some of your nice drawings for my sister-in-law because she has stomach ulcers."

Those annoyed by Thurber's art probably find his women the most offensive. The Thurber cartoon woman has been described as "a fiercely aggressive female with the figure of a potato sack, a face which is a cross between a weasel's and a swordfish's, and the final indignity, perfectly straight and stringy hair."[12] Dorothy Parker reports that a heckler once said that Thurber women have no sex appeal, to which Thurber replied: "They have for my men."[13] (Elsewhere this reply is attributed to Marc Connelly.) Thurber was not always so hard on the fair sex; in some of his pictures he attempted to draw shapely women with well-groomed hair. Occasionally he turned out pictures of proper little old Victorian ladies with their hair done up in neat top knots. But, since he claimed he could not draw a beautiful woman successfully, he made the most of his flair for the graceless type.

In any case, Thurber's men are not exactly matinee idols. They are usually either large and lumpish or small, flabby, and worried-looking, sometimes wearing a pince-nez represented by a slash line across the nose. When asked how to tell a Thurber man from a Thurber woman, Marc Connelly answered, "The Thurber women have what appears to be hair on their heads."[14] Though the men are usually hairless, they are not necessarily bald, for the boys have no hair either; it seems to be missing only so that Thurber could draw heads with a simple rounded stroke. For this reason many of his figures lack chins as well.

For a while, Thurber costumed his people in the styles then current, but since the mid-1930's, he deliberately drew them wearing the attire of the early 1920's—the ladies with flat hair styles, long formless gowns, helmet-type hats, and long wrap-around coats with big fur collars; the men with derbies, bow ties, and styleless suits. His birds have a much more raffish plumage as well as a more impressive physiognomy. But the handsomest creature in the drawings is the hound, who Thurber said has "an austere and pensive Rodinesque posture" and "resembles a Supreme Court Justice gravely submitting to the indignity of being photographed."

Men, women, and dogs—all are immediately recognizable as Thurber's. "The artist has gone into the language," writes Dorothy Parker. "How often we say, 'He's a Thurber man' or 'Look at that woman—she's a perfect Thurber,' . . ." And of course Thurber's dogs have become a distinct artistic breed. "If I were Mr. Thurber," Dorothy Parker goes on to say, "I should rather have my name used that way even than have it bracketed, as it has so often been, with that of Matisse."[15]

Thurber's drawings reached their height of technical accomplishment about 1933-40. During these years he produced *The Last Flower* and *Fables for Our Time and Famous Poems Illustrated* plus many of the drawings for *Men, Women and Dogs,* which show his art at its best. In addition he illustrated five books by other authors. The first of these, Alice Leone Moates's *No Nice Girl Swears* (1933), is a book on practical etiquette. The second, Don Marquis' *Her Foot Is on The Brass Rail,* was printed privately in 1935. Perhaps the best drawings are for *How to Raise a Dog: in the City . . . in the Suburbs* (1938), written by Dr. James R. Kinney and Ann Honeycutt. This volume is humorously informative like Thurber's reportorial essays on bloodhounds and police dogs. Thurber's pictures for the book are a delight and make the reader wish that dogs and people were always as likeable in real life. In 1939, Thurber illustrated two other books: *Men Can Take It,* by Elizabeth Hawes, and *In a Word,* by Mrs. Margaret Samuels Ernst. The argument of the first is that men's clothing is uncomfortable, senseless, and ridiculous (especially that of clergymen, judges, and military officers), and that it should be changed radically. The book is written with a humorous touch but is inconsequential and already has passed into obscurity. Only the negative side of its argument would carry much weight with Thurber, who claimed that no amount of sartorial effort could make him look elegant. *In a Word* concerns a subject closer to Thurber's heart—the comic etymology of words. The text of both books received mixed critical comment, but Thurber's pictures were praised with unqualified enthusiasm. Within the confines of his style, Thurber achieved technical perfection plus an irresistibly humorous manner. This excellence of style continues in *The Last Flower* and *Fables for Our Time*. Art critic William Murrell states that, "A great style in graphic humor as in the other arts, is a composite of technical excellence and a mature but by no means cynical world-outlook. . . . There are, broadly speaking, two main types of humorous drawing; that which makes humor an end in itself, the light humor of episode or situation; and the other, the humorous statement of a political, social, or personal viewpoint by means of ridicule. The whole purpose of the first is to provoke laughter; the purpose of the second is to awaken perception through laughter."[16] In his illustrations for books by others, Thurber performed the first type of drawing; in his picture parables, cartoons, and illustrations for the *Fables*, he did the second and quite memorably.

Just as Thurber reached his fullest development as draftsman, his remaining eye went bad; and a series of operations restored only temporary threshold vision. For long intervals he was unable to draw; and, during those periods when he could do so (on huge sheets of yellow paper, with the aid of powerful magnifying lenses), the number of his pictures necessarily was greatly curtailed. In 1946, he told Earl Wilson, "My sight comes and goes in cycles. . . . A mist covers the eye part of the time. In a couple of months it should move away, and I'll try to draw some more. I haven't even tried to draw for a month." His deficient eyesight did not, however, impair the quality of his work. Some of the cartoons in his best collection, *Men, Women and Dogs* (1943), were done after his operations, as were his fine animal pictures for *The Beast in Me*. Thurber's visual problems had no relation to the technique of his art. His drawings were most devoid of detail when his sight was strongest; and his later illustrations, even after the operations, have considerably more detail than the earliest ones.

As his sight continued to weaken, Thurber tried various visual devices, including a special drawing board that lit up from behind and a mechanical aluminum pencil manufactured in Czechoslovakia that produces a line glowing like neon, but even this became inadequate. After a three-year interval, he began in 1950 doing the cartoons again in white chalk on black paper; but, after 1951, he had to give up drawing altogether. His last picture was the cover of the July 9, 1951, issue of *Time*. For a while, he and Harold Ross would reverse old pictures and use new captions or cut drawings up and rearrange them. From *Thurber Country* on,

his books were illustrated in this way. He also used to send captions
to *The New Yorker* for cartoons by other artists such as Whitney
Darrow. "You mustn't think I grieve about not being able to
draw," he explained. "If I couldn't write, I couldn't live, but drawing to me is a little bit more than tossing cards in a hat."[17]

Both before and after his operations, the speed with which
Thurber executed his drawings was a constant source of amaze-
ment. Seldom did a picture take more than ten minutes, and
most were done in far less time. Thurber explained that he drew
for relaxation and usually sketched without any preconception;
he evolved the idea as his pen moved over the paper, one detail
or figure suggesting another, in a sort of incremental composition.
He believed that his cartoons done for a caption were usually
inferior to those done with nothing in mind, and he commented
that "His drawings . . . sometimes seem to have reached comple-
tion by some other route than the common one of intent." When
a picture thus drawn failed to satisfy him, he did not correct it
but discarded it and began another. Thus there may have been
many rejected trial-and-error attempts before he was satisfied with
an illustration, but no one picture took more than a few minutes.
As a result his drawings have a spontaneous, unlabored appearance. Even after his eye operations, *Life* clocked Thurber as
completing a cartoon and caption from scratch in six and a quarter
minutes. Even more phenomenal is the fact that he wrote an
entire book, *The Last Flower* (with fifty-three drawings, some of
them crowded with figures), in about two hours.

He was equally fast at doing murals and in two hours produced
a ninety foot long snow scene in white chalk on a blackboard surface for the Cafe Français at Rockefeller Center. On another
memorable and less formal occasion, he covered a wall of Tim
Costello's Third Avenue Saloon with drawings (for drinks) in
ninety minutes. Costello was so fond of these that, when he moved
to a new location, he took Thurber's wall along. One night in
Los Angeles, Thurber did an unauthorized mural (not a dirty one,
he insisted) in the men's room of Chase's Restaurant. The next
morning the proprietor was congratulating himself and planning
ways to make the men's room the main feature of his establishment,
when a scrub woman told him she had taken two whole hours
washing off some idiot's crazy cartoons. Later, the restaurant commissioned Thurber to do two large wall panels. (Once Franklin
Delano Roosevelt requested him to do a cartoon about a bowl of
Brussels sprouts; Thurber found the sprouts diabolically difficult
to draw, especially with his failing eyesight, but he finally managed
a satisfactory rendition.)

Thurber recalled that his pictures encouraged many parents to send in their children's drawings: "Some people thought my drawings were done under water; others that they were done by moonlight. But mothers thought that I was a little child or that my drawings were done by my granddaughter. So they sent in their own children's drawings to *The New Yorker,* and I was told to write these ladies, and I would write them all the same letter: 'Your son can certainly draw as well as I can. The only trouble is he hasn't been through as much.' "[18]

II   *Thurber the Inscrutable*

Thurber debunked the attempts to explain his drawings by Jung, Freud, or other elaborate interpretations. Spoofing psychoanalysis, he divided his cartoons into various categories. The first is the Unconscious or Stream of Nervousness, by which the artist was thinking of something else while his hand was guided by the Unconscious or Subconscious. As an example of this Thurber cited the cartoon captioned, "With you I have known peace, Lida, and now you say you're going crazy." Then there is the second classification: the cartoon created in the realm between the Purely Accidental and Haphazard Determination. In the cartoon, "For the last time, you and your horsie get away from me and stay away!" the man riding another was supposed to be standing erect; but, as his head was drawn too high and too small, Thurber put him on another man's shoulders. The third category is a variant on the second. The bloodhounds in "The father belonged to some people who were driving through in a Packard" were intended to be merely a group of dogs; the interior, people, and caption grew up around them. A fourth category consists of pictures drawn for captions contributed by other people. Finally there is the Intentional or Thought-Up Category. "If you want to," Thurber said, "you can cut these drawings out and push them around on the floor, making your own categories or applying your own psychological theories: or you can even invent some fresh rumors. I should think it would be more fun, though, to take a nap, or baste a roast, or run around the reservoir in Central Park."

While many of Thurber's pictures are wildly original, quite a few have a similar basic drawing of a couple conversing, and the humor and originality come from the caption. Rather than clarifying his cartoons, the captions often add to the confusion. Usually they are not jokes or punch lines but such enigmatic comments as, "Think of it, Madam! I was only sixteen at the time," or, "Don't you remember? I was here three nights ago with a lady who beat me up." Some are inscrutable, such as, "What's come over you since Friday, Miss Schemke?" or, "While you were out of the room I lost my mind." Some are deflated, like "The magic has gone out of my marriage. Has the magic gone out of your marriage?" Others are exuberantly uninhibited: "See how beautifully your *wife* has caught the spirit of nudism, Mr. Spencer." And what is one to make of the kangaroo that is brought into the courtroom to refresh the defendant's memory?

Just as metaphors sometimes appear ludicrous if taken too literally, some cartoons simply cannot be given a rational explanation and still retain their humor. There is a story that some psychologists once used Charles Addams' famous cartoon of the skier who has made one ski track around each side of a tree, to test a group for their aptitude in appreciating humor. The subjects attempted to give logical explanations as to how the skier could have avoided hitting the tree and yet make tracks on both sides of it, and so they completely lost the comedy of the cartoon situation. Similarly it does no good to give explanations as to how the first Mrs. Harris happens to be crouched on a bookcase and what she is doing there while the second Mrs. Harris is being introduced to some guests in one of Thurber's most famous cartoons. *The New Yorker* asked if she were dead or stuffed, and one might wonder whether Thurber had Browning's "My Last Duchess" in his subconscious. But the humor lies in the fact that there is no explanation for the first Mrs. Harris; she is simply there.

CHAPTER 9

Literature and Language

THOUGH HE DREW with great rapidity, Thurber wrote with extremely painstaking care. In contrast to many of his contemporaries who experimented in narrative by indirection, obscure symbolism, turgid rhetoric, cryptic compressions, or semi-delirious stream-of-consciousness, Thurber's prose is notable for clarity, lightness, and precision. "Humor cannot afford the ornaments and indulgences of fine writing, the extravagance of consciousness-streaming, or lower case unpunctuation meanderings," Thurber explained in a letter to Malcolm Cowley. "You can't blunt the edge of wit or the point of satire with obscurity."[1] Cowley observes that Thurber "prefers the familiar words that would be used in conversation without a self-conscious pause. His art consists in arranging them so that they give the impression of standing cleanly and separately on the page, each in its place like stones in a well-built wall."[2] Or, in Thurber's own words, "I like the perfectly done, the well-ordered, as against the sprawling chunk of life."[3] Nevertheless, he said that he did not prefigure his work. "I don't bother with charts and so forth . . . I don't believe the writer should know too much where he's going. If he does, he runs into old man blueprint . . . old man propaganda."[4]

I *Thurber's Early Writing*

Thurber began writing seriously at Ohio State, where he edited the student monthly and reported for the daily campus paper. His views on English composition were strongly influenced by the teaching of Joseph Russell Taylor, one of his favorite professors. Taylor "brought impulsive feeling, rather than cold mental analysis, to everything he touched," Thurber recalled, "but he had the good writer's dissatisfaction with imperfect statement." He insisted that "Art is revision," and Thurber learned this lesson so well that he rewrote *The White Deer* twenty-five times and *The 13 Clocks* twenty-two times.

Another person who early influenced Thurber's writing was Robert Ryder, columnist for *The Ohio State Journal*. Thurber relates: "In my teens I was more interested in Ryder than in Sir Walter Scott or Cicero, and one winter I wrote a monthly column for the East High *X-Ray* in bold imitation of the old master." He praised Ryder's style for being clear, precise, and unaffected, observing that good paragraphers like Ryder, "slaved over their paragraphs the way a poet slaves over a sonnet . . . and can make something that was ground out sound as if it were dashed off." Thurber's writing seems equally effortless, yet he polished until he secured just the right word and phrase.

As a boy, Thurber was fond of melodramatic nickel novels—adolescent "Westerns" and detective fiction of the Nick Carter variety—and later he read the fiction popular at the turn of the century: John Fox, Jr., Charles Major, Booth Tarkington, O.Henry, and various other historical and sentimental romancers. At Ohio State his professors introduced him to James, Cather, Conrad, Meredith, and other novelists of sensibility; and he began to see wider literary horizons. But his taste at this time was still uneven and largely conservative. Professor Taylor favored the Romantic and Victorian poets and novelists, and Thurber doubted that he would have cared for the new literature of the 1920's except for Willa Cather's. Thurber's short story teacher, William Graves, wished his students to imitate De Maupassant, Fannie Hurst, Hugh Walpole, Richard Harding Davis, Robert W. Chambers, and Quiller-Couch; he was distressed by four-letter realism and dissonant prose; and he later spoke distastefully of Hemingway and would have disapproved of Maugham's Sadie Thompson.

The taste of the times, as well as his professors, influenced Thurber's early literary judgments. Looking back at his 1923 book reviews for the Columbus *Dispatch*, he was amused and a bit appalled at his youthful views. In writing disparagingly of Joyce, Eliot, Gertrude Stein, and D. H. Lawrence, he had attacked their experimental language and symbolism and denounced the "sordid" sexuality in some of their work. He complained that Sherwood Anderson and Sinclair Lewis "hysterically maligned" the Midwest, and he asked for a return to the "civilized romanticism" of Willa Cather. In poetry he was enthusiastic about Housman and Henley and disliked the experimentation of modern verse, though he wrote admiringly of E. E. Cummings.

Later, of course, as the 1920's revolution in taste and morals became a *fait accompli* and as he left Midwestern provincialism and finished his literary apprenticeship, his tastes matured. He became a friend or admirer of many of the authors he had previously disliked. Mrs. Thurber writes that among his closer contemporaries he knew and liked Hemingway and Faulkner, "although Faulkner's tortured style was not his favorite style of writing. Still, he was a Henry James man, and how tortured can you get?"

In light of his later work, Thurber's undergraduate notes for stories are interesting; some of them are preserved in endpapers of his text, Walter B. Pitkin's *The Art and Business of Story Writing,* in the Thurber collection of the Ohio State University Library.

A girl who suspects that the man to whom engaged has begun to love another girl forces admission from him.

. . . .

A crook watching a younger pal undergoing 3rd degree out of pity assumes other man's guilt

. . . .

A soldier who has successfully bluffed his comrades into belief he is a brave man, in an incident of trench warfare yields to his innate feeling of cowardice.

. . . .

A young step-mother overcomes the cold aloofness of her husband's daughter who has resented her coming into the home.

. . . .

A girl who has allowed a flirtation on her part to result in a serious affection from man confesses her fault to him and seeks forgiveness.

. . . .

An aging actress, recognizing her shortcomings, yields her place to an understudy whom she has hitherto jealously shut out of any opportunity. Indicate gesture, emotion, choose one of two as dominant, seq. report, throw thing into high relief.

. . . .

Fanny Brent is a stenographer 28 years old, intelligent and attractive. She lives alone with her invalid mother. She has had an offer of marriage from Geo. Irvin, fairly prosperous busy man, about her own age whom she loves but whom her mother does not like. She knows that he will insist upon taking her to a home of their own sans her mother.

But how does one begin to make a living from literature? Thurber's newspaper work for the Columbus *Dispatch* may have helped him write compactly and economically, but there was the danger of journalistic jargon and slickness. Fortunately, Norman Kuehner, his editor, insisted that he write precisely, pruning extraneous material and removing elaborate circumlocutions. Kuehner was suspicious of college men and objected violently to "literary" efforts. Thurber finally managed to write news to Kuehner's satisfaction, but he told of a recurrent dream in which the clock in the city room is frozen at fifteen minutes past the deadline, while Kuehner stands forbiddingly over his shoulder. (Thirty years later this scene reappears in *The 13 Clocks,* where the wicked duke's clocks are frozen at ten minutes to five.)

Eventually Thurber's work expanded from the city-hall beat to include movie reviews and his own Sunday halfpage, "Credos and Curios," which gave him a chance to try creative criticism and humor. Departments of these early "Credos" included "The Book End," "Dad Dialogues," and "The Cases of Blue Ploermell," a burlesque detective series in which Blue the sleuth is always eating animal crackers—his favorite is a Newfoundland dog. The "Credos" also contained Thurberian editorials, light verse, and fiction, some of which foreshadow his later work. "The Menace of the Mystery," for instance, looking at *Hamlet, Lear, Caesar,* and *Macbeth* as mystery plays on the order of *The Bat,* anticipates "The Macbeth Murder Mystery" fourteen years later. Another piece in which Thurber's father and brothers fight a bat in the living room is a dry run for *My Life and Hard Times.* Thurber also wrote editorials eulogizing Henry James; the *Dispatch* was doubtless, in 1923, the only paper in the country that urged James upon its readers. One character in the early "Credos" says to Thurber: "You can't take ten sentences without bumping into Henry James, hanging on his neck and praising him in the maudlin tone of an inebriate to whom every passerby is bes' fr'en ev' had."

When his wife urged him to go to New York to try freelancing, Thurber was afraid he couldn't support them. But in 1924, when a friend offered his cottage in New York state, Thurber accepted and quit the *Dispatch.* Not succeeding in his literary endeavor, he returned to Columbus after three months without cash or confidence. The *Dispatch* refused to take him back, so he worked briefly as a free-lance press agent. Then he and his wife returned to France in May, 1925, first to Paris and then to a farmhouse near Granville, where he worked for six weeks on a novel about his school days. When he had written himself out in the first chapter and was without an income, he found work on the Paris and then the Nice edition of the Chicago *Tribune* at $12.00 a week. The "Lost Generation" was at its zenith, but Thurber did not mingle with the literary expatriates. Still he persisted at creative writing and sold several short pieces to *Sunset Magazine,* the *Detroit Athletic Club News,* and "The Lion's Mouth" of *Harper's Magazine.*

In April, 1926, he returned alone to the States, planning to write a book and earn enough to go back to France. Deciding that humor was his forte, Thurber wrote a twenty-five thousand word parody of Paul de Kruif's *Microbe Hunters* and of George Amos Dorsey's *Why We Behave Like Human Beings.* Thurber's book, *Why We Behave Like Microbe Hunters,* was rejected in every way, shape, and form by the publishers. Once more without an income, Thurber landed a job at $40.00 a week as reporter on the New York *Evening Post,* writing overnight feature stories of a thousand words or less. He did get to interview Edison, Ambassador Herrick, General Pershing, Valentino, and the widow of Houdini. In his off-duty hours he wrote sketches, poems, and stories with which he bombarded *The New Yorker* and other humor publications with meager success. He had written for *Harper's,* the Sunday *Times,* the New York *World,* the *Herald Tribune,* the Kansas City *Star,* and *Vanity Fair,* and he had been offered editorial jobs on *Liberty* and *Time;* but none of these offered him the sort of creative outlet he wanted. By this time he was thirty-two years old and had not yet gotten an encouraging start as a writer. But he had undergone a thorough apprenticeship; when he got a break, he was ready for it.

II *Ross, White, and* The New Yorker

The break came in February, 1927, when he met E. B. White, who was already a mainstay of the two-year-old *New Yorker.* Thurber had met White's sister on shipboard; and, since he had finally sold some poems to *The New Yorker,* he went to its offices to see White. White introduced him to Harold Ross, the editor-in-chief; and Ross, thinking that Thurber was a long-standing friend of White's, hired him immediately as managing editor. He quickly succeeded in being demoted to the writing staff.

Knocking around as a journalist had given him little job security and forced him to do creative work in his spare time. Now *The New Yorker* offered him a stable base of operations, some stimulating associates, and let him devote full time to his own writing.

The magazine helped also by freeing him from the daily deadlines of rapid-fire reporting. Afraid journalism might make him a sloppy stylist, he was mixing "journalese" with Henry James to create prose alternately abrupt and elaborate. E. B. White's example straightened him out and taught him, he said, to write simple declarative sentences. Thurber, who wrote many tributes to White's influence, stated: "The precision and clarity of White's writing slowed me down from the dogtrot of newspaper tempo and made me realize a writer turns on his mind, not a faucet."[5] Editor Harold Ross not only encouraged clarity but insisted on it: "he was a purist and perfectionist and it had a tremendous effect on all of us; it kept us from being sloppy."[6] Thus in "The American Literary Scene," Thurber satirized the critic who complains of "the exasperatingly lucid and understandable prose of *New Yorker,* in which one may never find comfort for even a moment in a weirdly managed construction. . . ." Wolcott Gibbs, who praised the fine precision of Thurber's own syntax, wrote that, "Among other things, Mr. Thurber is a grammarian's wit."[7]

To achieve this precision, he revised relentlessly. For "The Secret Life of Walter Mitty," which is about four thousand words long, he worked steadily for eight weeks and did about fifteen complete rewrites. (An early version of "Mitty" had a scene in which Mitty got between Hemingway and an opponent in a Stork Club brawl, but Thurber cut this at Mrs. Thurber's suggestion that the story should contain nothing topical.) His method was to put everything down in a burst of energy and then go over it again and again. He explained that his first drafts appeared to have been done by a charwoman but weren't supposed to be any good; "the whole purpose is to sketch out proportions. I rarely have a very clear idea of where I'm going when I start. Just people and/or a situation. Then I fool around—writing and rewriting—until the stuff jells."

Even after it jelled he was reluctant to stop. He recalled that, during the tryout of *The Male Animal,* Herman Shumlin told him, "You're obviously dissatisfied. What do you want to do?" "Spend another year on the play," said Thurber. Shumlin barked, "Dammit, we open next Monday in New York."[8] There is a well-known story that, after a number of painstaking efforts were rejected, Thurber dashed off his first *New Yorker* story, "American Romance," in forty-five minutes. This is true, but it was not his usual pace. He dictated "File and Forget" and "Afternoon of a Playwright" in an afternoon each, but most of his pieces took weeks of work.

In a letter to Malcolm Cowley in 1954, Thurber wrote: "I have been trying to finish a book I started, or a long piece rather, just a year ago in Williamsburg. I have spent a thousand hours on it, although it won't exceed fifteen thousand words when it's finished, and I've done about thirty complete rewrites, but have run into the well known blank wall."[9] This book had been announced for publication for the spring of 1954, as *The Sleeping Man;* then, for the fall of that year, as *The Secret Dream of Stanley Caldwell;* it was postponed again; later it was announced as ready to appear in the spring of 1956 as *The Train on Track Six.*

Thurber worked on the book for about two years, but it did not turn out as he wanted it to and so was not released for the press. He explained: "It was a *tour de force* of twenty thousand words, most of it taking place in a dream, or series of dreams. It started out as a fairy tale, involving the dream of W. H. Caldwell, an engineer, and ended up, on the twentieth re-write, without the fairy tale and a new dreamer named Farland, a publisher. I have lifted out quite a lot from this story, mainly situations or phrases, to use in my new book of fables."[10]

In the fall of 1957, it was announced that he was again at work on this book, now titled *The Train on Track Five,* but it never materialized. Neither did several other projects in his last decade. Rather than rush through a piece, Thurber would put it aside, sometimes for years if it ceased to hold his interest. Thus he left three more unfinished fantasies, including twenty-five overlapping versions of one called *The Spoodle.* There was also *The Grawk* (retitled *The Nightinghoul*), a satire on Midwestern politics, and one unsatisfactory version of *The Lamplighter's Daughter* or *The Ugly Princess.*

Slaving over his work to get every word right, Thurber found "le mot juste" with amazing accuracy. Malcolm Cowley comments: "Some of Faulkner's most involved and longest sentences were written most rapidly. The slow writers are often the deceptively smooth writers; the best of their stories, like Thurber's, appear to be very simple until you read them a second time. Other writers can learn a great deal from Thurber. . . ."[11]

Thus, in surveying books published in 1952, Lon Tinkle chose *The Thurber Album* as "the stylistic delight of the year" from among a list that included Hemingway's Pulitzer Prize winning *The Old Man and the Sea.* Praising Thurber's style, Mr. Tinkle wrote that he "can still sandpaper down a sentence as well as Hemingway, and make his phrase vibrate with its concentration of precision and point."[12] (Incidentally, Hemingway—who was among Thurber's admirers and who called *My Life and Hard Times* "superior to the autobiography of Henry Adams"—seems in "The Fable of the Good Lion" to have been influenced by Thurber's fables.)

Thurber's style is one of the great achievements of his art. With a masterful sense of rhythm, tone, and diction, he developed a highly effective prose, as supple as a whip and just as biting when necessary. Always relaxed, it was at first comparatively plain but became increasingly subtle and poetic over the years. Thurber wrote of Fitzgerald's "jeweled prose," and the description equally fits his own.

Like much American humor, Thurber's writing often has an oral quality. "He should be read leisurely and aloud," wrote S. T. Williamson. Thurber himself remarked that "The Night the Bed Fell" makes a better recitation than a piece of writing. In this and other reminiscences he used the manner of a yarn spinner or raconteur. Friends called him one of the greatest conversationalists in America, and Hemingway said, "If Thurber can talk as well as he writes he must be one of the greatest and least boring talkers."[13] After his blindness, he had to resort to dictation, and his shift "from being an eye writer to being an ear-writer" caused him to omit visual effects and to make his later stories almost pure conversation. He explained to Henry Brandon: "There's something about voice that is destroyed if you are watching the expression of the face. It will mislead you sometimes. Everybody looks at the eyes and expression, but I concentrate on inflection, intonation, and dropping and raising the voice."[14] The dialogue became increasingly good in his work of the 1940's and 50's and that of "Am Not I Your Rosalind," "The Waters of the Moon," "The Case of Dimity Ann," "Teacher's Pet," and "The Interview" is some of the best in contemporary prose.

This achievement is not mere accident but the result of long and sometimes painful effort. Elliott Nugent said that Thurber was a perfectionist.

> I think sometimes about an afternoon many years ago just before I went out to Hollywood to act in and direct pictures. Jim was rather critical of this, and over a couple of glasses of beer we began to talk about the values of Greek philosophy and the classes we had been in together, and our purposes in life, what is the "Magnum bonum." I think I admitted that I was willing to accept a sort of Platonist philosophy, trying to achieve a well-rounded life, with a little money, a little success, using what ability I had to some avail I hope. But I also wanted to enjoy life and have a family and play some tennis. Thurber was pretty disgusted with this. He told me quite clearly, and meant it, that he wanted to be a great writer, and that success or monetary considerations or security for himself, or even for his family, should not stand in the way of that goal.

Thurber was always a perfectionist. He commented that before his blindness, he was a visual writer. "I liked the shape of words and phrases, and I liked clean copy. I never turned in a page with a single mistake on it. I always copied it over. Naturally, when you copy you make changes and you improve your copy."[15]

Even when blind, he continued to revise extensively but developed new methods of composition. For a while he scrawled in pencil, about twenty words to a large page. Thanks to his total recall he could write complete stories in his head and remember verbatim as many as three complete versions. "I can remember a 3,500 word story without missing a punctuation mark," he said in 1953. Eight years later, he told W. J. Weatherby: "Most memories begin to go in the middle forties. But I can still recall a whole scene. I write in bed at night and I can recall as much as 2,000 words which I have gone over and over and rewritten in my mind. Next day I dictate it, leaving out the phrases I have thrown out."[16]

With fewer distractions in his blindness, he would also write in his mind at meals and at parties if the conversation lagged. He explained that, thanks to his memory, he did not "have to do the sort of thing Fitzgerald did with *The Last Tycoon*—the voluminous, the tiny and meticulous notes, the long descriptions of character. I can keep all these things in my mind."[17] But research projects posed a problem. For *The Thurber Album* he wrote over five hundred letters during a four-year period to inquire about information or to verify details about his biographical subjects. For *The Years with Ross*, though he could recall scenes and dialogue with the vividness of a Boswell, he was given the use of a *New Yorker* office and a secretary. He also had the Ross correspondence of some thirty thousand letters available to him.

Before his eye operations, Thurber's fiction had a fair amount of action and a good many visual details. His later situations are more sedentary and depend more upon sound and dialogue. Thurber always had a good ear; and, after his vision deteriorated to a point approaching blindness, he became keenly attuned to sounds, especially the cadences of human speech. "It is no illusion," he wrote, "that the blind become equipped with the ear drums of an elk hound. I can hear a pin drop on a carpet. It makes two sounds— a sharp plop when it strikes the carpet and a somewhat smaller sound, a faint thip! when it bounces and strikes again."

Sometimes Thurber provided an audio accompaniment for his stories. An excellent example is "The Whip-poor-will," the already discussed account of Mr. Kinstrey's increasing neuroticism that ends in murder. While Kinstrey's cup cackles idiotically in its saucer, the high-strung call of the whippoorwill, like a nerve vibrating shrilly, is an undercurrent and stimulus to rising madness. It prophesies doom not like a tolling bell but like the violin's scraping that shatters a glass.

Sound becomes dominant in his fairy tales and some of the later fables. Many passages break into irregular rhyme and meter embellished with alliteration, assonance, consonance, onomatopoeia, and frequent puns. Many of Thurber's verbal devices were used by James Joyce, another blind writer who became preoccupied with words for their own sake; but, where Joyce became increasingly obscure, Thurber's language illuminates with its clarity. Still, he tended to treat words as three-dimensional objects so that *reason* is six-sevenths of *treason* and a *t* added to *Haiti* makes *Tahiti.* Thus in *The Wonderful O,* when the letter o is banned:

> "When coat is cat, and boat is bat, and goatherd looks like gathered, and booth is both, since both are bth, the reader's eye is bothered."
>
> "And power is pwer, and zero zer, and, worst of all, a hero's her." The old man sighed as he said it.
>
> "Anon is ann, and moan is man." Andrea smiled as she said it.
> "And shoe," Andreus said, "is she."
> "Ah, woe," the old man said, "is we."

Thurber often used his virtuosity to parody the style and content of both subliterary and serious authors. During his first eight years on *The New Yorker,* he wrote a great many of these burlesques, most of which are so ephemeral that he did not bother to include them in his collections. Amusing though many of them are, they are essentially imitative and lead to a literary dead-end. A few erupt with mad inspiration, such as "If Grant Had Been Drinking at Appomattox," but it is perhaps fortunate that Thurber did not expend a major part of his productivity in pastiche. At best, the parodies serve satirically as criticism of literary absurdities and mannerisms. They also indicate Thurber's versatility in his treatment of Galsworthy ("One More April"), Kipling and G. K. Chesterton ("The Man Who Was Wetly"), Erskine Caldwell ("Bateman Comes Home"), James M. Cain ("Hell Only Breaks Loose Once"), Henry James ("Recollections of Henry James," "The Beast in the Dingle"), and—for a real *tour de force*—a fusion of James's *The Ambassadors* with Willa Cather's *A Lost Lady* ("A Call on Mrs. Forrester"). Once at least, in "The Secret Life of Walter Mitty," parody contributes to his finest work, for he managed to catch superbly the clichés and tone of extravagant understatement in the tight-lipped adventure fiction that forms the substance of Mitty's daydreams.

III *The Lesson of the Master*

On close reading, a good many of Thurber's pieces reveal the influence of Henry James, whose nervous nuances and refined Gothicism are altered to humorous focus. James's frustratingly fastidious, ineffectual, and hypersensitive characters are Victorian grandparents of Thurber's middle-aged man on the flying trapeze; and the narrator of such pieces as "The Breaking Up of the Winships," "Something to Say," and "A Final Note on Chanda Bell" is a Jamesean confidant. A James story like "Maud-Evelyn," the perplexing account of one Marmaduke's delicately deranged court-ship and marriage to the deceased daughter of his patrons and his eventual death of bereavement, needs only a slight touch of burlesque to become Thurberian fantasy. Thurber owned the thirty-five-volume London edition of James, and Clifton Fadiman called him "a true expert on Henry James" who "could remember characters . . . that I think even professionals in the James field had forgotten. He had a creative sense of the immediate past, and I think cultivated with the kind of combined sadness and irony, what Henry James called 'the sense of the past.'"

However, too much can be made of the Jamesean influence. Otto Friedrich, in a perceptive criticism, perhaps overstates the case when he claims that James's effect on Thurber was all pervading:

James as a literary figure is the implied object of most of Thurber's later critical writing, just as the ideal of James' writing is implicit in most of Thurber's best fiction. As Thurber's critical writing broadens out to cover all "the literary life," James thus becomes increasingly the central figure. . . . Dominated by such an imposing figure as James, Thurber's essays on The Letters of James Thurber and The Notebooks of James Thurber seem to reflect a deep sense of inadequacy, and this sense of inadequacy develops into an increasing preoccupation with the image of the literary master surrounded, imitated, and annoyed by a tribe of pygmies.[18]

Although these essays contain several Jamesean allusions, their purpose is not to reveal the author's sense of personal inadequacy (Mr. Friedrich here fails to distinguish between Thurber and his fictional self) but to deflate the self-conscious pomposity with which some writers (not necessarily James) condescend to bestow their private papers upon the world.

"The Notebooks" and "Letters" are minor pieces that hardly justify Friedrich's sweeping statement, but Friedrich also holds that Lockhorn, the author in "The Interview," "represents a synthesis of James and Thurber, combined in fiction as they could not be combined in 'The Letters' and 'The Notebooks of James Thurber.' "[19] If so, the portrait is hardly flattering to either; for Lockhorn is arrogant and enjoys embarrassing Price, who has come to interview him. Lockhorn is a cynic and an alcoholic, thrice divorced. He is saddled with a nagging fourth wife, who apologizes for his work; but, at the same time, he is an imprecating husband. At one point Lockhorn does call James "The greatest master of them all," but later he states that "Henry James had the soul of an eaves-dropper. . . . Everything he got, he got from what he over-heard somebody say. No visual sense, and if you haven't got visual sense, what have you got?" This may be an oblique comment on Thurber's blindness; but, if anyone in this story represents Thurber's view, it is probably Price, the inoffensive onlooker who is both sympathetic to and repelled by Lockhorn's situation.

Despite his enthusiasm for James, Thurber was too eclectic and original to take any author as an exclusive model. He alluded frequently to Shakespeare, Wordsworth, and Browning; and he said in 1940 that he was interested in the writings of George Milburn, William March, Robert M. Coates, John O'Hara, Conrad Aiken, Edmund Wilson, Hemingway, and Fitzgerald. One quite un-Jamesean influence is O. Henry, whom Thurber praised as one of the best humorists America produced. Thurber stated that James was "an influence you had to get over. . . . I have the reputation for having read all of Henry James. Which would argue a misspent youth *and* middle-age."[20] Thurber's clarity of style, though the result of intensive rewriting, has a spontaneity lacking in the mannered circumlocutions and overelaborate analysis of James's later work. While the sentences of James's late period are often labyrinthine, Thurber could (as David McCord put it) tighten up his paragraphs as with a spanner.

By the 1950's Thurber began to qualify his enthusiasm for James. He imagined that if James were still alive and writing a preface to a novel about our age, he would get so lost in its implications that he wouldn't care to read it over to find his way out again. "That's the trouble with James," observed Thurber. "You get bored with him finally. He lived in the time of four-wheelers, and no bombs, and the problems then seemed a bit special and separate."[21] And Thurber tried to imagine James approaching Brigitte Bardot with "awe and embarrassment and helplessness." In 1958, he told Henry Brandon that he greatly admired James as a craftsman. "But the more I reread Henry James, the more I realize he didn't have a great deal to say except in skill and in the relationships of sensibilities—rather than the clash of anything more important."[22]

IV *Laundering Stuffed Shirts*

Certainly there are too many good writers for any one to be the high priest of prose, and neither James nor Thurber anywhere propounds literary dogmas. Thurber was a writer of integrity but seemed to think that some artists and critics became pompous and unnatural by taking themselves too seriously. He wrote, for instance, that the elaborate published correspondence of some intellectuals has a studied and disingenuous tone like an exchange of essays written to be filed and printed some day. It is too pretentious and calculated. Thurber's own letters may consist of little more than notes reading, "Will you please for God's sake come back with my shoes?" but they are not coldly formal. Pricking pomposity, he stated: "The effect of Thurber's letters on his generation was about the same as the effect of anybody's letters on any generation; that is to say, nil. It is only when a man's letters are published after his death that they have any effect and this effect is usually only on literary critics." Mocking the critical jargon of ponderous literary studies, he sarcastically divided his career into "Part I: the Youthful Years"; "Part II: Sturm und Drang"; "Part III: The European Phase"; and "Part IV: The Challenging Years." But he said that his publishers regarded as a "major deterrent" the loss of seventy-one letters written from abroad that had been intended to make up Part III.

Thurber burlesqued the attempt of some critics to find deep significance in every action of an author, and the author's attempt to make every movement seem profound. Parodying critical jargon, he remarked that his own notes are rarely "instinct with a sense of affirmation"; instead they are smudged, crumpled, and stained with cider. The notes from his university days are disordered and covered with doodles and such memos as: "drill cap, white gloves, gym suit. See G. Packer. Get Locker." They are not deliberately calculated to impress. "If my friends ever set out to locate my letters," he wrote, "they will come upon old college yearbooks, dance programs, snapshot albums, and the works of John Fox, Jr., and probably lose interest in the original subject of their search."

Thurber tried to show that an author can lead a reasonably normal life. Despite the dedication that Nugent mentioned, he objected to total obsession with art to the exclusion of enjoyment. Consequently, a fair amount of his work deals with trivia—draw-

ings of dogs, humorous casuals on word games and mispronunciations (such as the nurse's reading to him of "That first fine careless rupture" while he was hospitalized), and sundry amusing
episodes of no world-shattering significance. Otto Friedrich took
Thurber to task for this. "Mr. Friedrich thinks that preoccupation
with trivia is unbecoming in a writer who belongs to the Solemn
if not, indeed, the Sombre tradition of American letters," commented Thurber. He replied that "Trivia Mundi has always been
as dear and as necessary to me as her bigger and more glamorous
sister, Gloria. They have both long and amicably inhabited a
phrase of Coleridge's, 'All things both great and small,' and I like
to think of them taking turns at shooting albatrosses and playing
the bassoon."

Thurber also found that trying to give his thoughts the semblance
of importance merely made them a little stuffy. He explained:

I enjoy a drinking evening that begins with light cocktail talk,
goes into serious discussions, ends with imitations of Ed Wynn and
W. C. Fields and the singing of "Linger Awhile" and "Bye, Bye
Blackbird." On such a planless plan have my days and nights and
years been organized or disorganized. Out of trivia often grows the
serious, after the serious often comes the trivia, after the labor of
writing came the relaxation of my drawings or there wouldn't be
any. This, to me, makes up the Human Comedy and the un-
methodical system of the serio-comic writer or artist. I consider
some of my best journalistic pieces important, and clashed mildly
with Leon Edel recently at lunch when I called his Foreword to
"Guy Domville" the work of a fine journalist while he insisted on
literary historian. Humor is counter-balance, not balance."[23]

Much of Thurber's earlier trivia is quite transitory; but the
later work, even when superficial, has such a brilliant surface and
dazzling display of language that it cannot be dismissed as wit
wasted. In some of his later fables, fantasies, and language pieces,
the style surpasses the substance yet has such a fusion of figurative
thought and verbal grace as to be authentically poetic. A category
all their own, they might best be considered analogous to musical
divertimentos, etudes, fantasies, and rondeaux that form a legitimate
counterpart to oratorios, symphonies, and missa solemnis.

Despite his linguistic experiments, Thurber wrote considerable
satire about avant-garde writers who, in breaking too sharply
from tradition, might erect a new tower of Babel, or whose efforts
seemed to be more pretension than performance. And so in "Here
Come the Tigers," when two drunken acquaintances burst in at
midnight with the glorious news that they had discovered a new

literary dimension, Thurber was not overly enthusiastic. Hayes announced the key to this dimension—that the mood and tone and color of a word are echoed in its component parts.

> "There are lips in pistol
> And mist in times,
> Cats in crystal,
> And mice in chimes."

I stared coldly at Jordan's transfigured face. "Is this the spear-head of the New Beauty?" I asked.

Jordan globbered his drink down, ran his hand through his hair, and glared at me demoniacally. "Shows what What's-his-name of 'Christabel' and Keats of 'Eve of St. Agnes' could have done if the goddam fairy casements had opened on this lovely dimension! he shouted . . . "It's like little boxes, one inside each other," Jordan was saying . . . "You lift out concentric meanings of practically identical mood and tone. Yet people have let the component parts of words go for a thousand years."

Thurber was willing to play word games for fun, but he refused to make them significant. When he made some objections to the new system, the visitors accused him of having "the obscurantism of the explicit." "You got to feel it like a child," said Jordan. But Hayes was no longer so sure; it seemed a little thin "when you get to thinking of the hare twisting in the frozen grass and the mastiff bitch in the moonshine cold." " 'What the hell's he talking about?' Jordan almost wailed." " 'What's-his-name and Keats,' I said."

"A Final Note on Chanda Bell" continues the satire of the new dimensional artist, for Miss Bell, though her works were bafflingly cryptic, was a high priestess of the modern novel and ruled her admirers with haughty mockery. "Praise me!" she would command. In this story Thurber assumed the role of a critic proud of meriting intellectual intimacy with her by his penetrating analysis of her work. He became lost in the "brilliant wilderness" of Chanda Bell's prose but by a "process of equation, synthesis, and integra-tion . . . was able to reveal the subtle affirmation compounded of the double negative of her unmeaning and her unmethod." A fusion of Gertrude Stein and James Joyce, Chanda Bell had a habit of starting sentences in the middle and was fond of esoteric anagrams and "surrogate words with ambiguous meanings, like the words in dreams: 'rupture' for 'rapture,' 'centaur' for 'sender,' 'pressure' for 'pleasure,' and 'scorpio' for 'scrofula.' "

At first, Thurber, as the pretended critic, could venerate her writing; but he gradually began to fear her tortured novels were a major literary hoax intended to destroy the entire critical profession. What, for instance, could the explicator make of sentences like "Icing mellow moony on a postgate doves snow and love surrender"? "I could no longer tell," said Thurber, "whether it was beauty or balderdash. If it was balderdash, the book degenerated into the vivid cackling of a macaw, and my critique stood as a monument to a fatuous guillibility."

In "The Waters of the Moon" Thurber skewered another critical stuffed shirt. In the midst of a literary party, Thurber had broken away from an undulant discussion of kinetic dimensionalism and was talking with a lady chaoticist when his hostess dragged him off to meet the guest of honor, "a Mr. Peifer, editor of a literary review." " 'Holds his liquor beautifully,' my hostess said. 'Burns it up, I guess. He's terribly intense.' " Peifer explained that he was interested in the male American writer who peters out in his fifties. " 'Mr. Thurber is fifty-three,' my hostess said. 'He hasn't written anything since last April.' Peifer looked at me as if I were the precipitate of a moderately successful test-tube experiment." He announced that he wanted to get somebody to do a comprehensive treatise on the subject, including a study of the writer's decomposition, which he believed was to be found "in syphilophobia, prostatitis, early baldness, peptic ulcer, endentulous cases, true and hysterical impotence, and spreading of the metatarsals."

As a critic Peifer was purely clinical and utterly lacking in imaginative appreciation. "Peifer here," said Thurber, "would not have followed Bierce beyond the Rio Grande or Villon through the *porte* of St. Denis to see in what caprice or rondeaux their days came to an end." But Thurber was always following Bierce at least in imagination, and in "The Admiral on the Wheel" he contemplated taking off his glasses and wandering like Bierce into the unknown. He countered Peifer by answering him in his own jargon with an account of several imaginary and affected authors. There was Greg Shelby:

"He has never published anything," I said. "He is going to leave all his work to Harvard, to be published a thousand years from now. Greg's writing has what he calls Projected Meaning. He feels that in another millennium the intellectuals will understand it readily enough. I have never made head or tail of any of his stuff myself, but there is no missing the unique quality of the most exquisite English prose of our time."

Shelby's wife was an author too, but she wrote Gothic incantations "for the understanding of intellectuals a thousand years ago."

A great deal of Thurber's work is a critical commentary on literature and language. In his last ten years, he became increasingly obsessed with English as an expression of social values; and he protested—sometimes petulantly but more often sardonically —about slovenly usage, socio-political jargon, sloppy style, and sinister semantics. "My most intense dedication," he stated,

> is the defense of the English language against the decline it has suffered in this century and particularly since the end of the last war. My country has always cared little for exactness in language and has always depreciated good English as "book larnin'." Those of us who are dedicated to good English as the very basis of communication and understanding have been called everything from teacher's pet to egghead and nobody is more to blame than members of Congress.[24]

V *Linguistic Use and Abuse*

Language is a blind man's main contact with the world; it thus becomes increasingly a symbol of integrity, and the debasement of English into jargon or slovenly garble is not merely cause for complaint but a violation of that integrity. Perhaps it is more than coincidence that Thurber's concern intensified during the McCarthy era. Certainly Thurber felt that political terminologists helped make our vocabulary moribund. Through their influence, "Elephantiasis of cliché set in, synonym atrophied, the pulse of inventiveness slowed alarmingly, and paraphrase died of impaction. . . . We have become satisfied with gangrenous repetitions of threadbarisms, like an old man cackling in a chimney corner, and the onset of utter meaninglessness is imminent."

McCarthyism paralyzed the word "security" and caused it to lose its quality of affirmation by being "employed exclusively in a connotation of fear, uncertainty, and suspicion," but the Communists also contributed to this carcinomenclature. The inflexibility of their dialectic, Thurber felt, ruled out any stylistic grace and replaced it with bureaucratic jargon—as well as the dislocation of meaning in *1984*, where war is peace, freedom is slavery, and ignorance is strength. Thurber was concerned about "the smoke-screen phrases of the political terminologists" with their "menacing Alice in Wonderland meaningless." He was also uneasy about "the jargon of today's diplomacy, which so often seems content to settle for a phrase in place of a way out." Accordingly, he wished to "improve the process of communication, for precision of communication is important, more important than ever, in our era of hair-trigger balances, when a false, or misunderstood, word may create as much disaster as a sudden thoughtless act."

Science and sociology are also guilty of gobbledegook, and they helped force Thurber to create an imaginary psychosemanticist to rescue victims of psychic trauma caused by gibberish and polysyllabic monstrosities. "A word to the wise is not sufficient if it doesn't make any sense," he observed.

The preference for the unnecessary polysyllable, for abstract rather than concrete nouns, for the passive voice over the active, the ponderous movement of ideas caused by the excessive use of nouns to the neglect of verbs, and various forms of linguistic inflation all atrophy the language with dead wood; and the use of jargon provides stock phrases that make thinking unnecessary and seemingly undesirable. Such cancerous growth in the language is further malignant in its dehumanization. The passive construction omits the actor and leaves only the act, and for this reason is so widespread in bureaucracies where the impersonal office supersedes the individual official, who becomes simply another piece of mechanism. These breakdowns of verbal distinction show a confusion of values, a love both of bumblery and the short cut, and a wrenching of meaning that forebodes the impersonal, expressionless, thought-controlling language of Orwell's Newspeak. In his study of the rebel, Albert Camus wrote: "The mutual understanding and communication discovered by rebellion can survive only in the free exchange of conversation. Every ambiguity, every misunderstanding, leads to death; clear language and simple words are the only salvation from this death. . . . It is worth noting that the language peculiar to totalitarian doctrines is always a scholastic or administrative language."[25]

Another annoyance of Thurber's was degeneration of meaning into morbidity. After citing a number of examples, Thurber proceeded to invent his own semantic pejorations to match the perversity of the *Zeitgeist,* and he twisted old titles into macabre puns such as "The Pie-Eyed Peeper of Hamlin," "When Girlhood Was Deflowered," or "O won't you dismember Sweet Alice, Ben Bolt?" But as Matthew Arnold wrote, "one gains nothing on the darkness by being . . . as incoherent as the darkness itself"; and Thurber concluded that "I think we must learn to brighten the human idiom, as well as to make it communicable."

On a less somber level, Thurber protested against the linguistic muddle created by advertising coinages, journalistic short cuts, coyly misspelled brand names, the mannered clichés of Timen and Tiwomen in the Lucempire, "the tendency of tired American businessmen and statesmen to use slang and slogan," and generally careless usage. He charged the Madison Avenue men, "the men in the gray-flannel minds," with deliberately taking advantage "of all the slur and sloppiness, because when purists object, it simply

serves to spread the news of a product advertised in lousy English."
The vague and often dishonest diction of their commercials serves
to numb the critical intelligence.

But, by calling himself a purist, Thurber ran the risk of antagoniz-
ing some linguists who perhaps bend over backwards in stressing
popular usage as a reaction to the rigid rules and Latinate approach to English grammar that used to predominate in the
schools. Thus one woman "who proudly described herself as dis-
agreeable" wrote Thurber that if most people wanted "evening"
to mean "cat," then " 'evening' would properly *become* 'cat.' "
Technically, she is correct on the matter of usage; but the question still remains what legitimately constitutes usage, and whether
any advertising illiteracy, gossip columnist diction, or political
pronouncement should automatically be accepted. In his defense,
"bringing up the artillery of music and poetry, harmonics and
metre and melody, against those persons—those monsters of mind-
lessness—who believe that proper English usage should be deter-
mined by majority vote, as in the elections of the late President
Harding and Governor Long, of Louisiana," Thurber replied,
"Sunset and cat star, and one clear scat for you." Burlesquing the
confusion of the transitive and intransitive (his radio "listens fine
and travels and limpids the sound"), Thurber observed: "A living
language is an expanding language, to be sure, but care should
take itself that the language does not crack like a dry stick in the
process, leaving us all miserably muddling in a monstrous miasma
of mindless and meaningless mumbling."

"I hate writers," an old lady friend told Thurber. "They're such
Puritans about everything. You can't even use a figure of speech
the wrong way." Though his stylistic sense was offended by the
any-word-will-do people, he was bothered less by their language
per se than by the careless, confused thinking or bureaucratic
bumblery behind it; for, as George Orwell pointed out, "the sloven-
liness of our language makes it easier for us to have foolish
thoughts." For his part, Thurber sought "the direction of sense
and sanity," though it was increasingly hard to find: "A vital and
restless breed of men, given to tapping our toes and drumming
with our fingers, infatuated with every new crazy rhythm that
rears its ugly head, we have never truly loved harmony, the graceful structure of shapes and tones, and for this blindness and deaf-
ness we pay the awful price of continuous cacophony."

In his attacks on linguistic laissez-faire, Thurber was not so
much a purist as a stylist. He had never been an academic writer
and stated in his 1923 "Credos and Curios": "We don't give two
hoots about dictionary rules, because there are a lot of words and

phrases which Mr. Joseph Conrad and Mr. Henry James, for example, use constantly that no dictionary will stand for. But they are beautifully used." He wrote that, while on *The New Yorker*, he "was increasingly disturbed by Ross's insistence on super-clarity, overpunctuation, and strict rules of grammar and syntax and parsing." In "Here Lies Miss Groby" and "Ladies' and Gentlemen's Guide to Modern English" he poked fun at purism and pedantry. The grammatical confusion in the latter leads to misunderstood motives, mangled marriages, and social bedlam. Too intricate analysis causes anxieties, and it upsets and drives the would-be grammarian into indefensible positions until he breaks through the tangled web of rhetoric or else breaks something else like dinner plates and his engagement.

Actually, aside from the political prose, Thurber seems to have half enjoyed the language he complained about. A wily old fencer with lots of tricks left, he not only collected psychosematicisms but perpetrated his own. We can imagine a wicked expression of satisfaction on his face as he gave demented diction and tortured syntax another turn of the screw. He had a certain fondness as well as exasperation for the rarer flights of illiteracy and relished mispronunciations, grammatical grotesqueries, and startling non-sequiturs which stopped anyone else's conversation but encouraged Thurber to persevere in this form of oblique communication or booby-trapped colloquy even though he got nowhere faster than usual.

His linguistic conservatism was more than matched by the linguistic innovations of his later years. In 1945, Malcolm Cowley evaluated Thurber's style as "a sort of costly simplicity, like that of well-tailored clothes or good conversation." He added: "There is not much wit in Thurber's writing, although there is plenty of it in his conversation. Occasionally in a story he permits himself a relatively brilliant or sparkling metaphor."[25] But after his blindness, his comedy depended less on situation and became increasingly verbal. As a friend said, "Thurber sits alone in the dark chewing on words and letters." His final work is less humorous but much wittier; it becomes, in fact, almost too dazzling in verbal virtuosity and linguistic legerdemain. He became a master of metaphor, and Nathaniel Benchley found his similes incomparable. Alliteration and assonance ran riot, with the platypus in the pansies, the porcupine in the peonies, and Thurber playing at "pitching pennies with the Pittsburg Pirates in a pitter-patter of rain outside the Pitti Palace." He lay awake at night making up tongue-twisters like, "We supply wristwatches for witchwatchers watching witches Washington wishes watched."

"For years now," he wrote in 1959, "I have kept myself awake while courting unconsciousness by tinkering with words and letters of the alphabet and spelling words backward." "Ping-pong," for instance, becomes "gnip-gnop," and there is "the Sesumarongi, a backward tribe but a tribe that is all around us." When other words failed, he coined his own; his characters and creatures flobber and globber, zicker, flugger, gurble, and Black the pirate threatens to squck his parrot's thrug till all he can whupple is geep. There are also fabricated verb-nouns like "bragdowdy," "pussyfret," "shattermyth," and "dampenglee." Thurber concocted blends, played with palindromes ("A man, a plan, a canal, Panama"), and was preoccupied with puns (for the vogue of adapting classics into Westerns, why not *Trelawney of the Wells Fargo, She Shoots to Conquer, Fanny's First Gunplay, The Sheriff Misses Tanqueray,* and *Have Gun, Will Shakespeare*).

Addicted to literary allusions, Thurber combined them with puns and sometimes came up with an esoteric masterpiece. When mistaken for Bing Crosby and asked how he was, he answered, *"Non sum qualis eram sub regno bony Sinatra."* He was never afraid to be literary, and he came to incorporate and alter quotations almost as much as the Eliot of *The Waste Land.* Some of the repartee of his last pieces sounds as if Eliot, Lewis Carroll, the later Henry James, E. E. Cummings, and the Joyce of *Finnegan's Wake* were all conversing over their cups. Kenneth Tynan said on the BBC that Thurber lived in "an interior universe, entirely inhabited by words, which he would play with, dismember, anatomize, dissect, reassemble in strange and odd combinations. His mind was a seething kind of kaleidoscope of word forms, word shapes, abused words, misused words, neologisms, old coinages re-shaped."

Frank Getlein wrote: "Thurber is enchanted by what can be done with words and appalled by what is being done to them."[27] Perhaps the greatest tribute to his art is the enchantment of his prose; for, even when his hero's foot is stuck in the piano stool, the music he plays has a rare beauty all its own.

CHAPTER *10*

Conclusion

INSTEAD of presenting a single approach, I have tried to give some indication of the rich complexity and variety of Thurber's work and of his unique qualities of thought and expression. Accomplished as a satirist, essayist, dramatist, cartoonist, and illustrator, and as a writer of fiction, fable, fantasy, and impressionistic biography, Thurber combined a perceptive insight and a sensitive imagination with consummate literary skill. Curiously, though he was tremendously respected by his fellow writers, he has received little serious critical attention. The Thurber bibliography is lengthy, but secondary material is mostly superficial. While numerous books and learned articles are written about Hemingway, Faulkner, Eliot, and even J. D. Salinger—as well as about contemporary writers of considerably lesser stature—Thurber has been almost completely ignored by scholars. He did not, of course, write primarily for the consideration of scholars, but then neither does any really first-rate artist. In any case, Thurber deserves more serious treatment than he has hitherto received. Many anthologies and college texts include one or two of his pieces, but too often the editors select trivial ones like "University Days." Moreover, he is usually given superficial comment and presented as an inconsequential dessert after a substantial meal of more somber writers.

I *The Case for Comedy*

In spite of his popularity (for in the eyes of some academicians an author is immediately suspect if his works are popular, and some critics disparage the popularity even of such distinguished figures as Dickens, Twain, Frost, and Hemingway), Thurber at his best did not accommodate his creativity to the demands of stereotyped magazine fiction. Far from being sophisticatedly slick, his style has genuine literary distinction. He offered authentic criticism of life, and he presented it in an imaginative, original way. "It is reality twisted to the right into humor rather than to the left into tranquillity," he explained; "In anything funny you write that isn't close to serious you've missed something along the line."[1]

Unfortunately, the humorist is often consigned to literary limbo. Even Otto Friedrich, one of the few critics to appreciate the substantial merit of Thurber's achievement, seemed to feel that the humor needed apology and that Thurber must be shown as actually a somber writer if his work was to receive recognition. Too many scholars, thinking like Matthew Arnold that really important literature must have "high seriousness," tend to dismiss Thurber as a "mere" humorist. Life is grim, life is earnest, and we must laugh only on holidays. Thurber said that he did not see many good humorists in the new crop of writers and thought the Depression was the cause by making students too grave and subdued. E. B. White, who has also been slighted by critics, explains:

> The world likes humor, but it treats it patronizingly. It decorates its serious artists with laurel, and its wags with Brussels sprouts. It feels that if a thing is funny it can be presumed to be something less than great, because if it were truly great it would be wholly serious. Writers know this, and those who take their literary selves with great seriousness are at considerable pains never to associate their name with anything funny or flippant or nonsensical or light."[2]

One of Thurber's virtues is that, while he took his art seriously as a meticulous craftsman, he did not consider himself with great solemnity; and so he avoided the fate of Humpty Dumpty. He spoke of his own "tiny corner of literature," but, if tiny, it is "a clean, well-lighted place." He was never a zany or a wag; his particular merit was his perception of the paradox of life in which comedy and tragedy are so closely interwoven that they may both exist in the same event. Some of his stories are grim, some undilutedly funny; but usually he achieved the difficult feat of showing those aspects of experience which lie upon the perilously narrow border between humor and catastrophe. Thus his writings have a rich complexity which can yield many layers of ironic meaning. At the same time his bifocal view of life gave him a sympathetic and unusual insight into the intricacies of human personality—one that is possessed by few writers of our time. It is no more just to classify Thurber as a "humorist" than to attach that label to Mark Twain. Thurber told J. E. Pollard, "I try to make as perceptive and helpful a comment on the human predicament as I can, in fables, fairy tales, stories, and essays. I am surprised that so few people see the figure of seriousness in the carpet of my humor and comedy."[3]

Complaining that "arrogant intellectual critics condemn humor and comedy," he insisted that "comedy is just as important, and often more serious [than tragedy] In its approach to truth, and, what few writers seem to realize or to admit, usually more difficult to write." Still, it must be admitted that a fair portion of Thurber's work is trivia—entertaining, but of no lasting interest. It is pompous to find this trivia unbecoming to him as an artist; such pieces are a welcome part of his personality, and the greatest of authors have had their *jeux d'esprit*. Better Thurber's skillfully amusing if sometimes casual wit than the ponderous or plodding minor productions of a Carlyle, Wordsworth, Ruskin, or Browning. Unfortunately, Thurber's trivia seems to obscure a full recognition of his masterpieces and to tempt readers into thinking him a featherweight. Like Twain, Thurber was sometimes exasperated by this reaction. He told W. J. Weatherby: "Anybody who thinks I have simply striven to entertain and amuse hasn't read me. I have written as many savage pieces as humorous ones. How many years will it take to convince people I am not a clown?"[4]

Otto Friedrich stated that Thurber's casual sketches "fulfill a constant need for money"; but such a charge, unsupported by any evidence, has no justification in fact. Actually, Thurber wrote for years for *The Bermudian* and refused to take any payment for his contributions, though the editor, Ronald John Williams, writes that "when Harold Ross lived he complained that Thurber was contributing more regularly to *The Bermudian* than to *The New Yorker* (the latter paid him handsomely, of course)."[5] Many of these pieces were so good that Thurber included them in his books. Since most of his pieces were published first in magazines, then reprinted in book form, and sometimes anthologized, he had a multiple income from them, for he controlled all reprint rights. Besides the original income from Broadway and Hollywood, *The Male Animal* still brings in royalties from amateur and professional productions. Thurber once turned down $3500 a week in Hollywood in order to write a Henry James parody. Hence he wrote trivia not to meet a pressing need for money but (as he explained) to sidetrack worrisome trains of thought by amusing himself and his public.

Thurber often complained that Americans didn't really want comic subtleties; they preferred "the loud laugh, the wow, the yak, the belly laugh, and the dozen other labels for the roll-'em-in-the-aisles gagerissimo." He refused to satisfy with this type of humor, for he maintained that "Humor is a gentle thing. That's why it is so necessary if our species is to survive."[6] He wrote that he praised and encouraged "all people of courage and sensibility"; and, accord-

ing to Eric Linklater, he "never defaced the human predicament. . . ." He did, though, feel that anger was sometimes a
necessary virtue for a satirist. In a moment of discouragement, he
commented: "Having tried for four decades to make some social
comment, it is something less than reassuring to discover that what
a jittery America wants is the boppo laugh or nothing." The
British, he thought, had humor in depth while too much of ours
was superficial. Thus Dylan Thomas' comment is relevant: "It is
still impossible to compare the shy and baffled, introspective
essays, fables, and fabulous reminiscences of Thurber, his cowering
terror before the mechanical gadgets, the militant neuroses, the
ubiquitous women, the democratic pitfalls and big-business bogies
of this modern Americanized Age; it is impossible to compare him,
class him, school him, with the glib Groucho zaniness of S. J.
Perelman. . . ."[7]

When *Credos and Curios* appeared posthumously, most reviews
were quite favorable, but a few critics turned on it with excessive
hostility, though their curt treatment failed to develop any
adequate arguments. John Updike in the New York *Times* was not
hostile but condescending; he dismissed most of Thurber's works
as unconvincing, uncomfortable, and less sensitive than Benchley
or Don Marquis. Updike's statement, however, was mere assertion
unsupported by analysis; and his review might best be explained
in view of his stories for *The New Yorker* as the ritual slaying of
the old king by the new.

II *Thurber's Limitations and Achievement*

However, Thurber's masterpieces (like Updike's) are on a small
scale; none of his individual writings has greatness of stature; but
his total production is impressive. He does not have the largeness
of conception of Cervantes or Twain. His heroes lack sufficient
tragic stature for their fall to be profoundly moving, nor do they
have the comic stature of Falstaff, Volpone, or Gulley Jimson.
His characters, in fact, are too much alike; one speaks of "Thurber
men" and "Thurber women" just as one speaks of a "Thurber dog"
when referring to that breed which unfortunately appeared only on
his drawing board. By writing short stories, he necessarily limited
his field for characterization. His people are not static; but in the
short story he could show them only in snapshot. Yet, since many
are variations on several basic personalities, we do get a complex
picture from different angles. The most individualized characters
are those in his reminiscences, and *The Thurber Album* does an
incisive job of presenting brief portraits. His book-length study of

Harold Ross is his most thorough characterization, but it consists mainly of brilliant, fragmentary glimpses of the editor.

For all his versatility, Thurber left out a great deal of human experience (though, on the other side of the fence, no more so than Hemingway). In his fiction there is practically no treatment of romantic love, death, religion, war (except in parables), childhood (except for antic adolescence), art, or working conditions. Many of his credos deal with these things, but they are not made a dramatic experience. Thurber dealt with life on a limited scale—mostly in the living room—but so do most critics of manners, including Jane Austen and Henry James.

In short, most of Thurber's works are vignettes. Perhaps he was not capable of sustaining a long effort, though he said he never felt the desire to do so. "Many writers feel a sense of frustration or something if they haven't, but I don't" he explained. "But brevity in any case—whether the work is supposed to be humorous or not—would seem to me to be desirable."[8] Thurber said that most of the books he liked were short; among them are *The Red Badge of Courage, The Turn of the Screw,* Conrad's short stories, *A Lost Lady,* Hergesheimer's *Wild Oranges,* Victoria Lincoln's *February Hill,* and *The Great Gatsby.*

> You know [he recalled] Fitzgerald once wrote Thomas Wolfe: "You're a putter-inner and I'm a taker-outer." I stick with Fitzgerald. I don't believe, as Wolfe did, that you have to turn out a massive work before being judged a writer. Wolfe once told me at a cocktail party I didn't know what it was to be a writer. My wife, standing next to me, complained about that. "But my husband *is* a writer," she said. "Why all I ever see is that stuff of his in *The New Yorker.*" In other words he felt that prose under 5,000 words was certainly not the work of a writer. . . . If you said you were a writer, he wanted to know where the books were, the great big long books.[9]

Thurber observed: "It seems to me you're going out on a limb these days to keep a book short."[10] But his short pieces have an economy, a sharpness, a crisp effectiveness lacking in many three-decker novels. He gave the details but seldom the broad sweep of experience. A lesser and kindlier Swift, he lacked the scope of creative vision which produced Gulliver. But he diagnosed his age and in part transcended it. Some of his satire will no doubt become obsolete as tracts for the times, but his best work penetrates deeper than the surface and should remain a valuable part of American literature.

Notes and References

Preface

1. Wolcott Gibbs, quoted in James Thurber, *The Years with Ross* (Boston and Toronto, 1959), p. 48.
2. E. B. White, quoted in James Thurber obituary, New York *Times* (November 3, 1961), p. 35.
3. James Thurber, letter to the author, June 23, 1959.

Chapter One

1. Al Capp, "The Comedy of Charlie Chaplin," *The Atlantic*, CLXXXV (February, 1950), 29-39.
2. Max Eastman, *Enjoyment of Laughter* (New York, 1936), pp. 341-42.
3. *Ibid.*, p. 342.
4. J. Bryan III, "Funny Man, A Study in Professional Frustration," *The Saturday Evening Post*, CCXII (September 23, 1939), 11, 93.
5. *A Subtreasury of American Humor*, ed. E. B. White and Katharine S. White (New York, 1946), p. 723.
6. Eastman, p. 341.
7. Harvey Breit, *The Writer Observed* (Cleveland and New York, 1956), p. 257.
8. Malcolm Cowley, ed., *Writers at Work* (New York, 1959), pp. 85-86.
9. Wolcott Gibbs, "In a Glass Darkly," *The New Yorker*, XXXI (March 19, 1955), 68.
10. Henry Brandon, *As We Are* (Garden City, 1961), pp. 257-58.
11. W. J. Weatherby, "A Man of Words," *Manchester Guardian Weekly* (February 9, 1961), p. 13.
12. Ruth White, "James Thurber, His Life in Columbus," Columbus *Dispatch*, March 10, 1940.
13. Kenneth MacLean, "James Thurber: A Portrait of the Dog-Artist," *Acta Victorana*, LXVIII (Spring, 1944), 5.
14. Weatherby, *loc. cit.*
15. John Gerber, quoted in *The Daily Iowan* (Iowa City, February 24, 1956), p. 5.
16. Brandon, p. 272.
17. James Thurber, "Thinking Ourselves into Trouble," *Forum*, CI (June, 1939), 310.
18. *Ibid.*
19. Brandon, p. 275.
20. J. Robert Nelson, ed., *The Christian Student and the University* (New York, 1952), pp. 13-14.
21. Thurber, "Thinking Ourselves into Trouble," *op. cit.*, p. 311.
22. *Ibid.*
23. *Ibid.*
24. *Ibid.*
25. *Ibid.*
26. Eastman, p. 343.

27. James Thurber, "Correspondence," *The Humanist* (October-November, 1951), p. 204.

28. *The Christian Student and the University*, p. 15.

29. Harvey Breit, "Mr. Thurber Observes a Serene Birthday," New York *Times Magazine* (December 4, 1949), p. 17.

30. "Priceless Gift of Laughter," *Time*, LVIII (July 9, 1951), 94-95.

31. Mark Van Doren, *The Autobiography of Mark Van Doren* (New York, 1958), pp. 255-56.

32. Brandon, p. 259.

33. Virginia Haufe, "Thurber Gives Advice to American Women," *Ohioana*, III (Summer, 1960), 36.

34. Edmund Wilson, "Books," *The New Yorker*, XXI (October 27, 1945), 92.

35. Kenneth MacLean, "Further Thurber," Typescript of Lecture at the University of Toronto, in possession of Mrs. James Thurber, p. 18.

36. Weatherby, *loc. cit.*

37. John Updike, "Indignations of a Senior Citizen," New York *Times Book Review* (November 25, 1962), p. 5.

38. Peter DeVries, "James Thurber: The Comic Prufrock," *Poetry*, LXIII (December, 1943), 151.

39. "Priceless Gift of Laughter," *op. cit.*, p. 88.

Chapter Two

1. Joseph Conrad, *Lord Jim* (The Modern Library, New York, 1931), pp. 415-16.

2. Joe Park, Letter to James Thurber, August 5, 1947, on file at the Alumni Office, Ohio State University.

3. F. Scott Fitzgerald, *This Side of Paradise* (New York, 1960), p. 25.

4. E. E. Cummings, *Poems 1923-1954* (New York, 1954), p. 345.

5. Edith C. Basso, *The Later Wordsworth* (Cambridge, 1933), p. 30.

6. Conrad, *Lord Jim*, p. 225.

7. C. P. Snow, *The Two Cultures and the Scientific Revolution* (New York, 1959), pp. 4-5.

8. Moody E. Prior, *Science and the Humanities* (Evanston, 1962), p. 38.

9. Raymond Dexter Havens, *The Mind of a Poet, A Study of Wordsworth's Thought with Particular Reference to The Prelude* (Baltimore, 1951), pp. 255-56.

10. William Wordsworth, *The Poetical Works of*, eds., E. De Selincourt and Helen Darbishire (Oxford, 1949), V, "The Excursion," IV, 11. 613-21.

11. Havens, p. 81.

12. Tennessee Williams, *The Glass Menagerie* (New York, 1945), pp. 3, 122.

13. Frederick Lewis Allen, *Since Yesterday, The Nineteen-Thirties in America* (New York and London, 1940), p. 161.

14. *Ibid.*, p. 75.

15. *Ibid.*, p. 63.

16. *Ibid.*, p. 327.

17. Kenneth MacLean, "The Imagination of James Thurber," *The Canadian Forum*, XXXIII (December, 1953), 201.

18. Robert Louis Stevenson, *The Works of* ("Pan's Pipes," *Virginibus Puerisque*), (London), XXII, 146.

19. Henri Bergson, *Laughter, An Essay of the Meaning on the Comic*, trans. Cloudesley Brereton and Fred Rothwell (New York, 1921), p. 128.

20. Thomas Wolfe, *Look Homeward, Angel* (New York, 1952), p. 450.

21. James Thurber, letter to Patricia Stone, March 24, 1949.

22. W. J. Weatherby, "A Man of Words," *Manchester Guardian Weekly* (February 9, 1961), p. 13.

23. D. W. Brogan, *The American Character* (New York, 1950), p. 72.

24. William E. Bohn, *I Remember America* (New York, 1962), p. 129.

25. Walter Blair, *Horse Sense in American Humor* (Chicago, 1943), pp. 293-94.

26. *The* [London] *Times Literary Supplement* (November 3, 1945), p. 520.

27. Francis Downing, "Thurber," *Commonweal*, XLI (March 9, 1945), 519.

28. Sigmund Freud, *The Basic Writings of Sigmund Freud*, trans. and ed. Dr. A. A. Brill (New York, 1938), pp. 663, 665.

29. Bergson, p. 181.

30. *Ibid.*, p. 115.

Chapter Three

1. Henry Adams, *The Education of Henry Adams* (New York, 1931), p. 442.

2. *Ibid.*, p. 447.

3. Malcolm Cowley, "James Thurber's Dream Book," *The New Republic,* CXII (March 12, 1945), 363.

4. Henry Bamford Parkes, *The American Experience* (New York, 1959), p. 259.

5. *Ibid.*, p. 262.

6. W. J. Weatherby, "A Man of Words," *The Manchester Guardian Weekly* (February 9, 1961), p. 13.

7. "Thurber, an Old Hand at Humor with Two Hits on Hand," *Life,* XLVIII (March 14, 1960), 108.

8. Virginia Haufe, "Thurber Gives Advice to American Women," *Ohioana,* III (Summer, 1960), 34, 36.

9. "Thurber, an Old Hand at Humor with Two Hits on Hand," *Life, loc. cit.*

10. Oswald Spengler, *The Decline of the West, Perspectives of World-History,* trans. Charles Francis Atkinson (New York, 1947), II, 328-29.

11. Henry Brandon, *As We Are* (Garden City, 1961), pp. 266-67.

12. W. H. Auden, "September 1, 1939," in *Another Time* (London, 1940), p. 114.

Chapter Four

1. Dorothy Parker, Introduction, James Thurber, *Men, Women and Dogs* (New York, 1943), p. x.

2. Kenneth MacLean, "The Imagination of James Thurber," *The Canadian Forum,* XXXIII (December, 1953), 200.

3. "James Thurber in Conversation with Alistair Cooke," *The Atlantic,* CXCIX (August, 1956), 40.

4. Harvey Breit, "Mr. Thurber Observes a Serene Birthday," New York *Times Magazine* (December 4, 1949), p. 17.

5. Romain Gary, *The Roots of Heaven,* trans. Jonathan Griffin (New York, 1958), p. 32.

6. Kenneth MacLean, "James Thurber: A Portrait of the Dog-Artist," *Acta Victorana,* LXVIII (Spring, 1944), 5.

7. Edward Wagenknecht, *Mark Twain the Man and His Work* (New Haven, 1935), p. 155.

8. Mark Twain, *The Mysterious Stranger and Other Stories* (New York, 1922), p. 50.
9. Fyodor Dostoyevsky, *The Brothers Karamazov* (New York), p. 247.
10. Cary, p. 99.
11. W. J. Weatherby, "A Man of Words," *Manchester Guardian Weekly* (February 9, 1961), p. 13.

Chapter Five

1. Walter Blair, *Horse Sense in American Humor* (Chicago, 1943), pp. 291-92.
2. Lon Tinkle, "Year of the Long Autumn," *The Saturday Review*, XXXV (December 27, 1952), 9.
3. T. E. Cassidy, "It All Began in Columbus, Ohio," *Commonweal*, LXI (June 20, 1952), 275.
4. Joseph Conrad, *Lord Jim* (New York, 1931), p. 43.
5. John Updike, "Indignations of a Senior Citizen," New York *Times Book Review* (November 25, 1962), p. 5.
6. F. Scott Fitzgerald, *The Stories of F. Scott Fitzgerald*, ed. Malcolm Cowley (New York, 1951), p. 388.
7. *The* [London] *Times Literary Supplement* (October 10, 1952), p. 658.
8. William Faulkner, *The Faulkner Reader* (New York, 1958), pp. 3-4.
9. F. Scott Fitzgerald, *Three Novels* (New York, 1953), p. 134.
10. "Priceless Gift of Laughter," *Time*, LVIII (July 9, 1951), 92.
11. Kenneth MacLean, "James Thurber: A Portrait of the Dog-Artist," *Acta Victorana*, LXVIII (Spring, 1944), 7.
12. Charles Brady, "What Thurber Saw," *Commonweal*, LXXV (December 8, 1961), 275.
13. George Meredith, *An Essay on Comedy and the Uses of the Comic Spirit*, ed. Lane Cooper (New York, 1918), p. 81.
14. James E. Pollard, "James Thurber," in *Ohio Authors and Their Books 1796-1950*, ed. William Coyle (Cleveland and New York, 1962), p. 633.
15. Malcolm Cowley, *The Literary Situation* (New York, 1954), p. 203.
16. *Ibid.*
17. "Jim," *Newsweek*, LVIII (November 13, 1961), 36.
18. Cowley, pp. 196-97.
19. *Ibid.*, p. 203.
20. Francis Hackett, *On Judging Books in General and Particular* (New York, 1947), p. 34.
21. *Ibid.*, pp. 34-35.
22. *Ibid.*, pp. 35-36.
23. *Ibid.*, pp. 37-38.

Chapter Six

1. Nelson H. Budd, "Personal Reminiscences of James Thurber," *The Ohio State University Monthly* (January, 1962), 13.
2. Joseph Wood Krutch, *The Nation*, CL (January 20, 1940), 81-82.
3. Otis Ferguson, "Curtain and Other Calls," *The New Republic*, CII (January 22, 1940), 116.
4. "Thurber, an Old Hand at Humor with Two Hits on Hand," *Life*, XLVIII (March 14, 1960), 108.
5. Rosamund Gilder, "Brain and Brawn, Broadway in Review," *Theatre Arts*, XXIV (March, 1940), 161.

6. Malcolm Cowley, ed., *Writers at Work, The Paris Review Interviews* (New York, 1959), p. 87.
7. John Gassner, ed., *Best Plays of the Modern American Theatre: Second Series* (New York, 1955), p. 267.
8. James E. Pollard, "James Thurber," in *Ohio Authors and Their Books 1796-1950*, ed. William Coyle (Cleveland and New York, 1962), p. 635.
9. *Theatre Arts*, XXXVIII (October, 1954), 15.
10. Harvey Breit, *The Writer Observed* (Cleveland and New York, 1956), p. 256.
11. Malcolm Cowley, "A Job to Do," in "Salute to Thurber," *The Saturday Review*, XLIV (November 25, 1961), 15.
12. *Ibid.*
13. Eugene Lyons, *The Red Decade, The Stalinist Penetration of America* (Indianapolis and New York, 1941), pp. 347, 350-51.
14. Malcolm Cowley, *The Literary Situation* (New York, 1954), pp. 221-22.
15. Breit, *loc. cit.*
16. Henry Brandon, *As We Are* (Garden City, 1961), p. 268.
17. *Writers at Work*, p. 97.
18. William S. Schlamm, "The Secret Lives of James Thurber," *Freeman*, II (July 28, 1952), 738.
19. Pollard, p. 635.
20. Breit, p. 257.

Chapter Seven

1. Louis Calta, "Thurber's Walter Mitty Dream Comes True in Performing Bow," New York *Times* (September 13, 1960), 14.
2. Kenneth MacLean, "James Thurber: A Portrait of the Dog-Artist," *Acta Victorana*, LXVIII (Spring, 1944), 6.

Chapter Eight

1. William Murrell, *A History of American Graphic Humor* (1865-1938) (New York, 1938), II, 237.
2. *New Statesman and Nation*, XVIII (December 23, 1939), 936.
3. Dorothy Parker, "Introduction," James Thurber, *The Seal in the Bedroom and Other Predicaments* (New York, 1932).
4. James Thurber, *The Years with Ross* (Boston and Toronto, 1959), p. 154.
5. Parker, *loc. cit.*
6. James Thurber, letter to Patricia Stone, July 14, 1948.
7. Henry Brandon, *As We Are* (Garden City, 1961), p. 263.
8. Letter to Patricia Stone, July 14, 1948.
9. W. H. Auden, "The Icon and the Portrait," *Nation*, CL (January 13, 1940), 48.
10. James Thurber, letter to Harvey Breit, November 25, 1949.
11. C. Lester Walker, "The Legendary Mr. Thurber," *Ladies Home Journal*, LXIII (July, 1946), 122.
12. "That Thurber Woman," *Newsweek*, XXII (November 22, 1943), 84.
13. Parker, *loc. cit.*
14. "James Thurber in Conversation with Alistair Cooke," *The Atlantic*, CXCVIII (August, 1956), 38.

15. Dorothy Parker, "Introduction," James Thurber, *Men, Women and Dogs* (New York, 1943), p. ix.
16. Murrell, II, 262-63.
17. Brandon, pp. 262-63.
18. "James Thurber in Conversation with Alistair Cooke," p. 39.

Chapter Nine

1. Malcolm Cowley, "Lions and Lemmings, Toads and Tigers," *The Reporter*, XV (December 13, 1956), 42.
2. *Ibid.*
3. James Thurber, quoted in Fred B. Millett, *Contemporary American Authors* (New York, 1940), p. 613.
4. Malcolm Cowley, ed., *Writers at Work*, (New York, 1959), p. 87.
5. "Jim," *Newsweek*, LVIII (November 13, 1961), 35-36.
6. Cowley, *Writers at Work*, p. 91.
7. Wolcott Gibbs, "In a Glass Darkly," *The New Yorker*, XXXI (March 19, 1955), 68.
8. Arthur Gelb, "Thurber Intends to Relax Till '61," New York *Times* (March 28, 1960), p. 35.
9. Malcolm Cowley, *The Literary Situation* (New York, 1954), p. 192.
10. James Thurber, letter to the author, April 9, 1956.
11. Cowley, *The Literary Situation*, p. 193.
12. Lon Tinkle, "Year of the Long Autumn," *The Saturday Review*, XXXV (December 27, 1952), 7, 9.
13. Ernest Hemingway, interviewed by George Plimpton, "On the Art of Writing," *Horizon*, I (January, 1959), 133.
14. Henry Brandon, *As We Are* (Garden City, 1961), p. 280.
15. James Thurber, quoted by John Ferris, *The Columbus* [Ohio] *Citizen* (November 8, 1953).
16. W. J. Weatherby, "A Man of Words," *Manchester Guardian Weekly* (February 9, 1961), 13.
17. Cowley, *Writers at Work*, p. 87.
18. Otto Friedrich, "James Thurber: A Critical Study," *Discovery*, V (January, 1955), 175-76.
19. *Ibid.*, pp. 178-79.
20. *Writers at Work*, p. 92.
21. *Ibid.*, p. 93.
22. Brandon, p. 281.
23. James Thurber, letter to the author, June 23, 1959.
24. Brandon, p. 276.
25. Albert Camus, *The Rebel* (New York, 1957), p. 283.
26. Malcolm Cowley, "James Thurber's Dream Book," *The New Republic*, CXII (March 12, 1945), 362.
27. Frank Getlein, "Thurber's Last Collection," *The New Republic*, CXLVII (December 22, 1962), 25.

Chapter Ten

1. Cowley, *Writers at Work*, p. 95.
2. E. B. and Katharine S. White, eds., *A Subtreasury of American Humor* (New York, 1946), p. xviii.

3. James E. Pollard, "James Thurber," *Ohio Authors and Their Books 1796-1950*, ed. William Coyle (Cleveland and New York, 1962), p. 635.

4. W. J. Weatherby, "A Man of Words," *Manchester Guardian Weekly* (February 9, 1961), 13.

5. Ronald John Williams, letter to the author, April 25, 1962.

6. James Thurber, quoted by Rod Nordell, "James Thurber–Lightness and Light," *The Christian Science Monitor* (November 3, 1961).

7. Dylan Thomas, *Quite Early One Morning* (New York, 1954), p. 159.

8. *Writers at Work*, p. 94.

9. *Ibid.*

10. *Ibid.*, p. 95.

Selected Bibliography

This bibliography lists most of Thurber's identifiable writings in print, including a series of articles he wrote under the pseudonym of Jared L. Manley. It is not definitive, for it does not include his undergraduate contributions to *The Sun-Dial* and *The Lantern* at Ohio State University, his anonymous early newspaper work, nor all of his column for Ralph Ingersoll's *PM* in 1940-41. For eight years, Thurber helped write *The New Yorker's* "Talk of the Town": the best of his contributions are collected in *The Beast in Me*, and the rest of them are anonymous. There are several hundred uncollected and unindexed cartoons and drawings in *The New Yorker*, plus an unknown number of original, unpublished Thurber drawings owned by his friends. Thurber wrote thousands of letters, and Mrs. Thurber is editing his correspondence for publication. Most of his pieces first appeared in *The New Yorker* and other periodicals before being reprinted in his books, and many have been often anthologized; in such cases I have listed only the book as the handiest reference.

The secondary bibliography is highly selective. There are hundreds of journalistic articles and brief reviews, most of them rather trivial. I list only the most useful, including those by his colleagues and collaborators.

PRIMARY SOURCES

A. *Books*

Alarms and Diversions. New York: Harper & Brothers, 1957.

Amorocco, A Two-Act Musical Comedy. Registered by the Scarlet Mask Club of Ohio State University, A675990, December, 1925.

The Beast in Me and Other Animals, A New Collection of Pieces and Drawings about Human Beings and Less Alarming Creatures. New York: Harcourt, Brace and Company, 1948.

Cream of Thurber, Skimmed from the Following Writings and Drawings: My Life and Hard Times, The Owl in the Attic, The Middle-Aged Man on the Flying Trapeze, Let Your Mind Alone. London: Hamish Hamilton, Ltd., 1939.

Credos and Curios. New York: Harper and Row, 1962.

"Elliott Nugent," in *Ohio Authors and Their Books 1796-1950.* William Coyle, editor. Cleveland and New York: The World Publishing Company, 1962.

Fables for Our Time and Famous Poems Illustrated. New York: Harper & Brothers, 1940.

Further Fables for Our Time. New York: Simon and Schuster, 1956.

The Great Quillow. New York: Harcourt, Brace and Company, 1944.

Is Sex Necessary? or Why You Feel the Way You Do (with E. B. White). New York: Harper & Brothers, 1929.

Lanterns and Lances. New York: Harper & Brothers, 1961.

The Last Flower, A Parable in Pictures. New York: Harper & Brothers, 1939.

Let Your Mind Alone! and Other More or Less Inspirational Pieces. New York: Harper & Brothers, 1937.

The Male Animal (with Elliott Nugent). New York: Random House, 1940.

Many Moons. New York: Harcourt, Brace and Company, 1943.

Many Moons, A Musical Comedy in Two Acts. Words and music by W. W. Havens, William Haid, R. E. Fidler and others. Registered by the Scarlet Mask Club of Ohio State University, A656649, January, 1922.

Men, Women and Dogs, A Book of Drawings. New York: Harcourt, Brace and Company, 1943.

The Middle-Aged Man on the Flying Trapeze. New York: Harper & Brothers, 1935.

My Life and Hard Times. New York: Harper & Brothers, 1933.

My World—and Welcome to It. New York: Harcourt, Brace and Company, 1942.

Nightingale. Registered by the Scarlet Mask Club of Ohio State University, D690000, October, 1924.

Oh My! Omar (with Hayward M. Anderson). The Scarlet Mask Club of Ohio State University, 1920.

The Owl in the Attic and Other Perplexities. New York: Harper & Brothers, 1931.

The Seal in the Bedroom and Other Predicaments. New York: Harper & Brothers, 1932.

Tell Me Not. Words and music by R. L. F. McCombs, Ralph L. Wolf, and others. Registered by the Scarlet Mask Club of Ohio State University, A675990, December, 1925.

The 13 Clocks. New York: Simon and Schuster, 1950.

The Thurber Album, A New Collection of Pieces about People. New York: Simon and Schuster, 1952.

A Thurber Carnival (Revue). New York: Samuel French, Inc., 1962.

The Thurber Carnival. New York: Harper & Brothers, 1945.

Thurber Country, A New Collection of Pieces about Males and Females, Mainly of Our Own Species. New York: Simon and Schuster, 1953.

Thurber's Dogs, A Collection of the Master's Dogs, Written and Drawn, Real and Imaginary, Living and Long Ago. New York: Simon and Schuster, 1955.

A Thurber Garland. London: Hamish Hamilton, 1955.

A Twin Fix (with Hayward M. Anderson). Registered by the Scarlet Mask Club of Ohio State University, A697418, January, 1923.

"What the Animals Were Up To," in *While You Were Gone, A Report on Wartime Life in the United States*. Jack Goodman, editor. New York: Simon and Schuster, 1946.

The White Deer. New York: Harcourt, Brace and Company, 1945.

The Wonderful O. New York: Simon and Schuster, 1957.

The Years with Ross. Boston and Toronto: Atlantic Little, Brown and Company, 1959.

B. *Books Illustrated or Introduced by Thurber*

HAWES, ELIZABETH. *Men Can Take It*. James Thurber, illustrator. New York: Random House, 1939.

KINNEY, JAMES R., V. M. D. AND ANN HONEYCUTT. *How to Raise a Dog: in the City . . . in the Suburbs*. James Thurber, illustrator. New York: Simon and Schuster, 1953.

MARQUIS, DON. *Her Foot Is on the Brass Rail*. James Thurber, illustrator. 200 copies privately printed in 1935.

Selected Bibliography

MIAN, MARY. *My Country-in-Law.* Introduction by James Thurber. Boston: Houghton-Mifflin and Company, 1946.

MOATED, ALICE LEONE. *No Nice Girl Swears.* James Thurber, illustrator. New York: Alfred A. Knopf, 1933.

SAMUELS, MARGARET. *In a Word.* James Thurber, illustrator. New York: Alfred A. Knopf, 1939.

SAYRE, JOEL. *Persian Gulf Command.* Introduction by James Thurber. New York: Random House, 1945.

C. Uncollected Pieces

Eighth grade class prophecy, Douglas School, 1909, included as Appendix A in Samuel Bernard Baker, *James Thurber: The Columbus Years,* Unpublished M.A. Thesis, The Ohio State University, 1962.

"Credos and Curios," 36 weekly pages for the Sunday Columbus *Dispatch,* 1923. Mrs. Thurber has photostats of these, and some are included as Appendix B in the Baker thesis.

"Quick, the Other Side, Some Hints for the Well-Dressed Man Who Plans to Travel in France," *The Detroit Athletic Club News,* November, 1925.

"Sock on the Jaw, French Style," *Harper's,* CLII, February, 1926, 384-86.

"Villanelle of Horatio Street, Manhattan," *The New Yorker,* II, February 26, 1927.

"Street Scene," *The New Yorker,* II (February 26, 1927).

"An American Romance," *The New Yorker,* III (March 5, 1927).

"News of the Day," *The New Yorker,* III (April 2, 1927).

"Portrait of a Lady," *The New Yorker,* III (April 9, 1927).

"Youngsters as Crickets," *The New Yorker,* III (April 30, 1927).

"More Authors Cover the Snyder Trial," *The New Yorker,* III (May 7, 1927).

"My Trip Abroad," *The New Yorker,* III (August 6, 1927).

"Polo in the Home," *The New Yorker,* III (September 17, 1927).

"Literary Meet," *The New Yorker,* III (September 24, 1927).

"Memoirs of a Wreath-Layer," *The New Yorker,* III (October 15, 1927).

"Breakfast with the President," *The New Yorker,* III (November 12, 1927).

"Visit from St. Nicholas" (parody of Hemingway), *The New Yorker,* III (December 24, 1927).

"How to Acquire Animal Crackers," *The New Yorker,* III (December 24, 1927).

"Chronicle of a Crime [Written after an Evening Spent in Reading *The Nation*]," *The New Yorker,* V (January 21, 1928), 58-59.

"Cross-Country Gamut," *The New Yorker,* III (February 11, 1928), 40-42.

"The Story of a Superfilm [as Told in Advertisements]," *The New Yorker,* III (February 18, 1928), 20.

"As Europe Sees Us," *Sunset,* LX (March, 1928), 17.

"Not Together [A Fragment from the Theatre]," *The New Yorker,* IV (March 3, 1928), 73.

"How It Feels to Kill a Man," *The New Yorker,* IV (March 10, 1928), 27-28.

"Advice to American Ladies Who Are Preparing to Travers the Atlantic in the Style of Miss Leslie's Household Book, 1854," *The New Yorker,* IV (June 16, 1928), 28.

"Camera vs. St. Bernard," *The New Yorker,* IV (June 30, 1928), 17-18.

"Profiles—Master of Ceremonies, Myron T. Herrick," *The New Yorker,* IV (July 21, 1928), 19-22.

"Duet," *The New Yorker,* IV (November 17, 1928), 34.

"Bachelor Burton," *The New Yorker,* IV (November 17, 1928), 34.

"Topics of the Day," *The New Yorker,* IV (November 24, 1928), 25.
"I Burn My Bridge Behind Me," *The New Yorker,* IV (December 1, 1928), 31-32.
"The Spirit of St. Louis," *The New Yorker,* IV (December 8, 1928), 27.
"Business Outlook Is 97,000,000!" *Magazine of Business,* LV (January, 1929), p. 49
"On Tearing into Business," *Magazine of Business,* LV (March, 1929), 267.
"This Week's Miracle from the Inner Shrine of Signem and Boostem Publishers," *The New Yorker,* V (April 6, 1929), 25-26.
"Bad Boy," *The New Yorker,* V (April 13, 1929), 34.
"The Psyching of Mr. Rogers," *The New Yorker,* V (April 27, 1929), 22.
"Let's Have a Set of Rules for Our Testimonial Industry," *Magazine of Business,* LV (May, 1929).
"Two Ships Bring Americans of Note and English Author [By Our Own Ship-News Reporter]," *The New Yorker,* V (June 8, 1929), 18.
"Gang War, 1940 [From a Newspaper Account of That Day]," *The New Yorker,* V (July 13, 1929), 16.
"Little Joe [Suggested by the Latest Gunman Fiction, and Several Other Things]," *The New Yorker,* V (September 7, 1929), 24-25.
"Burglar Proof—Maybe," *The New Yorker,* V (September 14, 1929), 72-80. Under pseudonym of James Grover.
"What Love Did to Us, One Man's True Confession," *The New Yorker,* V (February 1, 1930), 16-17.
"News Is Stranger than Fiction [An Impression, Gained from Reading the Minor Crime-and-Disaster Items in a Morning Paper]," *The New Yorker,* VI (March 22, 1930), 21-22.
"Memoirs of a Banquet Speaker," *The New Yorker,* VI (March 29, 1930), 17-18.
"A Reporter at Large—Cop into College Man," *The New Yorker,* VI (March 29, 1930), 43-48.
"Literary Tea [After Milling Around at Five or Six of Them]," *The New Yorker,* VI (April 12, 1930), 22.
"Spring Rehearsal," *The New Yorker,* VI (April 26, 1930), 19-20.
"A Little Episode," *The New Yorker,* VI (May 24, 1930), 20.
"Dorothy and Harry [A Story for Children, Written in Collaboration with Sally Morrison, Aged Five, Who Was Bored to Tears by All the Nice Storybooks She Got for Her Birthday]," *The New Yorker,* VI (June 14, 1930), 20.
"The Future of Psychoanalysis [More or Less in the Manner of the Science Itself]," *The New Yorker,* VI (July 19, 1930), 16-17.
"An Outline of the Byrd Report," *The New Yorker,* VI (July 26, 1930), 22-23.
"Answers-to-Hard-Questions Department," *The New Yorker,* VI (August 2, 1930), 17-18.
"Are Women Getting Anywhere? [A Profound and Searching Article, a Whole Lot Like Some of Those in 'Scribner's,' 'Harper's' the 'Atlantic Monthly,' etc.]," *The New Yorker,* VI (September 6, 1930), 17-18.
"Mr. Higgins' Breakdown," *The New Yorker,* VI (September 20, 1930), 19-20.
"North America in Ferment, South American Contagion Spreads," *The New Yorker,* VI (September 27, 1930), 27-28.
"Broadway Bulletin [With All of the Confusion of the Theatre Columns in the Papers]," *The New Yorker,* VI (October 4, 1930), 25.
"So You're Going to a Hotel," *The New Yorker,* VI (November 1, 1930), 16-18.

"Thumbs Up," *Harper's*, CLXII (December, 1930), 123-24.

"Subscriber's Nightmare," *The New Yorker*, VI (January 7, 1931), 19.

"The Burning Deck," *The New Yorker*, VI (February 7, 1931), 16-18.

"Late Afternoon of a Patrolman," *The New Yorker*, VII (April 11, 1931), 19-20.

"Some Notes on the Married Life of Birds," *The New Yorker*, VII (June 27, 1931), 13-14.

"Cholly," *The New Yorker*, VII (September 19, 1931), 17-18.

"The Future of Element 87," *The New Yorker*, VII (October 31, 1931), 17.

"Why Mr. Walker Went to California [If Everything that You Heard Was True]," *The New Yorker*, VII (December 5, 1931), 23.

"Mr. Hoover on Mr. Coolidge [A Resume of the Letters to the Editor Which Will Appear in the 'Herald Tribune' During the Next Few Months, Compiled So that You Won't Have to Read Them All]," *The New Yorker*, VII (January 30, 1932), 13.

"Listen to This, Dear," *Harper's*, CLXIV (January, 1932), 250-52.

"Thoughts from Mr. Tierney," *The New Yorker*, VII (February 13, 1932), 13-14.

"Voices from a Box," *The New Yorker*, VIII (February 20, 1932), 20-21.

"No More Biographies," *The New Yorker*, VIII (March 19, 1932), 16.

"The Advent of Mr. Moray," *The New Yorker*, VIII (April 16, 1932), 15-16.

"A Farewell to Florida [Or Hello to All This]," *The New Yorker*, VIII (April 30, 1932), 15-16.

"The Crosstown Bus Situation," *The New Yorker*, VIII (May 14, 1932), 20-21.

"Isn't Life Lovely! [If Some Prominent Autobiographers Had Written Their Memoirs the Way Elsie Janis Recently Wrote Hers!]," *The New Yorker*, VIII (June 25, 1932), 15-16.

"The Flaw in the Jewel," *The New Yorker*, VIII (July 9, 1932), 18-19.

"The Bright Emperor," *The New Yorker*, VIII (August 20, 1932), 16-17.

"This Little Kitty Stayed Cool," *The New Yorker*, VIII (September 10, 1932), 17-18.

"A Reporter at Large—Blushes and Tears," *The New Yorker*, VIII (September 24, 1932), 34-39.

"Letters from Roger," *The New Yorker*, VIII (November 12, 1932), 19-21.

"Kiddies' Hour at the Surrogate's [After Reading Reports of Surrogate O'Brien's Speech, 'A Kiddy in Every Home,' and the One on 'Keep the Kiddies in School']," *The New Yorker*, VIII (November 18, 1932), 20.

"The Great Sheet Scandal," *The New Yorker*, VIII (December 17, 1932), 15-16.

"A Farewell to Santa Claus, or Violins Are Nice for Boys with Chins," *The New Yorker*, VIII (December 24, 1932), 12.

"A Reporter at Large—Georgia vs. the World," *The New Yorker*, VIII (December 31, 1932), 25-29.

"What Price a Farewell to Designs?" *The New Yorker*, IX (March 18, 1933), 13.

"Tom, the Young Kidnapper, or, Pay Up and Live," *The New Yorker*, IX (June 10, 1933), 14-16.

"Recollections of Henry James," *The New Yorker*, IX (June 17, 1933), 11-13.

"Behind the Statistics," *The New Yorker*, IX (July 1, 1933), 21-23.

"The Threefold Problem of World Economic Cooperation," *The New Yorker*, IX (August 5, 1933), 19-20.

"Is the Allure of Glamour Cloying? (After Reading all the Movie Magazines to Find Out)," *The New Yorker*, IX (October 21, 1933), 20.

"The Happier Beast," from "Paunch," *The New Yorker*, IX (January 13, 1934), 21.

"One Man in His Time," *The New Yorker*, IX (January 20, 1934), 11-12.

"How to Tell a Fine Old Wine," *The New Yorker*, X (February 24, 1934), 17-18.

"Odyssey of Disney," *Nation*, CXXXVIII (March 28, 1934), 363.

"How to Relax While Broadcasting," *The New Yorker*, X (May 5, 1934), 25-26.

"Notes for a Proletarian Novel," *The New Yorker*, X (June 9, 1934), 15-16.

"How to Trace a Fish," *The New Yorker*, X (August 1, 1934), 13-14.

"Has Photography Gone Too Far?" *The New Yorker*, X (August 1, 1934), 13-14.

"A Fairly Interesting Envelope (With Apologies to Mr. R. A. Barry's Column about Interesting Stamps and Envelopes, in the Herald Tribune)," *The New Yorker*, X (August 25, 1934), 20.

"Thirteen Keys," *The New Yorker*, X (September 8, 1934), 23-24.

"And the World Laughs with Them," *The New Yorker*, X (September 29, 1934), 15-16.

"The Wizard of Chitenango," *The New Republic*, LXXXI (December 12, 1934), 141.

"More Ice Added to U.S. as Thousands Cheer," *The New Yorker*, X (December 22, 1934), 13-14.

"The Japanese Naval Situation," *The New Yorker*, X (January 12, 1935), 15-16.

"The International Spy Situation," *The New Yorker*, X (January 19, 1935), 15-16.

"Producers Never Think Twice," *The New Yorker*, XI (February 16, 1935), 17-18.

"The Old Friends," *The New Yorker*, XI (March 23, 1935), 16-18.

"Why Not Die?" *The New Yorker*, XI (September 21, 1935), 21.

"Essay on Dignity," *The New Yorker*, XI (January 4, 1936), 19-20.

"My Day (With Apologies to Eleanor Roosevelt)," *The New Yorker*, XI (February 15, 1936), 17.

"Voices of Revolution" (Review of *Proletarian Literature in the United States*, ed. Granville Hicks), *The New Republic*, LXXXVI (March 25, 1936), 200-1.

"Where Are They Now?" written under pseudonym Jared L. Manley, *The New Yorker*, XII (April 18, 1936), 23-27; (April 25, 1936), 20-23; (May 23, 1936), 22-25; (June 6, 1936), 18-20; (July 4, 1936), 19-24; (August 15, 1936), 21-24; (September 5, 1936), 20-25; (December 5, 1936), 29-33; (December 19, 1936), 22-25; (January 23, 1937), 21-27. XIII (March 27, 1937), 22-25; (June 26, 1937), 26-29; (August 14, 1937), 22-26; (December 25, 1937), 23-25.

"Merry Christmas to All" *The New Yorker*, XII (December 26, 1936), 16-17.

"Tempest in a Looking Glass," *Forum*, XCVII (April, 1937), 236-38.

"Men, Women, and Dogs," *The New Yorker*, XIII (April 17, 1937), 19-20.

"Is It True What They Say About Connecticut?" *Forum*, XCVII (June 1937), 363-66.

"The Man Who Knew Too Little," *The New Yorker*, XIII (December 4, 1937), 29-30.

"Pepper for the Belgians," *The New Yorker*, XIII (December 18, 1937), 20.

"Final Orders Given by a Very Ill Country Gentleman to His Grief-Stricken Secretary," *The New Yorker*, XIV (April 23, 1938), 19.

Selected Bibliography

"The Character of Catastrophe," *The New Yorker*, XIV (May 28, 1938), 17-18.
"Look Out for the Warelians!", *The New Yorker*, XV (April 1, 1939), 17-18.
"Unfamiliar Misquotations," *The New Yorker*, XV (May 30, 1939), 18.
"Thinking Ourselves into Trouble," *Forum*, CI (June, 1939), 309-11.
"Thurber Reports His Own Play, *The Male Animal*, with His Own Cartoons," *Life*, VIII (January 29, 1940), 27-28.
"Bermuda for Debts?", *The Bermudian* (April, 1940).
"The Story of the Bicycle," *The Bermudian* (May, 1940).
"Meet Mr. Curvey," *The Bermudian* (September, 1940).
"Taps at Assembly" (Review of F. Scott Fitzgerald, *The Last Tycoon*), *The New Republic*, CVI (February 9, 1942), 211.
"What Price Conquest?" (Review of John Steinbeck, *The Moon Is Down*), *The New Republic*, CVI (March 16, 1942), 370.
"Correspondence," *The New Republic*, CVI (March 30, 1942), 431.
"The Light that Fails" (Review of Aldous Huxley, *The Art of Seeing*), *The New Republic*, CVII (November 30, 1942), 719-20.
"1776 and All That," *The New Yorker*, XIX (April 24, 1943), 15-16.
"Cherboors," *The New Yorker*, XX (August 5, 1944), 17.
"Memoirs of a Fairly Old Timer," Columbus *Dispatch Magazine* (October 28, 1945), pp. 6-8.
Speech on Robert Ryder to be read at the Ohioana Library Association Meeting, October, 1946, in the Thurber collection at the Martha Kinney Cooper Ohioana Library, Columbus.
"Goldwyn vs. Thurber," *Life*, XXIII (August 18, 1947), 19-20.
"Notes on Talking and Homing Dogs," New York *Times Magazine* (February 8, 1948), pp. 18-19+.
"Case of the Laughing Lady," *The New Yorker*, XXV (September 24, 1949), 24-28.
"Comparable Max: a Quandary," *The New Yorker*, XXV (September 24, 1949), 34-35.
"How I Reclaimed the Catbird Seat," *Publishers' Weekly*, CLVI (October 8, 1949), 1671.
"Letter from the States," *The Bermudian*, October, 1949, through April, 1951; June, 1951 to March, 1952.
"The Telephone and I," *Holiday*, IX (January 14, 1950), 83-84.
"James Thurber," New York *Herald Tribune Book Review* (October 8, 1950), p. 4.
"Don't Fire Through the Front Door," *MacLean's Magazine*, LXIV (May 1, 1951), 26.
"Jottings of a Journalist," *The Bermudian* (May, 1951).
"Penicillin for Sweet Molly," *MacLean's Magazine*, LXIV (May 15, 1951), 48.
"Notes of an Old Reporter," *The Bermudian* (June, 1951).
"Correspondence," *The Humanist* (October-November, 1951), p. 204.
"Notes in May," *The Bermudian* (May, 1952).
"Michael, Son of Adam," *The Bermudian* (June, 1952).
"Dark Suspicions," New York *Times* (July 27, 1952), II, 1.
"Thurber to Hobson to Thurber," *The Saturday Review*, XXXV (November 8, 1952), 24.
"When Chic Harley Got Away," early poem reprinted in the Columbus *Dispatch*, November 5, 1953, 1B.
"How to Be Sixty," *The Bermudian* (June, 1954).
"Ad for *Webster's New World Dictionary*," *The Atlantic*, CXCIX (June, 1957), 86.

"State of the Nation's Humor," New York *Times Magazine* (December 7, 1958), pp. 26-27+.

"Harmonica Man," *Echo Magazine*, I (1959).

"Proper Care of the Eyes Is Vital," the Columbus *Dispatch* (January 17, 1960), p. 45B.

"Advice from a Blind Writer," *Newsweek*, LV (February 1, 1960), 48.

"The Quality of Mirth," New York *Times* (February 21, 1960), X, 1, 4.

"Dedication Speech for Denney Hall, April 1, 1960," *The Ohio State University Monthly*, LI (May, 1960), 6-7.

"State of Humor in the States," New York *Times* (September 4, 1960), X 3.

"The Thurber Method of Acting," New York *Times Magazine* (October 16, 1960), p. 28+.

"The Time of My Life," written for the AP and reprinted in *The State Journal* ([Lansing, Michigan] August 21, 1961), p. 13.

"Letter to *Saturday Review* drama critic Henry Hewes, September 21, 1961," *The Saturday Review*, XLIV (November 25, 1961), 18.

"Thurber Looks Back," Columbus *Dispatch* (October 1, 1961), pp. 14-16.

D. *Interviews*

Interview with Harvey Breit, "Mr. Thurber Observes a Serene Birthday," New York *Times Magazine* (December 4, 1949), p. 17+.

Interview with R. T. Allen, "Women Have No Sense of Humor, But They Don't Seem to Know It," *MacLean's Magazine*, LXIV (June 1, 1951), 18, 19+.

Interview with Harvey Breit, "Talk with James Thurber," New York *Times Book Review* (June 29, 1952), p. 19. Reprinted in Harvey Breit, *The Writer Observed*. Cleveland and New York: The World Publishing Company, 1956.

Interview, "Says Superwoman Will Force Peace," AP News (August 22, 1953). Reprinted in Columbus *Dispatch* (August 23, 1953), p. 7.

Interview with George Plimpton and Max Steele, "The Art of Fiction," *The Paris Review*, X (Fall, 1955), 35-49. Reprinted in *Writers at Work*. Malcolm Cowley, editor. New York: The Viking Press, 1959.

"James Thurber in Conversation with Alistair Cooke," *The Atlantic*, CXCVIII (August, 1956), 36-40.

Interview with Maurice Dolbier, "A Sunday Afternoon with Mr. Thurber," New York *Herald Tribune Book Review* (November 3, 1957), p. 2.

Interview with Henry Brandon, "Everybody Is Getting Serious," *The New Republic*, CXXXVIII (May 26, 1958). Reprinted in a fuller version as "The Tulle and Taffeta Rut" in Henry Brandon, *As We Are*. Garden City: Doubleday and Company, 1961.

Interview with Eddy Gilmore, "James Thurber Isn't Sure He's Funny," London (August 2, 1958). Reprinted as AP News in the Cincinnati *Enquirer* (August 3, 1958), p. 47, and in other papers that day.

Interview with Carol Illig, "Hear Your Heroes," *Seventeen* (January, 1960), pp. 88-89.

Interview with Arthur Gelb, "Thurber Intends to Relax Till '61," New York *Times* (March 28, 1960), p. 35.

Interview with Virginia Haufe, "Thurber Gives Advice to American Women," *Ohioana*, III (Summer, 1960), 34-36.

Interview with W. J. Weatherby, "A Man of Words," *The Manchester Guardian Weekly* (February 9, 1961), p. 13.

Interview with Eddy Gilmore, "American Male No Panther, He's a Pouncer," London (May 6, 1961). Reprinted as AP News in the Salt Lake Tribune (May 7, 1961), W 19, and in other papers that day.

SECONDARY SOURCES

A. *Books*

BAKER, SAMUEL BERNARD. *James Thurber: The Columbus Years.* Unpublished M.A. Thesis, Ohio State University, 1962.

The Best Plays of 1939-40 and the Year Book of the Drama in America. Burns Mantle, ed. New York: Dodd Mead and Company, 1940. Data on *The Male Animal.*

The Best Plays of 1959-60. Louis Kronenberger, ed. New York and Toronto: 1960. Contains data on *A Thurber Carnival.*

BLAIR, WALTER. *Horse Sense in American Humor.* Chicago: University of Chicago Press, 1943. Considers Thurber as an example of cynical modern humor.

BOHN, WILLIAM E. *I Remember America.* New York: The Macmillan Company, 1962. Contains a brief but perceptive essay on Thurber as an unreconstructed individualist.

COWLEY, MALCOLM. *The Literary Situation.* New York: The Viking Press, 1954. Contains a letter from Thurber and discusses Thurber's methods of composition.

Current Biography, Who's News and Why. Maxine Block, ed. New York: H. W. Wilson Company, 1940.

Current Biography 1944. Anna Rothe and Helen Demarest, eds. New York: H. W. Wilson Company, 1944.

EASTMAN, MAX. *Enjoyment of Laughter.* New York: Simon and Schuster, 1936. Attempts to define Thurber's tragi-comedy.

HACKETT, FRANCIS. *On Judging Books in General and Particular.* New York: John Day Company, 1947. Includes a perceptive essay on Thurber's Romantic nonconformity.

HERZBERG, MAX. *The Reader's Encyclopedia of American Literature.* New York: T. Y. Crowell Company, 1962.

KRAMER, DALE. *Ross and The New Yorker.* New York: Doubleday and Company, 1952. A rather pedestrian study, with some anecdotes about Thurber.

KUNITZ, STANLEY AND HOWARD HAYCRAFT. *Twentieth Century Authors, A Biographical Dictionary of Modern Literature.* New York: H. W. Wilson Company, 1942.

KUNITZ, STANLEY AND VENETA COLBY. *Twentieth Century Authors: First Supplement.* New York: H. W. Wilson Company, 1955.

MILLET, FRED B. *Contemporary American Authors, A Critical Survey and 219 Bio-Bibliographies.* New York: Harcourt, Brace and Company, 1940.

MURRELL, WILLIAM. *A History of American Graphic Humor* (1865-1938). New York: The Macmillan Company, 1938. Discusses Thurber as a cartoonist.

POLLARD, JAMES E. "James Thurber," *Ohio Authors and Their Books 1796-1950.* William Coyle, ed. Cleveland and New York: The World Publishing Company, 1962.

RYBERG, CHARLES LEWIS. *Humor and Pathos in James Thurber's Short Stories.* Unpublished M.A. Thesis, Southern Illinois University, 1959.

STONE, PATRICIA. *Thurber as a Comic Artist.* Unpublished M.A. Thesis, University of Florida, 1949.

STROUD, BEVERLY JEAN. *An Analysis and Production Book of The Male Animal by James Thurber and Elliott Nugent.* Unpublished M.A. Thesis, Ohio State University, 1950.

A Subtreasury of American Humor. E. B. and Katharine S. White, ed. New York: Tudor Publishing Company, 1946.

VAN DOREN, MARK. *The Autobiography of Mark Van Doren.* New York: Harcourt, Brace and Company, 1958. A discussion of Thurber's blindness and pessimism by a distinguished scholar who was Thurber's friend and neighbor.

B. Serials and Pamphlets

ARNOLD, OLGA. "James Thurber, Humorist." *Amerika,* Number 7 (December 4, 1956), pp. 1-18. For U.S. Information Agency.

AUDEN, W. H. "The Icon and the Portrait," *Nation,* CL (January 13, 1940), 48. Essay on *The Last Flower.*

BENÉT, WILLIAM ROSE. "Carnival with Spectres," *The Saturday Review of Literature,* XXVIII (February 3, 1945), 9. Review of *The Thurber Carnival.*

BRADY, CHARLES. "What Thurber Saw," *Commonweal,* LXXV (December 8, 1961), 274-76. A perceptive summing up after Thurber's death.

BUDD, NELSON H. "Personal Reminiscenses of James Thurber," *The Ohio State University Monthly,* LIV (January, 1962), 12-14. Includes a note from Thurber on *The Male Animal.*

COATES, ROBERT M. "Thurber, Inc.," *The Saturday Review of Literature,* XXI (December 2, 1939), 10-11+. A critical survey by a friend and author Thurber admired.

COWLEY, MALCOLM. "James Thurber's Dream Book," *The New Republic,* CXII (March 12, 1945), 362-63. A review of *The Thurber Carnival.*

———, "Lions and Lemmings, Toads and Tigers," *The Reporter,* XV (December 13, 1956), 42-44. Review of *Further Fables for Our Time,* with observations on Thurber's Joycean use of language.

DEVRIES, PETER. "James Thurber: the Comic Prufrock," *Poetry,* LXIII (December, 1943), 150-59. Perceptive criticism by a fellow humorist whom Thurber introduced to *The New Yorker.*

ELIAS, ROBERT H. "James Thurber: the Primitive, the Innocent, and the Individual," *The American Scholar,* XXVII (Summer, 1958), 355-63. A scholarly analysis by an expert on Dreiser.

FRIEDRICH, OTTO, "James Thurber: a Critical Study," *Discovery,* Number 5 (January, 1955), pp. 158-92. A lengthy study stressing Thurber's role as a literary critic dominated by the image of Henry James.

GILDER, ROSAMUND, "Brain and Brawn, Broadway in Review," *Theatre Arts,* XXIV (March, 1940), 158-62. Review of *The Male Animal.*

"James Thurber, Aphorist for an Anxious Age," *Time,* LXXIII (November 10, 1961), 81. Obituary.

KRUTCH, JOSEPH WOOD. "Review of *The Male Animal,*" *Nation,* CL (January 20, 1940), 81-82.

MACLEAN, KENNETH. "Further Thurber," Typescript of Lecture at the University of Toronto, in possession of Mrs. James Thurber.

———. "James Thurber–a Portrait of the Dog Artist," *Acta Victorana,* LXVIII (Spring, 1944), 5-6.

Selected Bibliography

————. "The Imagination of James Thurber," *The Canadian Forum*, XXXIII (December, 1953), 193, 200-1.

McCord, David. "Anatomy of Confusion," *The Saturday Review*, XXXVI (December 5, 1953), 33. Review of *Thurber Country*.

"Men, Women, and Thurber," *Time*, XLII (November 15, 1943), 38.

Morsberger, Robert E. "The World of Walter Mitty," *Utah Academy Proceedings*, XXXVII (1960), 37-43. Analysis of frustration and fantasy in Thurber's fiction.

Moynihan, Julian. "No Nonsense," *New Statesman*, LXIV (December 14, 1962), 872. An obituary analysis of Thurber's work.

Nugent, Elliott. "James Thurber of Columbus," *Ohio Valley Folk Publications*, New Series, Number 95 (April, 1962). Reminiscences by a friend and collaborator.

"Priceless Gift of Laughter," *Time*, LVIII (July 9, 1951), 88-90+. A journalistic but perceptive critical survey.

"The Private Life of James Thurber," *The World of Books*, BBC Home Service Broadcast, December 2, 1961, script in possession of Mrs. James Thurber. (A critical symposium by literary friends and associates.)

"Salute to Thurber," *The Saturday Review*, XLIV (November 25, 1961), 14-18+. Reminiscences and criticism by E. B. White, Malcolm Cowley, Peter DeVries, and others.

Schlamm, William S. "The Secret Lives of James Thurber," *Freeman*, II (July 28, 1952), 736-38. A reactionary piece attacking Thurber for his criticism of Senator McCarthy.

Taylor, Wilfrid, "James Thurber," *Rothmill Quarterly* (Autumn-Winter, 1958), pp. 94-101. Appreciation by a British critic.

"That Thurber Woman," *Newsweek*, XXII (November 22, 1943), 84-86. A report on Thurber's battle of the sexes.

"Thurber Amuses People by Making Them Squirm," *Life*, XVIII (February 19, 1945), 12-14.

"Thurber, an Old Hand at Humor with Two Hits on Hand," *Life*, XLVIII (March 14, 1960), 103-8. Contains some significant comments by Thurber about his aims and objectives.

"Thurber and His Humor. . . . Up with the Chuckle, Down with the Yuk," *Newsweek*, LI (February 4, 1957), 52-56. Discusses some of the subtleties of Thurber's satire.

Walker, C. L. "The Legendary Mr. Thurber," *Ladies Home Journal*, LIII (July, 1946), 26-27+. A biographical and critical sketch.

Weales, Gerald. "The World in Thurber's Fables," *Commonweal*, LV (January 18, 1957), 409-11.

White, E. B. "James Thurber," *The New Yorker*, XXXVII (November 11, 1961), 247. *The New Yorker's* obituary, by an old friend and associate.

White, Ruth Y. "Early Thurber," *Life*, VIII (April 22, 1940), 108-9. Contains some biographical data.

Wilson, Edmund. "Book," *The New Yorker*, XXI (October 27, 1945), 91-94. Review of *The White Deer*.

C. *Newspapers*

Benchley, Nathaniel, "If There Is No Human Comedy, It Will Be Necessary to Create One," New York *Herald Tribune Book Review* (November 25, 1962), p. 3. Discusses the need of Thurber's humor for sanity and survival.

BENÉT, STEPHEN VINCENT and ROSEMARY, "Thurber: As Unmistakable as a Kangaroo," New York *Herald Tribune Book Review* (December 29, 1940), p. 6. Critical evaluation by the author of *John Brown's Body*.

BRANDON, HENRY. "Thurber Used Humor to Camouflage His Exasperations with the Human Race," Washington *Post* (November 3, 1961), B 4. Obituary by one of Thurber's better interviewers.

NUGENT, ELLIOT, "Notes on James Thurber, the Man, or Men," New York *Times* (February 25, 1940), X 3. Character sketch by the co-author of *The Male Animal*.

"Obituary," Columbus *Dispatch* (November 3, 1961), pp. 1, 6, 10B.

"Obituary," New York *Times* (November 3, 1961), pp. 1, 35.

UPDIKE, JOHN, "Indignations of a Senior Citizen," New York *Times Book Review* (November 25, 1962), p. 5. In a review of *Credos and Curios*, one of the leading younger writers dismisses most of Thurber's work as insignificant and unconvincing.

Much otherwise unavailable material can be found in collections of Thurberiana at the Martha Kinney Cooper Ohioana Library in Columbus, at the Ohio State University Library, and in Thurber's file at the Alumni Office of the Ohio State University.

Index